Partial Justice

Should the law be praised or cursed for what it has done to the American Indian? Using American legal history, politics and jurisprudence, this study considers the degree to which American courts have maintained their autonomy and withstood political pressure, when the sovereignty and property rights of Native American tribes were at issue.

In 1879, a chief of the Ponca tribe, when released from military custody by an order of a U.S. district court, pronounced the use of law "a better way" to redress Indian grievances. This study explores the development of legal doctrine affecting Native American tribes by courts and commissions in the United States beginning with seminal court cases of the early 19th century and continuing through to the 1980s. Whether the law ever was a better way for Native Americans is a question of fundamental importance not only with regard to the rights – or even the survival – of American Indian tribes but also with respect to the claim of the American legal system to be equally fair and just to all groups in society regardless of their economic and political power.

Petra T. Shattuck, at the time of her death in 1988, taught government at Harvard University Extension, and was an attorney associated with a Boston law firm.

Jill Norgren is Professor in the Department of Government, John Jay College of Criminal Justice, and also teaches in the Program in Political Science, Graduate Center, The City University of New York.

State, Law and Society

Series Editor: Andrew Altman

The series presents major authors in the continental, and particularly the German, tradition of legal and political theory. It is concerned with recent comparative work in the field of legal and political history, but it also makes available in translation some of the classics of this tradition.

Ernst-Wolfang Böckenförde, *State, Society and Liberty: Studies in Political Theory and Constitutional Law*

Franz Neumann, *The Rule of Law: Political Theory and the Legal System in Modern Society*

Anthony Woodiwiss, *Rights v. Conspiracy: A Sociological Essay on the History of Labour Law in the United States*

Partial Justice
Federal Indian Law in a Liberal
Constitutional System

Petra T. Shattuck *and* Jill Norgren

BERG
Providence / Oxford

First published in 1991 by
Berg Publishers, Inc.
Editorial offices:
221 Waterman Street, Providence, RI 02906, U.S.A.
150 Cowley Road, Oxford OX4 1JJ, UK

Paperback edition, 1993

Chapter 1 of this work is a revised version of Jill Norgren's article, "Protection of What Rights They Have: Original Principles of Federal Indian Law," which originally appeared in 64 *North Dakota Law Review* 73 (1988).

A CIP catalogue record for this book is available from the British Library.

Library of Congress Cataloging-in-Publication Data

Shattuck, Petra T.
    Partial justice : federal Indian law in a liberal constitutional
system /Petra T. Shattuck and Jill Norgren
        p.   cm.
    Includes bibliographical references and index.
    ISBN 0 85496 342 1 (paper)
    ISBN 0 85496 588 2 (cloth)
    1. Indians of North America – Legal status, laws, etc. – History.
    2. Indians of North America – Government relations – History.
    I. Norgren, Jill. II. Title.
    KF8205.S47   1990
    346.7301'3–dc20
    [347.30613]   90–39337
                                         CIP

Front cover photograph shows one of the many deputations of chiefs who went to Washington to state their grievances.

Printed in the United States by E.B. Edwards Brothers, Lillington, NC.

For our children
  Jessica, Becca, Peter, Tiana, and Anneka
And for
  Anneliese and Heinrich Tölle

And to the memory of Winnetou

Contents

Foreword   ix

Acknowledgments   xiii

Introduction: The Contradictions of Federal Indian Law   1

1. Original Principles of Federal Indian Law   23

2. Nineteenth-Century "Friends of the Indian" and the Rule of Law: Limits on the Use of Raw Power   78

3. The Transformation of Indian Law: Trusteeship, Plenary Power, and the Political Question Doctrine   109

4. The Indian Claims Commission: Politics as Law   141

5. Federal Courts, Tribal Sovereignty, and Indian Civil Rights   164

Conclusion: The Two-Tier Structure of Federal Indian Law and the Impossibility of Partial Justice   190

Select Bibliography   200

Index   204

Foreword

No matter how cynical they may sometimes appear, most lawyers fighting for the civil rights of racial and ethnic minorities, women, and the disabled in our courts share a deep and abiding faith in the evolutionary potential of the American Constitution. It is their fundamental conviction that, through their efforts, all Americans can expect, in time, to receive the full protection of a document that initially excluded all but a precious few from its conception of "We the People." There is much to justify their faith. One need only recall the *Dred Scott* decision's description of blacks as "so far inferior, that they had no rights which the white man was bound to respect" and then look at the degree to which blacks have, through constitutional amendments, federal statutes, and court decisions, gained increased rights and respectability in the intervening 133 years.

One can also witness today the growing integration of women into the workplace and compare that fact to a Supreme Court justice's view, in the 1873 *Bradwell v. Illinois* decision, that the "paramount destiny and mission of womanhood are to fulfill the noble and benign offices of wife and mother." Benefiting from the right to vote granted in 1920 and effective use of the ballot box and the courts, women have expanded significantly the range of opportunities open to them throughout society. Justice Oliver Wendell Holmes's comment in *Buck v. Bell*, a 1927 decision, concerning the disabled that "three generations of imbeciles are enough" must strike most of us today as shockingly insensitive, given the growing solicitude that federal courts and Congress have shown for the rights of the physically and mentally disabled in recent years.

Of course, that civil rights lawyers share this faith does not mean that they accept uncritically the current status of individual rights or do not lament the Herculean struggles that were necessary to bring American constitutional law to recognize racial and sex equality and to acknowledge that disabilities do not deprive one of his or her humanity. The case is quite the contrary. The consensus is surely that more should have been accomplished by now and that those still on the margins of society should not have to wait another day to enter the mainstream. Nevertheless, there still is an overall sense of forward momentum among this group; even in difficult times, it is a feeling that, though there may be some setbacks, the overall trajectory is upward and onward.

It is difficult to imagine anyone's faith in the evolutionary potential of the American Constitution not being profoundly shaken by the depressing, infuriating story that *Partial Justice* has to tell. Unlike blacks, other racial and ethnic minorities, women, and the disabled, Native Americans have not experienced an evolutionary growth of their rights and protections under the Constitution. Instead, they have, if anything, witnessed a gradual but ineluctable erosion of their status before the law since 1787. Consequently, while blacks, women, and the disabled look to Supreme Court decisions in the second half of the twentieth century as important milestones on their journey to equality, Native Americans are more likely than not to point to decisions in the 1830s as their greatest constitutional victories. *Partial Justice* traces this erosion in faithful detail, describing how the combined forces of lust for Native American land, a benign, yet misconceived, concern of some whites for Native American assimilation, and anachronistic concepts of separation of powers have left this segment of our society in constitutional limbo. It is not that Native Americans have lost all of their cases but rather that they have lost those that mattered fundamentally.

Partial Justice does not purport to provide any solution to the constitutional plight of Native Americans. However, this should be no reason for disappointment. Setting out as it does the origins and nature of the problem, this book makes an informed and, for that reason alone, much-needed contribution to public debate over the "Indian Question" in which one often encounters more heat than light. Nevertheless, one cannot help wondering about how a solution would look. At root, it will test the willingness of American institutions to acknowledge and respect difference. The contrasts are numerous. In a society in which industrialization and urbanization are regarded as hallmarks of progress, many Native Americans seek to adhere to rural and agrarian values. At a time when one is more likely to calculate his or her net worth in stocks, bonds, and certificates of deposit, ownership of land is the standard by which Native Americans measure their economic stability. Moreover, the wealth that we claim is usually individual, not communal. For Native Americans the reverse is true. In view of these contrasts, one would be inclined to think that affording Native Americans genuine independence from plenary federal control and direction would be a just answer. Their sovereignty as "domestic dependent nations," to use

Chief Justice Marshall's term, would finally be recognized.

If only the matter were so simple. Certainly the authors intended to invite the reader to compare Native Americans' lack of progress in the courts with the success of blacks in constitutional litigation as recounted in Richard Kluger's book, *Simple Justice*, the history of the 1954 *Brown* decision outlawing racial segregation in public schools. On another level, however, one has to be struck by the significant differences between the two groups' legal claims. In *Brown*, blacks were seeking protection under the Constitution against government-imposed burdens based upon their race. The case pitted individual rights against state sovereignty and the former prevailed.

In contrast, put in its most difficult context, Native Americans have sought recognition in the courts and in Congress of their national sovereignty to the disregard of what, in non–Native American cases, would be viewed as individual rights protected by the United States Constitution.

This is not to suggest, for it would be incorrect, that the erosion of Native Americans' rights as a group has been as a result of the courts' commitment to protecting the rights of individual Native Americans. Indeed, the Supreme Court's most recent pronouncement in a case presenting this conflict resolved the matter in the tribe's favor. Moreover, in most of the important litigation involving Native Americans, the tribes have sought to protect their interests, on behalf of their members, against encroachments by federal and state governments, as well as by private parties. Rather, it is designed to point up the fact that, for civil rights lawyers, the group described at the outset of this essay, recognition of Native American sovereignty presents a conundrum: Can that sovereignty be fully respected except at the expense of individual rights? Can the power of Native American tribes, acting as governments, expand without a concomitant contraction of the rights of Native American men and women?

It is a conundrum that truly taxes a faith in the evolutionary potential of the American Constitution. But one would hope that, as the five-hundredth anniversary in 1992 of Columbus's discovery of the New World approaches, we will begin in earnest the search for a means by which the first inhabitants of the American continent can live among us in dignity. That is what *Partial Justice* urges, plain and simple.

Drew S. Days III
New Haven, Conn.
September 1990

xi

Acknowledgments

In the late 1970s, Petra Shattuck and I began writing about Native American land claims cases. The more we wrote, the more we became absorbed with the question of whether, by laws of our own making, the United States's legal treatment of Native Americans had been fair and just. The opportunity to research a book on this topic arrived with the award of a fellowship from the Rockefeller Foundation. After a splendid year spent both at archives and in the field, we settled down for the long process of reading law and history, of exchanging thoughts and, finally, draft chapters. Our book was nearly completed when Petra Shattuck died suddenly in the spring of 1988. With encouragement from our families, friends, and colleagues, I have brought the project to a conclusion.

Many organizations and individuals helped with our research. These include tribal elected officials and spokespeople who were generous with their time and forthcoming in their answers to our questions. From the time of our earliest inquiries, the staffs of both the Native American Rights Fund and the Indian Law Resource Center nurtured and tutored us. In addition to the award of a Rockefeller Foundation Humanities Fellowship, we received generous financial support from The City University of New York PSC-CUNY Research Award Program. Petra Shattuck received a grant from the Fund for Investigative Journalism, and Jill Norgren completed research for chapter 2 with the help of a grant-in-aid from the American Council of Learned Societies and a teaching release-time award from John Jay College of Criminal Justice, The City University of New York. A fellowship from the National Endowment for the Humanities also permitted Jill Norgren to discuss various parts of the book with Professor Joel Grossman and members of his seminar, "Courts in American Society," at the University of Wisconsin. Both of us were grateful to President Gerald Lynch and Provost Jay Sexter for providing us with the sabbatical leave that permitted work to continue on this manuscript.
No manuscript awash in fact and footnote can possibly be

completed without the aid of library staff. At numerous institutions, we were fortunate to find help whenever we requested it. I would particularly like to thank my colleagues at the John Jay College of Criminal Justice library. In addition, the staffs of the Library of Congress, Pennsylvania State Law Library, Georgetown and Boston University Law School Libraries, and the National Archives came to our assistance both with expertise and good cheer.

It has been our great fortune to have advice and encouragement from many scholars and lawyers in the fields of Native American studies, federal Indian law, and civil rights and civil liberties. First, I want to express deep gratitude to Drew S. Days III who has been supportive of our work in so many ways over the years. Curtis Berkey, Reid Chambers, Robert T. Coulter, Richard W. Hughes, Thomas E. Luebben, and Steven M. Tullberg endured our questions while we were novices and suffered an even greater number as we discovered the complexity of federal Indian law. Numerous academic colleagues encouraged us, discussed the project with us, and offered valuable suggestions. These colleagues include Jane Cohen, Archibald Cox, Norman Dorsen, Robert F. Drinan, Martin Ginsburg, Sidney Harring, Frances H. Miller, Christopher Pyle, Aviam Soifer, Philippa Strum, and Jean Zorn. A number of individuals read the completed manuscript. Their suggestions and corrections have contributed in countless ways to this final version. My few words here cannot convey the gratitude that I offer to Andrew Altman, Frederick E. Hoxie, Richard W. Hughes, Nell Jessup Newton, John Shattuck, and Steven Tullberg. That there was a manuscript at all must be credited also to the research and administrative assistance we received from several people, including Carole Lee, David Lehman, Arthur Lewis, Janet Pickering, and Andrew Zelermyer.

Midway through this project Petra Shattuck added a law degree to her many other accomplishments. While continuing as a university teacher, she began to practice law. In that new career, several people mentored her and "talked law" – federal Indian and much more. The intelligence and practical insights of the Honorable Douglas Woodlock and John Taylor Williams, in particular, deepened her understanding of the law. Our work has also been affected by the attention of our friends, with whom we discussed the ideas for this project over the years and from whom we harvested new ones. These many good folk include Scott Armstrong, Dick and Eileen Balzer, Robert Borosage, Sheila and Michael Cole, Nancy Gertner, Curtis Gans, John and Ann Gearen,

Barbara Guss, Kay and Wil Kohl, Angela Lancaster, Ann Langdon, Stefi Markham, John Marks, Chuck Muckenfuss, Mark and Susan Munger, Serena Nanda, Deborah Salter-Klimburg, Phyllis and Eli Segal, Lee and Meg Sigal, Michael Shinagel, Michael Smith, Wendy and John Sommer, John and Susan O'Sullivan, Arnold Steinhardt, Dorothea von Haeften, Howard Weinberg, Deirdre and Mel Wulf, and the members of the Department of Government and the Department of Thematic Studies at John Jay College. Annegret Falter, sister and friend, discussed this project with us, buoyed us up, and cheered.

Petra's and my families have been extraordinarily fortunate in having Mrs. Laila Banks and Catherine Leong in our homes. Our collective five children have an energy level which could not have been corralled or coped with without their help. Coping has also been the great strength of our husbands, John Shattuck and Ralph Norgren: each has supported this book with loving commitment and boundless curiosity. Each is made of more than the right stuff.

And finally, I must acknowledge my great good fortune at having collaborated for thirteen years with a person of such formidible intellect and personal gentleness. Petra and I began as colleagues and ended as friends. I admired her as a colleague and delighted in her as a friend.

Jill Norgren
John Jay College of Criminal Justice,
The City University of New York
January 1990

Introduction:
The Contradictions of Federal
Indian Law

But where, some say, is the king in America? I'll tell you
friend . . . let a crown be placed thereon, by which the
world may know, that so far as we appove of
monarchy . . . in America the law is king.

Thomas Paine[1]

Law: A Better Way

After a federal district court judge in the Nebraska territory had
ordered the release of Standing Bear from military custody in
1879,[2] the jubilant chief of the Poncas went to thank his lawyers for
having found a "better way" of redressing Indian grievances. "You
have gone into court for us and I find that our wrongs can be
righted there! Now I have no more use for the tomahawk. I want to
lay it down forever."[3]

Whether the law ever was a better way for American Indians is a
question of fundamental importance not only with regard to the
rights – or even the survival – of American Indian tribes, but also
with respect to the claim of the American legal system to be equally
just and fair to all groups in society regardless of their economic
and political power. To the extent that federal Indian law validates
the claim to fair treatment of Native American tribes and provides a
moral context and legal basis for successful Indian resistance to
injustice it cements the legitimacy of liberal law. To the extent that
the legal fate of the American Indian proves the Ponca chief's faith
in the law mistaken it undermines the most crucial premise of the
liberal constitutional order: adherence of the legal system to its own
founding principles and promises.

The claim of the law to autonomy and integrity is put to its most
severe test by the legal and political history of Native American

1

affairs. Few historical relationships are marked by a starker imbalance of economic and political power than that which developed between the United States and Indian tribes. In the context of increasingly pervasive inequality, commitment to legal principles – original principles of federal Indian law – set down in the late eighteenth and early nineteenth centuries and guaranteeing the land and autonomy of Indian nations, had to conflict with powerful pressures to ignore these rights. As the imbalance of power between white and Indian grew, the demand and the temptation to subject the principles of law to the exigencies of power grew with it. Whether or not the law could be a "better way" for Native Americans thus turned on the ability of the American legal system to withstand economic and political manipulation of Indian rights.

The most powerful challenge to the autonomy of the law concerned Indian sovereignty and property rights. The original legal principles governing Indian land respected the tribes as national sovereigns. In addition, the law respected the Indians' rights of possession and occupancy of their lands, guaranteed their right to use it according to their own discretion,[4] and permitted extinguishment of Indian title only with tribal consent,[5] although acknowledging that conquest can extinguish Indian title.[6]

Taking Indian sovereignty and property rights seriously when Indian title to land began to stand in the way of the geographic expansion and material growth of white society could not but impose high political and material costs. Predictably the need for a continuing commitment to original legal principles of Indian sovereignty and land rights became subject to vehement political attack and controversy. The debate over which legal principles should govern Native American political power and property rights, or even whether they should be protected by law at all, caused conflicts challenging the autonomy of the legal system and led to changes of the original principles of Indian rights.

The outcome of that conflict raises two questions of federal Indian law. One is whether its principles contributed to the survival of Native Americans in the United States; the other is whether the same legal principles are responsible for the perpetual inferiority of Native Americans in their own land. More starkly, the question is whether the law ought to be praised or cursed for what it has done to the Indian.

Faith Mistaken

The legal history of Native American property rights and the struggle for self-determination hold neither a single nor a simple answer. Indians have both succeeded and failed in using the law "to right old wrongs." Legal victories and legal defeats stand side by side. Legal gains are negated in the political arena and political losses are reversed in judicial forums. There is notorious evidence of the failure of legal principles to protect Indian land from the predatory politics of non-Indian society. But there is also some evidence of the steadfastness of the law in protecting Native American rights from economic and political manipulation.

Standing Bear's legal victory proved futile in the Ponca's struggle to reverse the impact of their forcible removal from their homelands to the so-called Indian Country a thousand miles away.[7] Judge Elmer S. Dundy, who acknowledged the Indian as a *person* under United States law having the right of all persons to sue out a writ of habeas corpus and who ordered the Ponca chief released from what Dundy called arbitrary and unauthorized military custody, nevertheless affirmed in the most sweeping terms the unlimited power of the executive over Indian tribes.[8] Judge Dundy did not question the right of the United States to assert jurisdiction and to enter the territory of the Omaha Nation for the purpose of arresting Standing Bear. Dundy freed the Ponca only because the federal authorities had erred in procedure: the Ponca ought to have been turned over to civilian authorities. Standing Bear's faith in a law broadly protective of tribal sovereignty was mistaken.

Nearly a half century earlier, in the early 1830s, the Cherokee, too, had put their trust in the law in vain. First in appealing the murder conviction of tribal member Corn Tassel by a non-Indian court, and then in *Cherokee Nation v. Georgia*[9] and *Worcester v. Georgia*,[10] the Cherokee Nation sought the protection of the United States Supreme Court against the unprovoked aggression of the state of Georgia, which had asserted jurisdiction over the Cherokee and had determined to seize the Cherokee's well-cultivated lands and drive them from their home forever. Twice the Supreme Court acknowledged the Indians' "unquestionable and therefore unquestioned rights to the lands they occupy"[11] and confirmed the right of the Cherokee Nation to occupy its own lands for as long as it chose.[12] Yet although the Supreme Court, in 1832, found the law on the side of the Cherokee, it could not protect them or their land. President Jackson supported forced removal and state supremacy over Indians, a policy position reflected in the often repeated but probably apocryphal statement that the chief justice "go and enforce his own decision."[13] Regardless of Jackson's actual words, all of the president's actions proclaimed openly that in the Indians' case, power and politics must prevail over law. The Cherokee were rounded up by federal troops and state militia and driven off their ancient homeland to faraway and inhospitable lands west of the Mississippi.[14]

The Cherokee Nation never regained these eastern lands. Yet despite the toll of removal, the Nation rebuilt the Republic initiated under its preremoval constitution in territory newly assigned to it, maintaining a strong national identity, creating a viable economy and successful schools.[15] But the limits of tribal sovereignty to be tolerated by courts of the United States were quickly demonstrated. Little more than a decade after removal, the United States Supreme Court, no longer led by John Marshall – author of the earlier Cherokee decisions – expressed the opinion in *United States v. Rogers* that the Cherokee Nation, like other tribes, was subject to the "dominion and control" of the United States.[16] This decision was a prelude to later nineteenth-century decisions in which the Supreme Court repeatedly asserted congressional power over Native American governments and citizens. From the 1840s, the Cherokee Nation resisted United States judicial actions restrictive of its sovereign power and property rights.[17] By the end of the century, the Cherokee – still asserting treaties guaranteeing their land – were battling Washington for their corporate survival. They fought the passage of land allotment legislation designed by Congress to break tribal government and culture, end communal tribal land ownership, and pacify whites with "surplus" allotment lands,[18] but ultimately yielded to a negotiated policy of allotment rather than suffer a dictated agreement or again face United States force.[19] Original principles of federal Indian law had recognized the right of Native American nations not only to possess and occupy their lands but to use them as they wished. These principles recognized tribes as nations. The General Allotment Act and the supporting legislation that followed it negated these principles, destroying most tribal government by imposing new concepts of property ownership and legal title and promoting different patterns of land use and personal occupation.[20]

And still, in the 1980s, a century and a half after the Cherokee's forcible removal, the Western Shoshone found that legal action, far from helping them confirm title to their land, caused denial of tribal aboriginal title.[21] At the end of fifty years of litigation, which they had once hoped would confirm their aboriginal and treaty title to

Shoshone lands in Nevada, the Western Shoshone – like the Ponca and Cherokee before them – went to court only to find that the law would not protect them.[22]

The faith in the law of these Native Americans was mistaken. Their lands were taken despite court decisions and because of court decisions, despite legal commitments and treaties of peace and friendship – and they were taken without any wrongdoing on the Indians' part. Neither the Cherokee, nor the Ponca, nor the Shoshone nations were ever accused of having warred against the United States or of having attacked settlers or even of having broken any part of the treaties and agreements they had entered in good faith, trusting the white man's word and law. The United States never claimed to have conquered them. Their lands were nevertheless taken.[23]

The lands of the Cherokee, cultivated and prosperous, were taken simply because white settlers wanted them and because Andrew Jackson, the first president elected by popular vote and the first from the West, found it more politic to cater to the white clamor for Indian land than to enforce the Supreme Court's decision protecting the Indians' property rights.[24] The lands of the Ponca were taken by mistake in the course of federal policies that moved Indian tribes and people back and forth across the Western plains like so many pawns on a chess board.[25] No more than a footnote to the Sioux's misfortune, the Ponca's lands were inadvertently used to "pay off" the Sioux Nation, whose lands in the Black Hills had, in turn, been confiscated by congressional fiat in order to satisfy the demands of white settlers illegally roaming the treaty-guaranteed Sioux reservation in search of gold.[26]

The Shoshone lost the claim to their lands not because they were ever conquered, or because they sold it, or because they signed a treaty ceding it, or even because the government "stole it fair and square." Their lands were taken as a result of legal proceedings in which the Indian Claims Commission and the Court of Claims decided in 1979, and the Ninth Circuit affirmed in 1989, that the Indians' land must *somehow* have been taken in the course of the last century. The commission did not determine the facts of any single taking but relied on a stipulated average taking date, although no evidence existed that the Shoshone land was ever taken by anyone in any manner recognizable under the precedents and principles of federal Indian law.[27] What happened to the Cherokee, Ponca, and Shoshone is not unique in the annals of federal Indian law and it is not only a thing of the past.

The lands of the Comanche and Sioux were taken nearly a

hundred years ago by acts of Congress that unilaterally abrogated Congress's firm legal promises of only a few years earlier to protect and guarantee the two tribes' land forever.[28] The title of the Tee-Hit-Ton Band of Tlingit was extinguished three decades ago when Alaska became the last new frontier for American expansion and exploration.[29] The Comanches were barred from legal redress when the Supreme Court held Congress's unilateral abrogation of Indian treaties immune from judicial review.[30] Legal redress for the Tlingits was precluded when the Supreme Court held – for the first time in the history of federal Indian law – that the United States owed no compensation for the extinguishment of aboriginal title, no matter how valid and undisputed.[31] The property rights of no tribes proved immune from erosion once their land became the target of white demands, whether a century ago or now.

Faith Rewarded . . . Sometimes, and in Stated Ways

But the history of federal Indian law is not only the history of the legal disenfranchisement of Native American tribes; it holds more than examples of the pervasive disregard for Indian rights. There are cases where original legal principles were upheld despite political costs, where legal rules were interpreted to expand Indian rights and protect Indian property including natural resources, where judicial decisions have compensated Indian tribes for past moral and legal wrongs and defended vital economic tribal interests.

In the same period in which the Shoshone lost claims to their land in Nevada, two Maine Indian tribes succeeded in establishing their right to seek legal redress for the taking of millions of acres of their land nearly two hundred years ago.[32] The litigation became necessary when the Passamaquoddy and Penobscot Nations asserted that nearly twelve million acres, or two-thirds of the state of Maine, had been wrongly taken by treaties with the Commonwealth of Massachusetts (part of which later became the state of Maine) that had not been ratified by Congress as required by the 1790 Indian Trade and Intercourse Act. The tribes sued successfully to have a reluctant federal government, which has long asserted itself as guardian to Indian tribes, file protective suits on behalf of tribal land claims. In 1980, five years after a federal court of appeals upheld the trust responsibilities of the United States in this case, an agreement worked out by the tribes, the state of Maine, and the federal government established a multi-million dollar tribal trust fund, land-purchase fund, and resolved questions of jurisdictional powers.[33] The *Christian Science Monitor* described the settlement as the "biggest Indian victory since the Little Big Horn."[34]

Beginning with the passage in 1881 of a special jurisdictional act allowing the Choctaw Indians to sue the federal government for the wrongful taking of their land[35] and ending with the institutionalization of that principle through the establishment of the Indian Claims Commission (ICC) in 1946, a routinized claims procedure has made it possible for Indian tribes to sue the United States for uncompensated or otherwise unlawful or unconscionable takings of their land.[36] Altogether the ICC and the Court of Claims have paid Indian tribes close to one billion dollars for their claims.[37]

The process has been neither swift nor certain. After fifty years of litigation, first the United States Court of Claims, and then the United States Supreme Court acted to award the Sioux Nation more than one hundred million dollars – *but no land* – in compensation for the government's seizure of their Black Hills.[38] The taking of these lands occurred when General George Custer announced that there was gold in the Black Hills and white prospectors clamored to have the land taken away from its tribal owners. The Grant administration, which had only six years earlier in 1868 guaranteed the Sioux title to "absolute and undisturbed use" of the land by treaty, responded by first attempting to coerce the Indians to cede the Black Hills. When that failed, the government forced the Sioux out. Federal agents disarmed the Indians, took away their ponies, and finally threatened to cut off the government rations on which the Indians had become dependent after signing over much of their hunting grounds in 1868. When a majority of the Indians still refused to cede the Black Hills, Congress accomplished the land-grab by fiat in 1877.[39]

In awarding compensation to the Sioux in 1979, the U.S. Court of Claims found that the United States had practiced duress on the starving Sioux in expelling them from their land in order to open it up to gold prospectors. It characterized the actions of the United States as giving the Indians "the Hobson's choice of ceding the Black Hills or starving."[40] A year later the Supreme Court upheld both the award of seventeen million dollars in compensation (fair value of the land at the time of taking) and one hundred years' interest of one hundred million dollars. The Court's decision came in the face of the United States' argument, made by the deputy solicitor general, that its conduct toward Indian tribes is exempt from the constraints of constitutional standards and international principles of human rights and that the Congress has near absolute and unreviewable power over Indians.[41]

The Supreme Court rejected the argument that Congress had acted in perfect good faith, and with good judgment, in passing the Act of 1877 and that taking the tribe's land did not constitute "a mere change in the form of investment of Indian tribal property."[42] The justices found that the rations given to the Sioux after the seizure of this land, claimed by the United States to have added up to fair value for the land taken, were never intended to constitute fair equivalent for the value of the Black Hills,[43] that the rations were only an attempt to coerce the Sioux into capitulating to congressional demands,[44] and that these rations were provided in order to "ensure them a means of surviving their transitions from the nomadic life of the hunt to the agrarian lifestyle Congress had chosen for them."[45] The Court concluded that the United States had the obligation to make just compensation that "must now, at last, be paid."[46].

Courts have also pushed back attacks on tribal sovereignty, protecting Indian tribes in the right, acknowledged by the 1832 *Worcester* court, to be free from state power over them.[47] Federal courts have struck down laws attempting to impose state criminal jurisdiction without tribal consent. Federal courts have struck down state efforts to tax tribes and regulate businesses. And federal courts have rejected state regulatory schemes over Indian hunting and fishing on Indian land.

In a much heralded 1974 decision, United States District Court Judge George Boldt issued a landmark decision in which he agreed with fourteen Indian tribes and the United States government that treaty Indians had off-reservation fishing rights that were not being acknowledged by the state of Washington. Native American tribes in much of the United States had been in constant, often hostile, conflict with neighboring states over the question of state regulation of off-reservation fishing by treaty Indians. Both as commercial and sports activity, fishing represents an important economic asset in these communities. As a result, states have sought to apply licensing fees to Indians and to make them subject to fishing regulations concerning time, place, manner, and volume of the catch. But tribal members, including those who brought suit in *United States v. Washington*,[48] argue that treaties with the government of the United States guarantee the right to fish in "all usual and accustomed places" off-reservation free of the restraining power of state officials.

In the 1850s the United States sought large tracts of land from Pacific Northwest Indians. Reluctant to be confined to small reservations, various tribes negotiated treaties that *reserved* – not granted

– to their members the right to continue to fish beyond new reservation boundaries. Such fishing would take place in common with non-Indians. Historically, fishing figured centrally in diet, trade, and religious practice among Pacific Northwest Indians, but in the twentieth century state regulation grew and many Indians, intimidated, began to stay away from traditional off-reservation salmon and steelhead runs.

Concerned with the loss both of cultural and legal independence, in the mid-twentieth century some members of these tribes began to resist what they saw as the encroachment of state regulation and resumed using nonreservation waters. States like Washington responded aggressively. There was seizure and destruction of tribal members' fishing equipment, arrest, jailing, and an atmosphere characterized by Judge Boldt as one of "deep distrust and animosity on both sides."[49]

Prior to the Boldt decision, fishing rights doctrine was regarded as a legal thicket noted for perplexing, complex, and vague standards.[50] Judge Boldt's decision represented a bold effort to impose a clear standard. Admonishing the parties to, finally, get along, Judge Boldt told the state that "if at this time anything concerning treaty fishing rights should be beyond doubt or question, it is the basic principle that the treaty fishing of plaintiff tribes is a reserved *right*, not a mere privilege."[51] The decision enhances the sovereign position of tribes by stating that they are "entitled to exercise [their] governmental powers" to regulate the treaty right fishing of their members without state regulation. The decision does accept, however, a longstanding non-Indian judicial position that the state has "legal authority to regulate the exercise of Indian tribes' off-reservation treaty right fishing . . . to the extent necessary for conservation of fishing resources."[52]

In the most controversial part of this altogether controversial decision, Judge Boldt held that treaty Indians may harvest up to 50 per cent of the harvestable salmon and steelhead returning to the Indians' "usual and accustomed" places of fishing off-reservation.[53] By this rule, Judge Boldt dramatically altered the modern understanding of who should have access to considerable resources in a way that favors a poor minority group.

The Boldt decision does not end the ongoing controversy in the Pacific Northwest. Vocal, dissatisfied commercial and sports fishermen continue to seek legislative and judicial reversal of Boldt's ruling. Indeed, when the decision was upheld in 1979, the United States Supreme Court chose to repeat the observation of the federal court of appeals that "except for some desegregation cases,

9

the district court [in this case] has faced the most concerted official and private efforts to frustrate a decree of a federal court witnessed in this century."[54] But to date Judge Boldt's decision endures both in the articulation of specific standards where vagueness had reigned and as what one Seattle newspaper termed "the most carefully researched, thoroughly analyzed [ruling] ever handed down in a fishing-rights case."[55]

States and private groups have challenged tribal property and sovereignty rights in other economic and commercial areas, among them the rough terrain of taxation and the seemingly innocuous landscape of games of chance. Like many American religious organizations, entrepreneurs, and state governments, some contemporary Native American governments have turned to bingo and card games as a way of creating employment and raising revenues.[56] These games, often offering high money stakes, attract large numbers of off-reservation non-Indians. In 1987 the Supreme Court noted that more than one hundred such tribal enterprises currently operated "for the most part with the encouragement of the Federal Government."[57] Indeed, three federal departments have provided grants and loans to assist in the development of tribal gaming.[58] The tribal games, however, compete with games run by non-Indians who have brought pressure on state officials to prohibit them altogether or to subject them to state regulations concerning number of days of operation, volunteer rather than salaried staff, size and number of jackpots, and profits permitted the host organization.

Native American tribes argue that state regulation of tribal gaming businesses would be an impermissible infringement on tribal sovereignty and would hinder economic development.[59] Federal courts, including the Supreme Court, have agreed that the regulations, generally, were impermissible and that explicit congressional approval of state regulation had not occurred. In various opinions, the justices have concluded that where a neighboring state itself does not prohibit gambling entirely, tribal gaming can neither be criminalized nor made subject to state civil regulations. Specifically, the courts have not found express consent to state regulation of tribal gaming in either Public Law 280, a 1953 federal statute that enabled Alaska, California, Minnesota, Nebraska, Oregon, and Wisconsin to extend civil and criminal jurisdiction over Indian reservations within the state,[60] or the Organized Crime Control Act of 1982 (OCCA).[61] In the courts' view, state regulation would limit tribal government and the "congressional goal of Indian self-government, including the 'overriding goal' of encouraging tribal self-sufficiency and economic development."[62]

And again, in spite of and because of state and private action, recent federal courts have upheld a considerable – but not complete – tribal authority to regulate taxation on tribal land. These courts argue that Indian tribes have "always been considered as distinct, independent political communities" and that the "weaker power does not surrender its independence – its right to self government, by associating with a stronger, and taking its protection."[63] From this reasoning, federal courts have found tribal authority to tax an attribute of an inherent tribal power of self-government – although the power of Congress to legislate tax policy for tribes has also been strongly asserted by federal courts if and where Congress seeks it.

As early as 1867 the Supreme Court found itself standing between states of the United States and Native Americans on the question of a state property tax imposed on reservation lands. The Court held then that Indian lands were free of such real estate taxes because treaties and statutes protected their sovereign right not to be taxed.[64] More than a hundred years later, tribes continue to turn to federal courts for protection against state governments that seek to diminish tribal sovereignty and economic development with various state taxation schemes. Within the past two decades, the Supreme Court has reasoned that state taxation of a non-Indian trading-post owner's profits earned within the Navajo Nation was inconsistent with federal statutes and congressional intent that the Navajo should be free to govern the reservation without state interference.[65] The Court also rejected the imposition of an Arizona personal income tax on Navajo tribal members living and working in the Navajo Nation on the grounds that it violated Indian sovereignty doctrine and treaties and statutes leaving tribes free of state regulation.[66] The Court disallowed state cigarette taxes levied on tribal customers at tribal stores[67] and has barred county personal property taxes applied within reservation boundaries.[68]

The United States Supreme Court has encouraged a more positive climate for economic development and tribal revenue collection in yet other recent tax decisions. The outcome of litigation in 1980, for example, stimulates business by non-Indians with tribal customers by eliminating state taxation on the transaction.[69] Other decisions of this period acknowledge the "general authority, as sovereign," of tribes to impose a severance tax on non-Indian companies holding oil and gas leases as "a necessary instrument of self-government and territorial management,"[70] while at the same time rejecting a state tax imposed on tribal oil and gas royalties.[71]

Conclusion

At the signing of the Maine Indians Claims Settlement Act President Jimmy Carter said that the tribes had "placed their trust in the system that has not always treated them fairly."[72] Federal courts, part of the system to which Carter refers, have played their part by writing federal Indian law decisions that reveal increasingly complex tests and sharply contradictory and inconsistent holdings. The law summarized above is but a sample. Extending the sample would yield further contradictions: decisions that assert tribal civil regulatory jurisdiction over non-Indians on tribal lands[73] but deny tribes inherent criminal authority over non-Indians,[74] even while granting tribal power to exclude;[75] decisions that hold for exclusive tribal possession of aboriginal lands until that possession is transferred away or expressly extinguished by act of Congress,[76] while also concluding that an exact date of taking need not be established;[77] decisions that agree Congress may legislate in favor of Indians without violating equal protection obligations,[78] while also concurring that Congress may legislate in ways that disadvantage Native Americans;[79] decisions that establish the inherent sovereignty of tribes[80] while fixing tribes in a ward-guardian relationship to the United States,[81] leaving many tribal powers to federal approval and delegation.[82]

Contradictions of this sort explain why it is not simple to determine whether the law ever was or ever can be a "better way" for Native Americans and why that question remains the subject of harsh legal and political controversy. Against this backdrop, it is not surprising that federal Indian law is both praised for its protection of Indian rights and resources[83] and condemned for its failure to protect their land and autonomy.[84]

The case of Standing Bear illustrates the contradictions inherent in the legal treatment of Indians by the United States. The Ponca chief and his followers won their freedom in a decision that acknowledged procedural error, but nonetheless affirmed the unlimited power of the executive branch over Indian tribes. Before and since Standing Bear's time, the legal record is rife with such apparent contradictions. Our examination of this legal record rationalizes these contradictions by documenting the development of two levels, or layers, of legality that transformed the original principles of federal Indian law through adaptation and reformulation by the courts. The first, or higher, level asserted both that Indians were not covered by ordinary constitutional standards and procedures and that the federal government held plenary and trust powers over them. In addition, the courts failed to limit federal powers through any concept of inherent rights for Native Americans, external constitutional standards, or institutional restraints. Using the plenary power and trust doctrines, the United States government could, and did, make choices about the rights and resources of Indian people that were not bound by external standards or subject to judicial review.

The courts did not yield the field entirely to Congress and the executive branch. Although they did not limit the scope and substance of political choices available to the government, federal courts did impose a second, or lower, level standard of fairness and due process on the procedures. These standards were consistent with liberal principles of formal legal rationality and permitted the courts to scrutinize the implementation and administration of the policies that the federal government chose to pursue. The judicial decisions of the second tier suggest that law could be – as Standing Bear asserted – a "better way." Nevertheless, these decisions never breach the first tier of legality, which grants the federal government near unlimited power over the Indians. Thus, we conclude that the legal treatment of Native American tribes by the United States has resulted, at best, in partial justice.

Notes

1. *The Complete Writings of Thomas Paine* 29 (P. Foner ed.) (New York, 1945).
2. *United States ex. rel. Standing Bear v. Crook*, 25 F. Cas. 695 (C.C.D. Neb. 1879) (1879).
3. T. Tibbles, *The Ponca Chiefs: An Account of the Trial of Standing Bear* 114 (Lincoln, Nebr., 1972) (hereinafter cited as Tibbles).
4. *Johnson v. M'Intosh*, 21 U.S. (8 Wheat.) 543, 547 (1823).
5. *Worcester v. Georgia*, 31 U.S. (6 Pet.) 515, 544–45 (1832).
6. 21 U.S. (8 Wheat.) 543, 587–89 and 31 U.S. (6 Pet.) 515, 543. See also, Berman, "The Concept of Aboriginal Rights in the Early Legal History of the United States," 27 *Buffalo L. Rev.* 637, 642–56 (1978).
7. Tibbles, *supra* note 3, at 131–34, 136–37. The subsequent commission investigation ordered by President Hayes and the legislation enacting the commission's recommendations acknowledged wrongdoing by the United States. The solution, however, in keeping with the era, was to use the Ponca's misfortune to further the United States's policy of

allotment, an initiative intent upon destroying tribes as political and economic sovereigns.

8. *Standing Bear*, 25 F. Cas. 695, at 697 and 700.
9. *State v. George Tassels*, 1 Dud. 229 (1830) (Ga.); *Cherokee Nation v. Georgia*, 30 U.S. (5 Pet.) 1 (1831).
10. 31 U.S. (6 Pet.) 515. Newly uncovered letters to lawyer John Sergeant indicate that nationally prominent United States lawyers hired to litigate on behalf of the Cherokee Nation as well as a few Georgia attorneys continued to test questions of state jurisdiction well into 1834. See Jill Norgren, "Lawyers for the Cherokee Nation, 1828–1837" (forthcoming).
11. *Cherokee Nation*, 30 U.S. (5 Pet.) at 17.
12. *Worcester*, 31 U.S. (6 Pet.) at 554, 561.
13. C. Warren, I:759 *The Supreme Court in United States History* (Boston, 1922); J. Bassett, IV:430 *The Correspondence of Andrew Jackson* (Washington, D.C., 1929).
14. G. Foreman, *Indian Removal: The Emigration of the Five Civilized Tribes* (Norman, Okla., 1953).
15. G. Woodward, *The Cherokees* 242 (Norman, 1963) (hereinafter cited as Woodward). It is sometimes argued that the removal of Native Americans was an inevitable consequence of the clash of highly divergent cultures at very different stages of social and economic development. The nature of Cherokee society prior to removal, as well as after, refutes this theory. By the late 1820s, that nation had adopted a republican form of government with a constitution modeled upon those of nearby states as well as the United States Constitution; the Cherokee Nation operated schools and printed a bilingual Cherokee-English newspaper, the *Cherokee Phoenix*; many Cherokee citizens had accepted Christianity and lived by farming. Neither the Cherokee's stage of development nor resistance to assimilation provoked Georgia citizens or necessitated removal.
16. *U.S. v. Rogers*, 45 U.S. (4 How.) 567, 572 (1846). Specifically, the Court ruled that the grant of citizenship to a white American by the Cherokee Nation could never make him an *Indian*, subject only to the laws of Cherokee society. *Id.* at 569.
17. *The Cherokee Tobacco*, 78 U.S. 616 (1870).
18. The General Allotment Act (Dawes Act), ch. 119, 24 Stat. 388 (1887) (codified as amended at 25 U.S.C. §§ 331–58 (1976) initiated a new phase of alloting land in severalty as well as the termination of tribal government. Successive acts of Congress were required to move the policy along including "An Act for the protection of the people of the Indian Territory" (Curtis Act) ch. 517, 30 Stat. 495 (June 28, 1898) and "An Act to provide for the final disposition of the affairs of the Five Civilized Tribes in the Indian Territory" (Burke Act) ch. 1876, 34 Stat. 137 (April 26, 1906). On the constitutionality of the Curtis Act, see

Stephens v. Cherokee Nation, 174 U.S. 445 (1898); *Cherokee Nation v. Hitchcock,* 187 U.S. 294. Also, A. Debo, *And Still the Waters Run* 31–37 (Norman, Okla., 1984) (hereinafter cited as Debo).

19. Debo, *supra* note 18, at 31–32.

20. A 1989 decision of the Supreme Court, *Brendale v. Confederated Tribes and Bands of the Yakima Indian Nation,* 57 U.S. L.W. 4999 (1989) adds to this legacy of non-Indian control over land. The Court held that areas of heavily allotted Indian reservations in which a fair number of nonmembers live cannot be zoned by the tribe, thus leaving the area open to zoning by the county. The decision – one that has caused considerable concern among Native Americans working to maintain tribal sovereignty – strengthens a line of decisions permitting state and, now, local county sovereignty over tribes.

21. To date, in fourteen years of litigation in the Western Shoshone Dann sisters case, for example, there have been seven separate decisions on the merits. Decisions in contemporary Western Shoshone litigation include: *Western Shoshone v. United States,* 531 F.2d 495, 209 Ct. Cl. 43, *cert denied,* 129 U.S. 885 (1976); *Temoak Band of Western Shoshone Indians v. United States and the Western Shoshone Identifiable Group, Represented by the Temoak Bands of Western Indians,* 219 Ct. Cl. 346, 593 F.2d 994 (Ct.Cl.), *cert. denied,* 444 U.S. 973 (1979); *United States v. Dann,* 572 F.2d 222 (9th Cir. 1978) (Dann I); *United States v. Dann* 706 F.2d 919 (1983) (Dann II); *United States v. Dann,* 470 U.S. 39 (1985); *United States v. Dann,* 873 F.2d 1189 (9th Cir. 1989) (Dann III). In a brief on behalf of the Temoak, attorney Thomas E. Luebben argued, "[T]he United States Supreme Court *did not* hold in *United States v. Dann,* 470 U.S. 39 (1985), that Western Shoshone title was extinguished. The Supreme Court expressly limited its inquiry and its decision to whether 'payment' within the meaning of Section 22 (a) [of the Indian Claims Commission Act] has occurred. . . . At the very worst, as of December 19, 1979, Shoshones are precluded from asserting the tribal (national) aboriginal title of the Western Shoshone Nation as a whole (as distinct from local tribal or individual aboriginal title) based on continuous and continuing use and possession." Intervenors' Supplemental Brief on Due Process Issues and Suspension of Intervenors' Motion to Intervene at 5–6, Temoak Bands of Western Shoshone Indians of Nevada v. United States (March 11, 1988). The Ninth Circuit has rejected this – highly technical lawyer's – argument. A summary of the litigation and court decisions is contained in *United States v. Dann,* 873 F.2d 1189, 1191–94 (9th Cir. 1989). See *infra* note 22. See also Orlando, "Aboriginal Title Claims in the Indian Claims Commission: United States v. Dann and Its Due Process Implications," 13 *B.C. Envir. Aff. L. Rev.* 241 (1986).

22. After the Supreme Court's 1985 decision in *United States v. Dann,* attorneys John O'Connell and Thomas E. Luebben worked to keep

Shoshone land rights alive arguing that aboriginal title and treaty grazing rights had not been extinguished, that the government was liable for "misappropriation and mismanagement of trust monies, and that the Shoshone should recover hundreds of thousands of dollars in grazing fees paid by them to the United States. Intervenor's Reply Brief on Due Process Issues and Suspension of Intervenors' Motion to Intervene at 2, Temoak Bands of Western Shoshone Indians of Nevada v. United States (Ct. Cl.) (May 13, 1988) and Intervenors' Supplemental Brief (March 11, 1988), *supra* note 21, at 4–6, 23. For the response of the United States, see Defendant's Response to Intervenors' Supplemental Brief on Due Process Issues and Suspension of Intervenors' Motion to Intervene, Te-Moak Bands of Western Shoshone Indians of Nevada v. United States (April 8, 1988). In January 1989, the Ninth Circuit held that a taking of Western Shoshone land by the United States had occurred (although Judge Canby could not identify an actual taking date), that the Western Shoshone, having been awarded a claims judgment by the Indian Claims Commission in 1979 (despite the tribe's filing to stay the claims proceeding in 1976), no longer held aboriginal title, and that the Dann sisters held only an individual aboriginal land title and individual grazing rights to land occupied and animals grazed prior to passage of the Taylor Grazing Act in 1934. *Dann*, 873 F.2d 1189 (9th Cir. 1989).

23. Despite Chief John Ross's initial determination to keep the Cherokee Nation neutral during the American Civil War, factional differences among the Cherokee, the formal alliances of several Indian nations with the Confederacy, the excellent terms of a treaty offered by the Confederacy to the Cherokee, and major battle losses by the Union at Bull Run and Wilson's Creek, led to the Cherokee alliance with the Confederate States on October 7, 1861. This hostile posture occurred, of course, twenty-five years after the Cherokee lost their eastern lands and were forced to walk "the trail of tears." Woodward, *supra* note 15, at 253–89.

24. Burke, "The Cherokee Cases: A Study in Law, Politics, and Morality" 21 *Stan. L. Rev.* 500 (1969); Norgren and Shattuck, "Limits of Legal Action: The Cherokee Cases," 2 *Amer. Ind. Culture and Research J.* 14 (1978). Swindler, "Politics as Law: The Cherokee Cases," 3 *Am. Ind. L. Rev.* 7 (1975).

25. Tibbles, *supra* note 3, at 22–28.

26. *U.S. v. Sioux Nation*, 448 U.S. 371 (1980).

27. *Dann*, 706 F.2d 919, *reversed on other grounds*, 470 U.S. 39 (1985) and *supra* note 22.

28. *Lone Wolf v. Hitchcock*, 187 U.S. 553 (1903).

29. *Tee-Hit-Ton Indians v. U.S.*, 348 U.S. 272 (1955).

30. *Lone Wolf*, 187 U.S. 553.

31. Newton, "At the Whim of the Sovereign: Aboriginal Title Recon-

sidered," 312 *Hastings L. J.* 1215 (1980).

32. *Joint Tribal Council of Passamoquoddy v. Morton*, 522 F.2d 370 (1st Cir. 1975). See also, Vollman, "A Survey of Eastern Land Claims: 1970–1979," 31 *Me. L. Rev.* 5 (1979) (the Maine symposium on the Northeastern Land Claims) and P. Brodeur, *Restitution: The Land Claims of the Mashpee, Passamaquoddy, and Penobscot Indians of New England* (Boston, 1985).

33. Maine Indian Claims Settlement Act of 1980, Pub. L. 96–420, 94 Stat. 1785 (codified at 25 U.S.C. §§ 1721–35 (1982)).

34. Reprinted in Mohawk, "Maine: Nothing But A Money Grab," *Akwesasne Notes* 24 (Late Spring 1980). However, traditional members of the tribes did not approve of the settlement. Robert T. Coulter, attorney for these tribal members, labelled it a "sell-out" in which "all the fundamentals of Indian sovereignty, as popularly known, would be given up." Layton, "Attorney Calls Land-Claims Act 'Sell-Out'," *Bangor Daily News* (March 14, 1980).

35. Choctaw Claims Act "An act for the ascertainment of the amount due the Choctaw Nation," 21 Stat. 504 (March 3, 1881).

36. Indian Claims Act, 60 Stat. 1049 (1946).

37. *Final Report. Historical Survey. Indian Claims Commission* (Washington, D.C., 1978).

38. *Sioux Nation of Indians v. United States*, 601 F.2d 1157 (Ct. Cl.) (1979); *aff'd* 448 U.S. 371 (1980). The original attorneys under contract to the Sioux structured the litigation as a money claims case, rather than recovery of tribal land. Beginning in the 1970s, several of the Sioux Nation tribes made it clear that they would refuse a money settlement that did not include return of their land and later terminated contracts with attorneys who had not litigated for return of land. With new lawyers, among them Mario Gonzalez, an enrolled member of the Oglala Sioux Tribe, and attorneys from the Indian Law Resource Center (Washington, D.C.), Sioux Indian tribes have fought a limited, money, judgment. As a result, both the original one hundred million dollars from the 1980 judgment and the forty million dollars resulting from a second Sioux claims case have been placed in interest-bearing trust accounts that are under the control of the Interior Department.

But, in what the Court of Claims calls "an uncontrolled quagmire," the former attorneys and the United States government insist that the money judgment is final despite the failure of the original lawyers to obtain the consent of their former tribal clients to the settlement. In legal action stretching through the 1980s, Sioux tribes, including the Oglala and the Rosebud, have continued to argue for the return of their land and to question (with respect to the terminated attorneys) "whether . . . [they] were lawfully represented by counsel and whether counsel could lawfully agree to a settlement and final judgment without the tribes' knowledge or consent." Brief for Appellants at 2, Sioux Tribe of Indians v. United States, 862 F.2d 275 (Fed. Cir. 1988) (88–1236), *cert. denied*, 109 S. Ct. 2087 (1989). See also Petition For A Writ Of Certiorari To The United States Court of Appeals For The Federal Circuit, Oglala Sioux and Rosebud Sioux Tribes v. United States and Sioux Tribe (88–1380). In addition to legal action intended to withdraw tribes from the settlement, Senator Bill Bradley and other members of Congress have sponsored a comprehensive Sioux claims settlement bill (S. 705) that includes restoration of lands to the Sioux. There is also discussion of a federally appointed commission to examine and propose settlement terms.

39. "An act to ratify an agreement with certain bands of the Sioux Nation," ch. 72, 19 Stat. 254 (February 28, 1877).

40. *Sioux Nation of Indians*, 220 Ct. Cl. 442, 601 F.2d 1157, 1167.

41. Brief of the United States, *United States v. Sioux Nation* 448 U.S. 371 (1980).

42. *Sioux Nation*, 448 U.S. at 371–73, 423.

43. *Id.* at 418–19.

44. *Id.* at 419.

45. *Id.* at 422.

46. *Id.* at 424.

47. *Worcester*, 31 U.S. (6 Pet.) 559–61. ("The Cherokee Nation, then, is a distinct nation . . . in which the laws of Georgia can have no force.")

48. 384 F. Supp. 312 (1974), *aff'd* 520 F.2d 676 (9th Cir.) *affirmed in part, reversed in part, sub. nom, Washington v. Washington Commercial Passenger Fishing Vessel Association*, 443 U.S. 658 (1979).

49. *Id.* at 329. See American Friends Service Committee, *Uncommon Controversy: Fishing Rights of the Muckleshoot, Puyallup, and Nisqually Indians* (Seattle, 1975) (hereinafter cited as *Uncommon Controversy*) (outlining the history of the issue prior to litigation).

50. *Uncommon Controversy, supra* note 49, at 87; Johnson, "The States Versus Indian Off-Reservation Fishing: A United States Supreme Court Error," 47 *Wash. L. Rev.* 207, 208–9, and 227 (1972).

51. *Washington*, 384 F. Supp. 312, 336.

52. *Id.* at 342. Ralph Johnson makes several points with regard to tribal sovereignty and the conservation standard. First, he argues that "the Court should apply well-established principles of constitutional law and hold that off-reservation Indian fishing is not subject to state control until Congress expressly delegates such power to the states." Second, that, "if the Court persists in upholding state regulation, it should . . . recogniz[e] that conservation is only one of three goals now served by state management systems" (the others involve spreading the catch among number and types of users). *Johnson, supra* note 50, at 236.

Analysis of the decision by Rita Brunn also demonstrates the limits of Judge Boldt's acceptance of tribal sovereignty and cultural pluralism

– even as it has been the subject of virulent attack by anti-tribal organizations. Brunn writes that the management and reporting systems established by the Boldt decision serve to undermine the legitimacy of the very claims it is upholding. Treaty rights derive what legitimacy they have from recognition of the separateness and uniqueness of Indian culture. But in Brunn's view, Boldt could not, or would not, imagine a management program, cooperative or otherwise, that did not adhere to liberal values, e.g., efficient rule-centered management and accountability. Brunn, "The Boldt Decision: Legal Victory, Political Defeat," 4 *Law and Policy Quarterly* 271, 293–95 (July 1982).

53. In a decision otherwise upholding the Boldt decision, the Supreme Court left the way open for challenges to the 50 per cent figure: "It bears repeating . . . that the 50% figure imposes a maximum but not a minimum allocation." *Washington v. Washington State Commercial Passenger Fishing Association*, 443 U.S. 658, 686 (1979).

54. *Id.* at 696. In 1988 attorney Suzan Harjo testified to hate crimes and bumper stickers reading "Save a deer; shoot an Indian" and "Spear an Indian; save a salmon." Hearing before the United States Commission on Civil Rights, January 28, 1988, *Enforcement of the Indian Civil Rights Act*, at 121 (Washington, D.C., 1988).

Despite the Court's observation, its opinion contained language that startled tribes and their advocates: "It bears repeating . . . that the 50% figure imposes a maximum but not a minimum allocation. . . . If, for example, a tribe should dwindle to just a few members, or if it should find other sources of support . . . a 45% or 50% allocation of an entire run that passes through its customary fishing ground would be manifestly inappropriate because the livelihood of the tribe under those circumstances could not reasonably require an allotment of a large number of fish." *Id.* at 686–87. According to the Court in the same decision, "the central principle here must be that Indian treaty rights to a natural resource that once was thoroughly and exclusively exploited by the Indians secures so much as, but no more than, is necessary to provide the Indians with a livelihood – that is to say, a *moderate* living." *Id.* at 686 (italics added). Some observers find the principle of a population to income ratio egregiously anticapitalistic.

55. *Seattle Post-Intelligencer* (January 16, 1977) quoted in Quinault Education Project, *Understanding Indian Fishing Rights* (n.d.) at 1. A review of West's 57 *Federal Practice Index 3d* section 32.10 amply reveals the aggressive litigation posture adopted by citizens and officials of the state of Washington in response to the Boldt decision. Local attorneys in Washington State indicate that final grant of cert in *Washington v. Washington State Commercial Passenger Fishing Association*, 443 U.S. 658 (1979) was very political and followed, at least in part, from contempt of court on the part of non-Indian fishermen. They argue that the Supreme Court upheld the Boldt decision partially because of this

contempt posture. See also, S. 2163. Judge Boldt anticipated this resistance, maintaining jurisdiction after deciding the case, as well as appointing a fishery science management expert and a master (U.S. magistrate) to serve as mediators. Fifteen years later, the Court continues to hold jurisdiction and hundreds of orders have been entered in the case.

The effects of the decision were quickly felt with tribal catches of salmon, for example, increasing from 6 per cent prior to the decision to 15 per cent in 1976. *Joint Report* (to accompany S. 2163) at 2 and Quinault Education Project, 6 *Understanding Indian Rights* (Taholah, Wash., n.d.).

See also, Turner, "The Native American's Right to Hunt and Fish: An Overview of the Aboriginal Spiritual and Mystical Belief System. The Effect of European Contact and the Continuing Fight To Observe A Way of Life," 19 *N.M.L. Rev.* 377 (1989).

56. In one case, the Supreme Court noted, "[T]he games are a major source of employment for tribal members and the profits are the Tribes' sole source of income. . . . The Reservations contain no natural resources which can be exploited." *California v. Cabazon and Morongo Bands of Mission Indians*, 480 U.S. 202, 205, and 218 (1987).

57. *Id* at 214.

58. *Id.* at 217–18.

59. *Seminole Tribe of Florida v. Butterworth*, 658 F.2d 310 (1981); *Cabazon*, 480 U.S. 202.

60. Public Law 280, Act of August 15, 1953, ch. 505, 67 Stat. 588–90 (codified at 28 U.S.C. § 1360(a) (1982). For incorporation of Alaska into P.L. 280, see 18 U.S.C.A. § 1161 (West 1984) (criminal jurisdiction) and 28 U.S.C.A. § 1360 (West 1976 and 1989 Supp.) (civil jurisdiction). Tribal consent to state jurisdiction has been required since the passage of the Indian Civil Rights Act of 1968 [25 U.S.C. §§ 1321–22, 1326 (1982)].

61. OCCA, 18 U.S.C. S 1955 (1982). For the most recent congressional action pertaining to gambling in Indian country that occurred after this litigation, see 18 U.S.C.A. § 1166 (West Supp. 1989). This legislation expressly authorizes, in effect, state regulation of Indian gaming under certain circumstances.

62. *Cabazon*, 480 at 217–18.

63. *Merrion v. Jicarilla Apache Indian Tribe*, 455 U.S. 130, 159 (1982). Even as these decisions permit tribal authority in such matters, it must be noted that, in an explicit fashion, federal "checkpoints" constructed out of the doctrines of trust and congressional plenary power hang over these tax policy victories, as well as those in many other areas of Indian sovereignty, like the sword of Damocles. *Merrion*, at 155. For different reasons, many tribes and tribal lawyers accept broad federal power over tribes. This will presumably be the case until challenges to

this doctrine, rooted in *Lone Wolf v. Hitchcock*, 187 U.S. 553 (1903), succeed. See also, Martone, "American Indian Tribal Self-Government in the Federal System: Inherent Right or Congressional License?" 51 *Notre Dame Lawyer* 600 (1976) (an early analysis pointing to the Supreme Court's increasing insulation of tribes from state law using the doctrine of federal pre-emption rather than tribal sovereignty).

64. *The Kansas Indians*, 72 U.S. (5 Wall.) 737 (1866); *The New York Indians*, 72 U.S. (5 Wall.) 761 (1866). A parallel but sharply inconsistent line of decisions, beginning with *Thomas v. Gay*, 169 U.S. 264 (1898), has held that state taxation of non-Indian property on Indian land was not precluded by tribal immunity from state law. The authority of this line of cases has been felt in recent cases upholding, for example, state taxation of severance of Indian minerals by non-Indian companies, where the record contained no clear evidence that such tax was either passed on to the tribal owner or had a direct or significant impact upon tribal interests.

65. *Warren Trading Post v. Arizona Tax Commission*, 380 U.S. 685, 690 (1965). In *Warren Trading Post* evidence showed that the tax was passed directly to Indian consumers. This appeared to be the determinative factor for the court as in several later cases.

66. *McClanahan v. Arizona State Tax Commission*, 411 U.S. 164 (1973). Writing for the Court, Justice Thurgood Marshall did conclude, however, that Indian sovereignty doctrine had "evolved" during the 141 years since *Worcester* and that "the trend has been away from the idea of inherent Indian sovereignty as a bar to state jurisdiction and toward reliance on *federal pre-emption*." *Id.* at 172 (emphasis added). This first invocation of federal pre-emption as a bar to the assertion of state power, while holding back state power over tribes, potentially diminishes tribal self-determination, as pre-emption doctrine asserts the United States government, rather than Indian people, as ultimate decision makers. *Supra* note 65. More recently, Justice O'Connor relied strongly upon the *McClanahan* pre-emption doctrine in *Rice v. Rehner* [463 U.S. 713 (1983)] (upholding California State jurisdiction to regulate the sale of liquor on the Pala Indian Reservation). In addition, it is argued that the recent advent of an *ad hoc*, fact-specific balancing test (federal and tribal interests against state interests) has "heralded greater and greater state incursions into Indian affairs." Feldman, "Felix S. Cohen and His Jurisprudence: Reflections on Federal Indian Law," 35 *Buffalo L. Rev.* 479 (1986). But, see generally, C. Wilkinson, *American Indians, Time, and the Law: Native Societies in a Modern Constitutional Democracy* (1987) (arguing the period since 1959 has been marked by increasing court respect for tribal self-government). Justice O'Connor used a test balancing federal against state regulatory interests in *Rice*. 463 U.S. at 718–19.

67. *Moe v. Confederated Salish and Kootenai Tribes*, 425 U.S. 463, 475–81

(1976). However, both *Moe* and *Washington v. Confederated Tribes of the Colville Indian Reservation*, 447 U.S. 134 (1980) upheld the state's right to tax the sale of cigarettes to non-Indians at tribal shops. The Court's approval of state taxation raises an interesting legal question: In light of its ruling in *Santa Clara Pueblo v. Martinez* that tribes hold sovereign immunity [436 U.S. 49, 58 (1978)], if the tribe operates the cigarette shop need it permit the state to review its tax collection records? Core, "Tribal Sovereignty: Federal Court Review of Tribal Court Decisions – Judicial Intrusion Into Tribal Sovereignty," 13 *Am. Ind. L. Rev.* 175, 190–91 (n.d.).

68. *Bryan v. Itasca County, Minnesota*, 426 U.S. 373 (1976).
69. *Central Machinery Co. v. Arizona State Tax Commission*, 448 U.S. 160 (1980); *White Mountain Apache v. Bracker*, 448 U.S. 136 (1980).
70. *Merrion*, 455 U.S. at 137; *Kerr-McGee Co. v. Navajo Tribe*, 471 U.S. 195 (1985).
71. *Montana v. Blackfeet Tribe*, 471 U.S. 759 (1985). For a fuller presentation of tribal taxation cases before federal courts, see Kramer, "The Most Dangerous Branch: An Institutional Approach to Understanding the Role of the Judiciary in American Indian Jurisdictional Determinations," 1986 *Wis. L. Rev.* 989, 1015–27 (1986).
72. Native American Rights Fund, The Eastern Indian Land Claims, *Announcements* 6 (May 1981).
73. *Merrion*, 455 U.S. at 130.
74. *Oliphant v. Suquamish Indian Tribe*, 435 U.S. 191 (1978).
75. *Merrion*, 455 U.S. at 130.
76. *County of Oneida v. Oneida Indian Nation*, 470 U.S. 226 (1985).
77. *Temoak Band of Western Shoshone*, 593 F.2d. at 1000–1002.
78. *Morton v. Mancari*, 417, U.S. 535, 551–55 (1974).
79. *U.S. v. Antelope*, 430 U.S. 641, 645–47 (1977).
80. *Worcester*, 31 U.S. (6 Pet.) 515.
81. *Cherokee Nation*, 30 U.S. (5 Pet.) at 17.
82. *Cabazon*, 480 U.S. 202; *Merrion*, 455 U.S. at 155.
83. Cohen, "Original Indian Title," 32 *Minn. L. Rev.* 28 (1947).
84. Coulter, "Lack of Redress," *Civil Rights Digest* 30–37 (Spring 1978). Jerry Muskat and Rennard Strickland express the conundrum differently. Muskat has said that "law has been both lance and shield for the American Indian," while Strickland has written that "in the nineteenth century, law was a principal tool of genocidal extermination. In the twentieth century, law has become the major weapon in preservation and extension of Native culture and economy." Both quotes appear in Strickland, "Genocide-At-Law: An Historic and Contemporary View of the Native American Experience," 34 *U. Kansas L. Rev.* 713, 714–15 (1986).

1
Original Principles of Federal Indian Law

"Do you mean that you think you can find out the answer to it?" said the March Hare.

"Exactly so," said Alice.

"Then you should say what you mean," the March Hare went on.

"I do," Alice hastily replied; "at least – at least I mean what I say – that's the same thing, you know."

"Not the same thing a bit!" said the Hatter. "Why, you might just as well say that 'I see what I eat' is the same thing as 'I eat what I see'!"

"You might just as well say," added the March Hare, "that 'I like what I get' is the same thing as 'I get what I like'!"

Lewis Carroll[1]

Introduction

Early in the nineteenth century, United States federal courts began to adjudicate cases that required dealing with the nature of Native American land title and with tribal sovereignty. Led by Chief Justice John Marshall, the "mid-wife" of federal Indian law,[2] the United States Supreme Court developed the legal framework that underlies tribal property rights and political sovereignty according to the United States. These original principles of federal Indian law were spelled out by the Marshall Court in a series of Supreme Court decisions ending with *Worcester v. Georgia* in 1832.[3] The Marshall Court drew upon European and colonial precedent and authority. Nevertheless, the justices created their own legal understanding of United States-Native American relations.

These original principles govern federal Indian law to this day. However, by narrowing, distorting, and misapplying these legal principles, or making selective use of precedents, federal courts began to alter legal principles concerning tribal sovereignty and land title as early as the mid-nineteenth century.[4] Tribes, respected as separate nations at the beginning of the nineteenth century, were treated as "ignorant and dependent" wards of the federal government by the end of the century.[5] Half a century after the Supreme Court had held Indian occupancy rights to be "as sacred as the fee simple of whites,"[6] millions of acres of tribal land had been declared surplus land open for non-Indian settlement by simple congressional fiat and without judicial objection.[7]

The doctrinal changes that made these developments possible were gradual, and they did not break openly with earlier principles or precedents. Indeed, it was the special genius of the legal changes that occurred in the course of the nineteenth century that they appeared to be consistent with what went before. That formal consistency was, however, more apparent than real. In substance the legal rules that had evolved by the end of the century either undermined the power of the original legal principles by circumventing them through the creation of new legal doctrines inherently at odds with the original concepts or, alternatively, distorted the meaning and consequences of original principles by applying them in new contexts entirely different from those that gave rise to the original rule of law. The dramatic result, after a midcentury period of judicial uncertainty, was a metamorphosis of central concepts of federal Indian law including the sanctity of Indian possessory rights and plenary federal power. Whether law was a better way for the Indian came to be masked by a process in which legal protections appeared to be in formal harmony with established legal principle but were, by the beginning of the twentieth century, in substantive contradiction to them.

Law and the Europeans in the New World

The autonomy and sovereignty asserted by contemporary Native American governments rest upon historical facts, legal agreements, and ongoing political relations. The presence of Native Americans on the North American continent prior to the arrival of whites is basic to claims of sovereignty. The order of arrival stands as virtually the only undisputed fact of Indian-White relations. By the twentieth century, however, the order of arrival had become a curious piece of information – obvious but commonly dismissed. Nevertheless, as the basis of tribal sovereignty and aboriginal land title, it is the key to subsequent political events and legal principles.

24

The Europeans who colonized North America in the sixteenth, seventeenth, and eighteenth centuries came for a variety of purposes ranging from gold and trade to permanent settlement. They brought a common European ethnocentrism and a desire for wealth, but they dealt with aboriginal occupation of North American land in different ways.[8] Eventually, the European nations settled upon treating Native American nations as autonomous, though alien cultures. Through diplomatic – nation to nation – exchanges, land boundaries were outlined and trade relations encouraged. Western European nations also vied for political and military alliances with certain tribes, occasionally causing the Native Americans, ironically, to become agents in the Europeans' struggle to dominate the North American continent.

When the Unites States of America came into existence, a body of law already existed that incorporated many of the premises upon which the new nation built its legal and political relationship with the Native American governments of the continent. Indeed, the use of law in dealings with tribes was a central premise inherited from European colonial governments, but it was law thoroughly grounded in the preeminence of European values and ideas.

Europeans' use of law as one principle of foreign relations with non-Christians dates at least to the medieval period and the legal theories of the canon lawyer-pope, Innocent IV.[9] Scholars like Innocent offered persuasive ideas about the legal status and rights of non-Christian societies that later influenced the political and military actions of Catholic heads of state after contact with Native Americans in the New World. In the early years of exploration, the papacy functioned both to assign lands and to delimit a theological law of nations and relations with indigenous people.[10] Thus, shortly after the Spanish began explorations of the New World, the monarchy applied for, and obtained, an official document from the pope known as a papal bull – *Inter Caetera* of May 3, 1493 – by which the Spanish Crown received "forever" all that Columbus had discovered.[11] Throughout the sixteenth century, Spanish rulers also convened formal boards of inquiry, often composed of church scholars, to consider what, if any, rights were due the indigenous people of the New World. These inquiries focused upon what actions, including war and enslavement, could be properly pursued in the name of Christianity and the Crown.[12]

In the broadest sense, two positions developed out of these inquiries. One school argued that the so-called Indians were inferior or even inhuman and, thus, marked from birth for subjugation.[13] In contrast, even as they acknowledged the Indian as

25

a primitive nonbeliever in need of conversion, theologians and missionaries Franciscus de Victoria and Bartolome de Las Casas asserted a message of brotherhood and Indian sovereignty and property rights, although unequivocally within a European philosophical framework.[14]

Victoria's writings argued that the Indians were rational beings possessing inherent natural rights including the right to be recognized as the "true owners" of the lands they occupied, whose "dominion can not be denied to them."[15] His work, in particular his first lecture on this question, the 1532 "On the Indians Lately Discovered," set a critical tone in the debate. Victoria wrote that "even those who attribute lordship over the world to the Emperor do not claim that he is lord in ownership, but only in jurisdiction, and this latter right does not go so far as to warrant him converting provinces to his own use or in giving towns or even estates away at his pleasure."[16] Victoria's analysis granted that Europeans held a right to travel, trade, and declare the Gospel among the Indians under the law of nations and divine law, but he denied that discovery by the Spanish conveyed title to Indian land since the Indians already owned it.[17] Victoria also argued that barring a just war, as defined by the law of nations, the Spanish Crown could not wage war against Indians and therefore could not claim any rights by conquest.[18] His influence in Spain was considerable: by 1556 the Crown had abolished the oppressive *Requerimiento* by which Spain justified the enslavement of Indians and in 1573 a royal order mandated that only "peaceful methods" be employed when trying to convert Indians and bring them under Spanish rule. Victoria's opinions influenced the development of an international law of exploration in the following two centuries – a body of law that had to be reckoned with by the new government of the United States in the formulation of original principles of Indian law. That this new law of nations was attractive to the United States undoubtably followed from its complementary duality: on the one hand, heir to the Renaissance and Enlightenment, this law "secured for the Indians of the New World basic rights in European international jurisprudence," but at the same time this law – with its right to punish and duty to educate – provided a legal and ideological basis for European subjugation of Indians.[19]

By political example and legal treatise, the Dutch and then the British also influenced the early development of United States Indian law contributing, among other legal principles, the practice of acquiring Native American land by treaty. The Dutch followed this path in order not to antagonize Native Americans as trading partners.[20] Legal scholar Felix Cohen has argued that the Dutch practice of treating for Native American land expressed three critical premises, articulated in the early seventeenth-century document prepared for the Dutch West Indies Company that declared: (1) that both parties to the treaty were sovereign powers; (2) that the Indian tribe had a transferable title to the land under discussion; and (3) that the acquisition of Indian lands could not be left to individual colonists but must be controlled by the larger institution of government or the Crown itself.[21]

Great Britain also made efforts to acquire land by treaty, but British colonists, in particular the large landowners, generally were not cooperative. Roger Williams was one of the few who "dared to dismiss European claims to American soil as unjustified and illegal if the prior right of the Indian was not recognized."[22] Full title, according to the Rhode Island leader, resided in the tribe. Greed apparently prevailed, however, as defiant Englishmen negotiated illegal land deals creating chaos in Native American and colonial communities.[23] The Crown periodically attempted to assert direct central control of land policy in order to encourage the orderly growth of empire. It worried, for example, that the purchase of property within tribal territory by individual colonists placed these British subjects under tribal authority.[24] The British government also saw the legal instrument of treaties as a way of keeping peace with tribal governments and, thus, keeping the tribes out of the French political orbit.[25] Neither the British nor the French worried that indigenous systems of law held fundamentally different notions of, for example, land tenure.[26]

Revolutionary and Transition Years

The Americans of the United States had no doubts about the propriety of asserting Western law as the legal *lingua franca* of negotiations with Native Americans. That they felt the need for legal relations reflected acceptance of earlier colonial practice. The use of law also expressed an understanding of the power of the large North American tribes and of the new Republic's limitations. Physically exhausted from the war with England, lacking a national treasury, and still facing competition from European sovereigns, the early decades of the Republic were marked by a pragmatic appreciation of the utility and necessity of lawful and diplomatic relations with tribal governments.[27] The United States nonetheless ignored Native American systems of law and what they might have contributed to an international law of property and jurisdiction for the North American continent, proceeding rather with a Eurocentric inquiry – one that sought principles to allocate power and property among four sets of governments: the Indian nations, the United States and its state governments, and the European "competitors."

The European nations treated tribal governments as sovereign political communities. The Continental Congress adopted this principle of nation-to-nation diplomacy, seeking treaties of peace and friendship with tribal governments. Such relations were not easily accomplished, however, as the British had already drawn many tribes into alliances.[28] In addition, many tribes were "as reluctant as other nations to stake their future on an untried, radical 'new order'."[29] Nevertheless, the revolutionary government negotiated a small number of treaties of nonaggression and friendship, including one with the Delaware Tribe in September 1778,[30] and alliances with northeastern tribes whose fighting significantly affected the outcome of the war and ultimate land boundaries.

During this period the Continental Congress struggled to wrestle control of the surveying, sale, and governance of western lands (Indian lands) from both state governments and private land companies. Fears of lost revenue, as well as political hegemony, led the national government to establish a frontier policy. A policy was spelled out first in a 1783 proclamation of the Continental Congress,[31] and later in the 1787 Northwest Ordinance, by which the Congress sought to establish nationally directed Indian relations and to establish peace.[32]

As the first full policy statement governing relations with Native American governments, the Northwest Ordinance was critical to the development of a federal Indian law. The ordinance created what a United States commission subsequently described as a "principled 'bill of rights' for the Indian Tribes, declaring 'their property, rights and liberty' as being inviolate to unconsented invasions or disturbances."[33] It is notable that a 1537 papal bull was, almost word for word, the source of that part of the ordinance dealing with Native American relations.[34] Together with the treaties of peace and friendship, the Northwest Ordinance affirmed an early framework of relations built upon the laws of nations. It also underscored the central role of the national government, rather than state governments or private companies, in the conduct of diplomacy and law with tribal governments.

The same year, the Constitutional Convention confirmed this principle of national relations by assigning to Congress the power to "regulate commerce . . . with the Indian Tribes."[35] Assigning such power to the national government followed logically from earlier policy: in 1775 the incipient American government had divided "Indian country" into three departments for the purpose of nationally directed trade and diplomacy, and the 1777 Articles of Confederation specifically provided for the national direction of relations between the new confederation and tribal governments.[36] The U.S. Constitution similarly provided for national direction of relations with Native Americans explicitly in the commerce clause and implicitly in the treaty clause.[37] Congress quickly drew upon these constitutional grants of power enacting the Indian Trade and Intercourse Act in 1790. The legislation mandated federal approval of any purchase of tribal land[38] – a move meant to end the practice of state governments entering diplomatic relations with, and obtaining land cessions from, tribal governments.[39] To regulate the activities of American traders, which often destabilized and confounded United States-Native American diplomacy, the statute further initiated a trade licensing system. The Trade and Intercourse Act also codified existing treaties, a victory for those who argued the wisdom of applying the standards of international law to all dealings with Native American nations.

Thus, in laws of its own making the early United States government asserted the sovereign national status of Native American tribes. The United States sought out tribal governments for the purpose of treaties of nonaggression and friendship, as well as the legal transfer of land title. Read together, these treaties, the Northwest Ordinance, and the Trade and Intercourse Act expressed principles of an early federal Indian law. These principles represented a critical commitment to law over raw power at precisely the time when the pressure for more land among whites was growing and questionable land speculation deals were on the rise in the United States.

Land was a major source of capital for both the states and the new nation. Several states had financed their share of revolutionary war costs through the sale of Indian land grants.[40] In the first case discussed below, *Fletcher v. Peck*,[41] one reason the state of Georgia was anxious to accept the bid made by land speculators was her desperate need for funds with which to pay the militia.[42] The competition for tribal land among whites prompted the litigation that also required the High Court to address questions of tribal property rights and tribal sovereignty. When the Court entered this discussion, it was an institution of a nation whose leaders had not asserted the conquest of tribal governments. Quite to the contrary, men like Washington, Jefferson, and Knox respected, even feared, the large inland Native American tribes and assessed any attempt at subjugating Indians by force as too costly and too uncertain of success. The price of avoiding violent confrontation was respect for Indian land and tribal sovereignty. But, at the same time, as de Tocqueville observed in 1830, leaders of the United States well understood that the law need not be an impotent weapon in the pursuit of hemispheric political and economic goals.[43]

Enter the Court: The Development of Doctrine in *Fletcher*, *Wilson*, and *Johnson*

Supreme Court involvement in federal Indian law began with *Fletcher v. Peck*, the famous 1810 case best described as a squabble among thieves and best known in law as the case first used by the Court to extol the sanctity of vested rights in property and thus to secure broad meaning to the contract clause.[44]

The "Yazoo" case grew out of aggressive, and fraudulent, speculative schemes in western (Native American) land claimed by the state of Georgia. The litigation has been described as a "collusive suit . . . an arranged case between friendly 'adversaries'."[45] Legal action followed the passage of a law by the Georgia legislature repealing a statute by which the state had sold hundreds of thousands of acres to the New England Mississippi Land Company – of which John Peck was director. Peck had divided the land and resold it at considerable profit to, among others, Robert Fletcher. The repeal law called into question the legitimacy of all title alienated pursuant to the repealed statute.[46] Robert Fletcher sued John Peck in federal court, using the court's diversity of citizenship jurisdiction, for a "covenant broken" because he had sold him "that which he did not rightfully possess."[47] From the litigants' perspective, the validity of Georgia's action voiding the land grants formed the core issue in the suit. Men like Fletcher and Peck stood to lose considerable sums if the High Court upheld the repeal bill.[48] Invoking the sanctity of contract, however, the Court invalidated the repealing statute, thus satisfying both men's claims.[49]

Indian governments were not direct parties to the case. But because the land sold originally by Georgia had not been transferred from the tribes by treaty, and because it was not clear whether the disputed land fell within the boundaries of either the United States or Georgia, the Court addressed the question of the legal status of Indian land as it related to the issues of the Yazoo litigation.[50]

Marshall's opinion for the Court acknowledged a property right he described as "Indian title," establishing for the first time under American law at least a patina of judicial protection – a legitimate legal status for Indian land.[51] Possessing "Indian title," what specific rights did the tribes hold under the international law or the developing federal law of land tenure? The opinion described it as a title "certainly to be respected by all courts" until extinguished and urged only legitimate extinguishment of title.[52] Marshall thus affirmed the prerequisite of tribal consent to the extinguishment of Indian title, an important principle for the protection of Native American property rights dating to the earliest laws of the European colonies in North America, one incorporated by the United States in its Northwest Ordinance.[53]

It was conceded, however, to be only a title of occupancy.[54] In *Fletcher's* concluding sentence, Marshall wrote that the majority believed "Indian title . . . is not such as to be absolutely repugnant to seisin in fee on the part of the state."[55] The principle that Indian title was not one of fee simple but only occupancy drew upon the so-called doctrine of discovery.[56] The doctrine of discovery was generally understood as a rule initiated by European nations, at the time of exploration of the New World, to govern these new international relations. To avoid the possibility of overlapping and conflicting statements, the earliest discoverer obtained the preemptive right – against later arrivals – to acquire unoccupied land.[57] The doctrine was a distributional principle that had a succession of interpreters including Victoria, Vattel, Montesquieu, and Blackstone.[58] The doctrine came to be a rationale for the taking of land and, as such, has been described as an "alien European theor[y] that w[as] imposed on the native population."[59]

Adherence to the law of discovery offered the new American nation the significant advantage of legitimizing both its domestic and foreign policy goals. The sweeping legal principle of the paramount sovereignty of the discovering nation relieved the United States of the burden of establishing its dominion over each individual tribe by direct action. After defeating England the United States could simply succeed to English claims of sovereignty over the Indians. At the same time the assertion of paramount sovereignty over Indian tribes served to preempt the competing claims of European states to Indian lands and loyalty. Since compliance with the principle of preemption sanctioned America's claim to be the sole legitimate sovereign power on the North American continent, the doctrine of discovery supported the assertion of United States hegemony over the continent: this was formally invoked with the enunciation of the Monroe Doctrine in 1823.

In the view of the Supreme Court, as the legatee of discovery by earlier Europeans, the state of Georgia had obtained fee simple title and thus, for the purposes of the case, could grant patents to the land even though the state could not eject the tribes.[60] A host of practical and complex questions arose from this distributive formulation assigning dual, or split, property rights to the discoverer nation on the one hand, and Indian nations on the other, but the *Fletcher* opinion did not address them. This was apparently because the Court feared an examination of the political character of Indian nations and their land rights would distract from the more central discussion of the contract clause and federal judicial review of state legislation.[61] As the result of the dual property right assignment and the Court's failure to address the question of tribal dominion, the *Fletcher* Court's attempt to build a lexicon of tribal property rights can only be characterized as tentative and inconclusive. The justices, however, may have been well satisfied with the decision, which, from their perspective, simultaneously promoted interests of the national government, the states, and Indian nations.

Tilting toward the Republic, the Court outlined tribal land rights limited to occupancy, with no right of alienation and, therefore, compromised in the context of United States property law.[62] But on behalf of the tribes, Marshall's opinion asserted a legal right of occupancy that protected the residency of individual tribal members as well as the communal character of tribes.[63] *Fletcher* also invoked a tribal right of consent before the extinguishment of this occupancy title. But finally, looking to the interests of the states, the Court hazarded that Georgia was seised in fee for tribal land and, thus, also in possession of a significant property right.[64] Viewed together, this tripartite balancing of rights suggests a Court seeking safe but principled ground at a time when the position of the Supreme Court in the American political system was far from secure.[65]

Justice Johnson, however, sharply disagreed that the *Fletcher* majority had laid down acceptable principles of law with respect to Native American sovereignty and property rights.[66] His separate opinion minced few words in concluding that the majority had misapplied the law and misunderstood the true nature of tribal dominion and concomitant rights of property. Reluctantly addressing a question he characterized as one of "much delicacy . . . more fitted for a diplomatic or legislative than a judicial inquiry," Johnson argued that the "national fires" of the tribes in question had not been extinguished and they retained "absolute proprietorship of their soil."[67] Moreover, Johnson noted that "[i]nnumerable treaties . . . acknowledge [the Indians] to be an independent people, and the uniform practice of acknowledging their right to soil, by purchasing from them, and restraining all persons from encroaching upon their territory, makes it unnecessary to insist upon their right to soil."[68]

Directing his inquiry to the critical question, Johnson asked, "Can, then, one nation be said to be seised of a fee-simple in lands, the right of soil of which is in another nation?"[69] Having stated that the tribes were "absolute proprietors," Justice Johnson argued the position that would be established as a fundamental principle of federal Indian law twenty-two years later in *Worcester v. Georgia*: "Unaffected by particular treaties, [the discoverer's interest] is nothing more than what was assumed at the first settlement of the country, . . . a right of conquest, or of purchase. . . . All the restrictions upon the right of soil in the Indians, amount only to an exclsusion of all competitors from their markets . . . a pre-emptive right [of the discoverer]."[70] Then, in a curious twist of politics and jurisprudence, Justice Johnson – an appointee of Jefferson – disputed John Marshall's conclusion that this preemptive right could be vested in a state. Rather, he argued, it is a right vested only in the United States following the cession, "by the constitution, [of] both the power of pre-emption and of conquest."[71]

The next opportunity for Supreme Court analysis of tribal property rights and tribal sovereignty occurred two years after *Fletcher* in *New Jersey v. Wilson*,[72] a case again involving nontribal litigants. In 1758 a band of the Delaware Indians ceded a large parcel of land to the colony of New Jersey in exchange for tax-exempt, reserved lands. Forty years later the tribes sold this reserved land with the consent of the New Jersey legislature. The state subsequently resold the land and, a year later, repealed its tax exemption. The non-Indian purchasers appealed this change in tax status first to state courts and then to the United States Supreme Court.[73]

Marshall's opinion for the Court is most interesting for its near avoidance of the Indian question. Framing the issue as impairment of contract and discussing the constitutional implications of such a clause, the chief justice failed to examine directly the pressing question of tribal sovereignty or property rights, writing only that the original colonial purchase would quiet the title of the extensive claims of the Indians.[74] By its silence and by implication, the Court accepted that the rights of the new landowners were identical to those of the tribes originally granted the tax exemption – both mere landowners, neither sovereigns. Nothing in the Court's words challenged New Jersey's assertion that it need not have granted the exemption to the Delaware, supporting the conclusion that the justices believed the state to hold the ultimate fee or dominion of the tribe's territory.[75]

The third case in this sequence, *Johnson v. M'Intosh*,[76] has been called one of the "most misunderstood cases in the Anglo-American law."[77] It has become one of the most controversial in the field of federal Indian law.

As in *Fletcher* and *Wilson* a decade earlier, *Johnson* confronted the Marshall Court with the difficulties of outlining legal doctrine expressive of what the United States characterized as its "unique" relationship with Indian nations, unique because, unable to conquer the tribes, the United States continued its nation-to-nation political dealings while at the same time asserting an unmitigated racial and cultural superiority.[78] It is also argued that the *Johnson* decision was burdened with Marshall's interest in developing an "Americanized law of real property."[79] The opinion defined property rights – or possessory interests – and articulated principles of a newly limited tribal sovereignty. Unfortunately, this was accomplished in language that is vague and confusing in key passages. It is not surprising that *Johnson* is often misunderstood.

The controversy in *Johnson* involved land claimed by the plaintiffs as the result of direct tribal grants in 1773 and 1775 and by the M'Intosh faction as the result of a later United States patent obtained after the lands in question were ceded to the federal government by the same tribes. Whether because they did not share Western notions of ownership, or for other reasons, the tribes had sold the same land twice.[80] Although it involved no tribal litigants, the case required that the Court determine whether a grant of tribal land obtained by a non-Indian purchaser without the approval of the federal government conveyed a title to be respected in courts of the United States.[81] Regardless of the Court's decision, there would be no immediate tribal "losers" since either way title would be held by whites. In a larger sense, however, tribal prerogatives were very much at issue as the case posed the question of whether tribes could convey title without the consent of the discovering nation.

In *Fletcher* the Court had suggested that the state of Georgia, as legatee of discovery, held fee simple title to the land in question rather than the tribes who occupied it.[82] The opinion contained no further explanation of alienation rights or other questions of dominion. The *Fletcher* decision was, however, firmly grounded in the discovery principle. In *Johnson* the chief justice applied this previously enunciated doctrine in the Court's first full-blown interpretation of the nature of tribal sovereignty and tribal property rights under United States law.

As described, discovery had been a convention of intra-European diplomacy intended to keep colonial powers from overlapping land claims. In *Johnson*, Marshall undermined the original doctrine, transforming it into a principle of United States-Indian relations. Marshall now described the discovery doctrine as not only giving the discoverer the "exclusive right . . . to appropriate the lands occupied by the Indians,"[83] but also creating the "considerable" impairment of the rights of these original inhabitants. The Indians, he wrote, are "the rightful occupants of the soil, with a legal as well as just claim to retain possession of it, and to use it according to their own discretion . . ." but "their rights to complete sovereignty, as independent nations, were necessarily diminished, and their power to dispose of the soil at their own will, to whomsoever they pleased, was denied by the original fundamental principle . . . discovery."[84] *Johnson* thus stands for the principle that Indian title is not a property right including the right to alienate land – only the holder of fee simple title may alienate – and correspondingly, that tribal sovereignty has been diminished by this limitation upon tribal power.[85]

Yet even as the Court denied this ultimate alienation right to the tribes in favor of the discoverer and the patentee, the Court found that the discovery doctrine simultaneously conveyed the right of perpetual occupancy and "use according to their own discretion" to the holder of Indian title.[86] Because the Court extracted these dual political rights and property titles, *Johnson* has been called both a "brilliant compromise"[87] as well as an opinion "seiz[ing] upon this controversy to establish a judicial mythology that would rationalize the origin of land titles in the United States."[88]

Using legal concepts alien to tribal law, the Court also built a theory of land title sympathetic to the interest of the Republic.[89] Not only did the Supreme Court deny the validity of a transaction entered into by an Indian nation, but also by virtue of the chain of discovery rights, any property transaction that had occurred before the revolutionary war and the creation of the American Republic.[90] To achieve legitimacy for the real property claims of the Republic, Marshall devised prerogatives for the discovering nation that reached into tribal dominion and created a political power and a tribal land title of lesser force. Indian title became one of occupancy and use, not title absolute and complete.[91] In this calculus, however, neither had the United States obtained a title "absolute and complete" because its title, in turn, was subject to the Indian title of occupancy."[92]

The Court's opinion in *Johnson* fleshed out principles of federal Indian law at a critical moment in United States history. Facing increasing resistance to lands cession from eastern tribal nations, uncertain of new colonial ventures on the part of France, Spain, and Russia, and in need of a solidified American law of real property to protect the Republic against all these parties (not to speak of American investors), Marshall knew the political, economic, and moral stakes of the Court's work were indescribable.[93] For the first time, the *Johnson* Court had applied the principle of parallel property interests enunciated in *Fletcher*.[94] Yet the Court did not satisfy anyone's expectation of a thorough definition of either property rights or each sovereign's political powers. Perhaps, because the stakes were so high, the Court could not afford to be too precise.

Adding to the muddle of possessory rights versus ultimate property rights, halfway through the opinion the Court introduced dicta describing a theory of conquest of Indian nations presumably meant to ratify rights already asserted through the doctrine of discovery.[95] Asserting conquest of Native American nations stands as curious reasoning because it was unnecessary for purposes of claiming title. Moreover, it was not credible. The historical record shows clearly that most of the lands alienated to the United States were acquired by purchase rather than military action.[96] Marshall's dicta may, nonetheless, have been aimed at appeasing antitribal opinion in the United States. The reference to conquest may have been included as a conceit, a metaphor of European superiority. It permitted Marshall to discuss the Indian as a savage and to imply that, had conquest doctrine been used more fully as the basis of the opinion, tribal governments might have been granted even fewer rights.

It is also possible that the strongly nationalistic Marshall presented conquest as a salvo to accompany the Monroe Doctrine.[97] Apprehension had been high in Washington over a joint French and Spanish expedition into South America, as well as over the intentions of the Russians in the Northwest. While President Adams mulled his foreign policy options, the chief justice may have asserted conquest as an additional statement of American independence and hegemony in the New World.

The *Johnson* decision established, or extended from *Fletcher*, three interwoven principles of federal Indian law: the existence of Indian occupancy title, the discovering nation's exclusive right of extinguishing Indian title, and the requirement of Indian consent for such extinguishment. The decision did not assert any right to govern Native American internal affairs.

Considerable debate exists over the consequences of *Johnson* for Native Americans. On the one hand, it has been argued that in the *Fletcher-Johnson* sequence, "Marshall lent faint color to Jackson's aggression . . . [because] Indians could be deprived by a legal fiction of their title by 'discovery'."[98] It has also been stated, however, that the "consequences flowing to the status of Indian lands from [conquest] theory were nonexistent."[99] While it has been written that the decision left tribes with a title of "mere occupancy and use," others have urged that the opinion should not be clouded by the conquest dicta, negating the relatively small qualification of nonalienability.[100]

Assessing these varied readings requires both presumption and a review of the legal record. There could only be conjecture as to the immediate consequences for tribes of the *Fletcher-Johnson* sequence. No tribe was party to either case. While the decisions guaranteed occupancy title, they assumed implicitly – if not also explicitly – that tribes would shortly permit the "legal extinguishment" the Court demanded.[101] The two opinions can also be seen as encouraging Americans ready and willing to engage tribal governments aggressively in pursuit of Indian land.

It is also argued that Marshall had to deal with the apparent inconsistency of treating for tribal land given the assertion of intrinsic property rights on the part of the discoverer nation. Here it is argued that the Court understood treaties to constitute "legal extinguishment" representing the purchase of occupancy rights, or the removal of a "kind of lien on the discovering nation's sovereignty," not "basic proprietary and political rights in North America, for these flowed from discovery and [symbolic] possession."[102]

The Court's decision in *Johnson* has been called, "confusing and occasionally incoherent," its dicta "ponderous."[103] But it is necessary to consider the task before the Court: the creation and justification of property rights not for colonial possession but for a Republic several decades old. Unlike Victoria and Vattel, the Court was not arguing for a sovereign separated from her land by an ocean. Practical politics would not permit Marshall to declare that the Republic give back tribal land or pay a fair purchase price. Marshall's "brilliant compromise," granting simultaneous but incomplete interests to both the discoverer and the tribes, established the moral and political principle that Native American governments must be respected as to residential rights and the legal standard by which tribes might be separated from their land – legal extinguishment by the discoverer nation – namely, Indian consent. Because it denied full title to tribes, the decision may be viewed as corrupt. But, in fact, because Indians were not direct parties to this litigation, *Johnson* as well as *Fletcher* involved tribal rights only in the abstract. Given the political constraints on the Court and its, ultimately unfounded, optimism that the tribes would eventually sell their land, *Johnson* may be contemplated as the Court waiting for the future to happen – hoping to structure a future of United States-Indian relations informed by just and legal standards, but counting upon an ongoing tribal willingness to make land cessions so that the use of deceit and raw power would not be necessary.

A Critical Juncture: The Cherokee Cases

Whatever stance leaders in the United States maintained with respect to Indian property rights and sovereignty – and there did exist a considerable range in attitude – few believed that tribal governments would ultimately resist offers of land purchase. Regardless of their "momentary" differences, most whites were guided by the belief that it was only a matter of years before all the discussion would be but a moot issue and Native Americans would be gone from lands east of the Mississippi, which then constituted the border of the United States.[104] For this reason, in some negotiations the national government committed itself to Indian policies with tribes on the one hand, and states on the other, which proved contradictory, and ultimately, irreconcilable.

No case made this point more clearly than that of the Cherokee Nation and the state of Georgia – two sovereign populations that lived coterminously in the Southeast. The final insistence of the Cherokee, beginning in the late 1820s, on their legal right to refuse consent to Georgia's insatiable demands signaled what would happen to tribes that refused to accede to requests to trade their land. When the Cherokee leadership resisted entering into treaties relinquishing their land, the land was taken by deceit and fraud and, finally, by force. The outcome of the Cherokee's legal challenge to Georgia's – and the federal government's – disregard for the law made clear that power would prevail over law.

By the Treaty of Holston in 1791,[105] the United States secured lands and continuing legal and political jurisdiction to the Cherokee

Nation in return for certain land cessions. Following the Holston treaty, the United States supported the Cherokee Nation with foreign aid, subsidizing the work of white Protestant missionaries and teachers who contributed to the permanence of Cherokee settlements.

In 1802, however, the United States also entered into a compact with the state of Georgia by which the federal government promised that it would, at its own expense, extinguish Indian title to land "within" the boundaries of the state "as soon as it could be done peaceably and on reasonable terms."[106] For more than two decades, however, the national government faltered in the execution of the 1802 agreement as the Cherokees demonstrated a "fixed and unalterable determination . . . never again to cede *one foot more* of land."[107] The import of the Cherokee's resistance to further land cessions was unmistakable. Indian refusal to sell land entailed a lasting withdrawal of large areas from the real estate market at the very time when non-Indian demands for the acquisition of these lands grew. Legal guarantees for Indian occupancy threatened to become an insurmountable and permanent obstacle.

The contradictions of the 1791 and 1802 policies remained until President Andrew Jackson, early in his first term, announced support for a new Indian removal bill.[108] Encouraged by Jackson's stance, the Georgia legislature lost no time in pressing the issue to a hoped-for conclusion. It passed a series of draconian laws – completely violative of existing federal treaties – annulling the constitution and laws of the newly formed Cherokee Republic and substituting the jurisdiction of the state over all individuals living within the borders of the tribe.[109] With these laws Georgia served notice on Congress, and the Cherokee, that it intended an immediate resolution of the "Indian question" and that its actions would not be bound by the doctrine of "expansion with honor," that is, by law rather than force.[110]

The congressional legislation supported by Jackson, "An act to provide for an exchange of lands with the Indians residing in any of the states or territories, and for their removal west of the river Mississippi,"[111] required that the federal government arrange for the removal of southeastern tribes, including the Cherokee, to the western side of the Mississippi. Removal policy had become increasingly popular in the 1820s as an alternative to national policies of either military action against, or assimilation of, the Indian. As an idea, removal had originated with Thomas Jefferson at the time of the Louisiana Purchase.[112] The legal concept centered upon an "exchange" of aboriginal land title in eastern lands for fee simple title, guaranteed by treaty, in homelands to be west of the Mississippi, land that was not ancestral land, and land that was, critically, already occupied by western Indian nations. Guaranteed only by treaty, such title could be abrogated by Congress.

President Jackson very quickly aided, if not endorsed, Georgia's jurisdictional legislation by withdrawing the federal troops sent previously to protect the Cherokee.[113] The president further weakened tribal efforts to resist Georgia's aggressions, and to lobby against the Removal Bill, by withholding federal annuities owed to the Cherokee under land cession treaties. In a telling speech, Jackson spelled out the philosophy behind his support of the Removal Act:

> Philanthropy could not wish to see this continent restored to the condition in which it was found by our forefathers. What good man would prefer a country covered with forests, and ranged by a few thousand savages to our extensive republic, studded with cities, towns, and prosperous farms; embellished with all the improvements which art can devise, or industry execute . . . and filled with all the blessings of liberty, civilization, and religion![114]

The Removal Bill provoked acrimonious debate that polarized the United States. Supporters stated that the unquestioned higher purposes of Western civilization demanded that whites have open access to all eastern lands. Congressmen in favor of the removal proposal argued that the United States had never recognized Indian nations as having any attributes of sovereignty and, therefore, any inherent property rights. A half century of formal diplomacy between the United States and Indian nations was summarily dismissed as something meant only to flatter "their vanity . . . by the acknowledgment of their name and rank."[115]

Opponents of the legislation, however, felt that other principles had consistently governed United States law with respect to the Indian nations. They labeled removal plans as open and rank assaults on Indian sovereignty. Prominent members of Congress characterized the bill as designed to flout firm and binding treaty obligations including the Treaty of Holston with the Cherokee. The speech of New York Whig Henry Storrs typified this position:

> The committee [on Indian Affairs] have suggested that we should not give much weight to "the stately forms which Indian treaties have assumed, nor to the terms often employed in them," but that we should rather consider them as "mere names" and "forms of intercourse." If

treating these Indian nations as proprietors of a qualified interest in the soil – as competent to enter into treaties – to contract alliance – to make war and peace – to stipulate on points involving and often qualifying the sovereignty of both parties, and possessed generally of political attributes unknown to individuals, and altogether absurd in their application to subjects, is nothing more than "mere names" and "stately forms," then this long pratice of the Crown, Colonies, the States, and the Federal Government, indeed, proves nothing. Words no longer mean what words import, and things are not what they are.[116]

Storr's speech suggested that the United States had been complicit by characterizing that sovereignty for the Indians who lacked an understanding of Western international law.[117] The congressman continued:

We have not only recognized them as possessed of attributes of sovereignty, but, in some of these treaties, we have defined what these attributes are. We have taken their lands as cessions – terms totally senseless if they are citizens or individuals. We have stipulated for the right of passage through their country, and for the use of their harbors, for the restoration of prisoners, for the surrender of fugitives from justice, servants, and slaves. We have limited our own criminal jurisdiction and our own sovereignty, and have disenfranchised our citizens by subjecting them to other punishments than our own. . . . You cannot open a chapter of Vattel, or any writer on the law of nations, which does not define your duties and explain your obligations. No municipal code reaches them. If these acts of the Federal Government do not show them to be sovereign to some extent, you cannot show that you have ever acknowledged any nation to be so.[118]

The antiremoval cause drew the support of other prominent members of Congress including Webster, Freylinghausen, and Clay, who were political antagonists of President Jackson and who supported national power over states' rights.[119] These men publicly attacked Georgia's actions and chastised Jackson for ignoring binding treaty obligations. But opponents of the Removal Bill were outnumbered. In a close vote the legislation passed. In the most explicit test of Indian sovereignty before the political branches of the United States government, Georgia prevailed, Jackson prevailed, and manifest destiny, already announced in the Monroe Doctrine seven years before, presented itself more clearly. Yet on the face of the law, formal principles had not been altered. The Removal Act articulated a *voluntary* process of removal to be agreed upon through a process of law.[120] Nevertheless, the tenor of proremoval debate and the very nature of the bill assaulted the sanctity of tribal sovereignty and aboriginal land title. As white population density increased and tribal willingness to continue land cessions diminished, the profound contradictions of the 1791 treaty and 1802 agreement could no longer be absorbed passively. Through the Removal Act the political branches acknowledged a new era in which the realities of this new Indian intransigence, together with their "occupancy and use" title, demanded an altered national policy. Removal was that policy, one that on paper appeared accommodating to all parties with its sanitary language of tribal choice and United States financial aid.[121] History was to prove the removal policy something quite the contrary.

With the passage of the Removal Act, the Cherokee's hopes for institutional political support in the United States ended; the political branches of both state and federal governments had united against them. It was at this point, in the summer of 1830, that the Cherokee Nation began to explore the possibility of litigation to untangle the increasingly confused and ambiguous web of text developing in federal Indian law.[122] Their options were not extensive. The failure of political attempts to protect their rights in the U.S. Congress left only war, or the courts. Unwilling to resort to force, reinforced by what they perceived to be the white man's respect for the law, they chose to put their case before the courts of the United States.

On the advice of anti-Jacksonian statesmen, the Cherokee leadership hired William Wirt and, later, John Sergeant to make a great test case at the Supreme Court.[123] The choice of legal counsel underlined the political significance of the case. Wirt, a regular before the Supreme Court and for many years the United States attorney general, and John Sergeant, a prominent Philadelphia lawyer, congressman, and adviser to the Bank of the United States, were central figures of the anti-Jackson establishment that had chosen to support the Cherokee cause. For them, Cherokee Nation litigation would serve to buttress their opposition to Jackson's narrow and restrictive view of the power of the national government. Although the Supreme Court was a critical forum for the Cherokee, it is possible that their lawsuit was, in large measure, merely an expedient means for anti-Jacksonians to foil the president's policies and prevent his reelection.[124]

An opportunity to put the issues of tribal sovereignty and property rights to the test presented itself when Georgia, acting upon its new jurisdiction laws, arrested and convicted a Cherokee citizen, George Tassels (Corn Tassel), on the charge of murder. Attorney

Wirt seized the opportunity to assert Indian immunity from state laws.[125] The case was appealed to the United States Supreme Court, which directed Georgia to show cause why a writ of error should not be issued against it.[126] The state deliberately ignored the High Court's order contending that "the interference by the chief justice of the supreme court of the U. States, in the administration of the criminal laws of this state . . . [was] a flagrant violation of her rights."[127] Corn Tassel was executed in this extraordinary expression of Georgia's contentious assertion of jurisdiction over citizens of the Cherokee Nation as well as of its continued resistance to federal judicial review of state criminal law.

Failing in its attempt to marshall the power of the United States judiciary against Georgia in the Corn Tassel case, the Cherokee determined to seek relief by filing a motion in the name of the entire sovereign and independent Cherokee Nation. In *Cherokee Nation v. Georgia*, the Cherokee brought suit as a foreign nation under the United States Supreme Court's original jurisdiction, filing to obtain an injunction and further relief, against Georgia, for property rights violations claimed under the treaties and laws of the United States.[128]

Cherokee Nation v. Georgia: They Are "Domestic Dependent Nations"

Even more explicitly than in the Corn Tassel case, the Cherokee hoped that raising the sovereign nation claim in *Cherokee Nation* would force the Court to clarify principles of federal law as they applied to the political and legal status of Indian nations. Raising these issues, as a direct party to the litigation, would seemingly present the Court with a far broader and more nettlesome question than either *Fletcher* or *Johnson*, which had only required a discussion of land rights. In particular, this litigation demanded that the Court speak to the recognition of tribal dominion as described by the United States in treaties *of its own writing*.[129] Unlike either the *Fletcher* or *Johnson* case, in this litigation the tribe was a direct party claiming legal injury, thus barring a purely abstract judicial consideration of aboriginal rights.[130] Specifically, it was hoped that a Supreme Court decision accepting the Cherokee's claim of sovereignty would prevent states from exercising jurisdiction over Indian tribes and from seizing tribal land.

Chief Justice Marshall's opinion for the Court in *Cherokee Nation*, however, denied the centerpiece of the tribe's case – the argument that the Cherokee Nation was, and should legally be considered, a foreign nation.[131] Instead, the opinion noted that the relation of Indians to the United States was unique, "perhaps unlike that of any other two people in existence."[132] The Court stated that Indian nations were not states within the United States, but it did not "comprehend" them in the "general term 'foreign nations'."[133] Therefore, the Court concluded that tribes like the Cherokee lacked standing to invoke the original jurisdiction of the Supreme Court under article three of the United States Constitution.[134]

Although failure to hear the case on its merits denied the Cherokee the immediate protection of the Court, Marshall's opinion was not a complete defeat for aboriginal rights. In dicta, the opinion specifically acknowledged a national character of Indian tribes, designating the Cherokee a domestic dependent nation rather than a foreign nation.[135] The Court noted that the relationship between the Cherokee and the United States "resemble[d] that of a ward to his guardian."[136] Marshall also described the Cherokee Nation as "capable of managing its own affairs and governing itself . . . a people capable of maintaining the relations of peace and war, of being responsible in their political character for any violation of their engagements."[137]

A sweeping interpretation of history, treaties, politics, and the doctrine of discovery led to Marshall's characterization of tribes as "domestic dependent nations:"[138]

> The Indian territory is admitted to compose a part of the United States. In all our maps, geographical treatises, histories, and laws, it is so considered. In all our intercourse with foreign nations . . . they are considered within the jurisdictional limits of the United States . . . They acknowledge themselves in their treaties to be under the protection of the United States. . . .
> They occupy a territory to which we assert a title independent of their will."[139]

Characterizing tribes as dependent domestic nations diminished the legal and political status of the tribes with respect to the United States. Marshall's opinion suggests, however, that the Court understood "unique" relations largely in terms of foreign affairs and did not support interference in matters of internal tribal governance.[140] That is, the United States as the discoverer nation had a vested property interest in tribal land and was asserting a protectorate status over tribal nations that was congruent generally with international law and, specifically, with discovery doctrine and the eight-year-old Monroe Doctrine:

They look to our government for protection. . . . They and their country are considered by foreign nations, as well as by ourselves, as being so completely under the sovereignty and dominion of the United States, that any attempt to acquire their lands, or to form a political connexion with them, would be considered by all as an invasion of our territory, and an act of hostility.[141]

Thus, while the characterization of tribes like the Cherokee as "domestic dependent nations" was problematic from the aboriginal point of view, the opinion did articulate principles of law that were not altogether destructive of tribal interests. In addition to asserting the national character of tribes, the Court's language of "protection" and "guardian" made explicit that it recognized federal and not state jurisdiction over Indian tribes. Moreover, the Court affirmed the Indians' "unquestionable, and, heretofore, unquestioned right to the lands they occupy," and clarified the ambiguity of *Johnson* on the subject of Indian consent by indicating that only voluntary cession would be honored in law.[142]

In not considering the case on the merits, the Supreme Court had in no way supported or condoned Georgia's assertion of jurisdiction over the Cherokee. While Marshall's opinion charted a fairly noncontroversial course hoping, no doubt, to avoid unnecessary confrontation with President Jackson and bumptious proremoval factions, Indian rights were not forsaken. If Marshall's opinion reflected the cautious approach with the chief justice writing that the restraint of the Georgia legislature and of the state's exercise of physical force savored "too much of the exercise of political power,"[143] at the same time he was not too intimidated to express the moral support of the Court: "If Courts were permitted to indulge their sympathies, a case better calculated to excite them can scarcely be imagined."[144]

The fine balancing of interests in *Cherokee Nation* was dictated not only by the politically explosive nature of the case given the passage of the Removal Act and Jackson's proremoval stance, but also by contemporary attempts by the Jacksonians to repeal the Court's appellate jurisdiction as described in Section 25 of the Judiciary Act of 1789 and to limit the term of office of federal judges.[145] Marshall would not make a decision on the merits of the case without estimating the consequences for the Court. In a calculus of politics and law, he fashioned a decision in some measure informed by the likelihood of further political attack on the Court.[146] Yet, while the chief justice asserted that the Cherokee had asked too much of the Court in this case, his closing text invited more circumscribed litigation selectively addressing the property right issue – in Marshall's words "a proper case with proper parties."[147]

If Marshall's opinion in *Cherokee Nation* was influenced by the political climate, the dissent written by Justice Thompson and signed also by Story, was not. Considering the complaint on the merits and drawing upon Evarts's essays and Justice Johnson's dissent in *Fletcher*, Thompson and Story argued that the Cherokee Nation constituted a foreign nation as understood by the works of Vattel, had never lost that status through conquest, and that it could, therefore, bring an original suit in the United States Supreme Court.[148] The dissent asserted that the Cherokee Nation properly claimed protection from Georgia's statutes under its treaties with the United States, statutes that if left untouched would "go the length of abrogating all the laws of the Cherokees, abolishing their government, and entirely subverting their national character."[149] The dissent concluded that the laws of Georgia, in violation of acknowledged treaties, were repugnant to the United States Constitution and therefore "void and inoperative."[150] Thompson and Story urged an injunctive writ be issued against the state of Georgia.[151]

Worcester v. Georgia: Law versus Raw Power

Even as the Court considered *Cherokee Nation*, Georgia continued her assault upon Cherokee sovereignty. Concerned with the pro-tribal support expressed by missionaries and other whites, late in December of 1830 the Georgia legislature had enacted a new statute prohibiting the passage of any white person onto Cherokee territory without the permission of the state.[152] Although most whites complied with the law, a handful of missionaries living among the Cherokee, including Samuel Worcester, defied the law, pronouncing it illegal, and were arrested.[153]

The case of northern missionary Samuel Worcester offered tribal attorneys the opportunity to fashion yet another challenge to Georgia's extension of state sovereignty over the Cherokee Nation – although not the property case suggested in Marshall and Thompson's opinions. The core question in this case, *Worcester v. Georgia*, continued to center upon the constitutionality of Georgia's actions and the right of Indian tribes, as nations, to be protected by the laws and treaties of the United States.[154] The legal posture of the case, however, which came to the Court on a writ of error from Georgia's superior court, had changed significantly because of the legal and political character of the plaintiff. As a white citizen and resident of Vermont, Worcester had standing to challenge the legality of the state laws. Marshall's brief review of the jurisdictional issues concluded that "it is . . . too clear for controversy, that the act of congress, by which this court is constituted, has given it the power, and . . . the duty, of exercising jurisdiction in this case."[155] In *Cherokee Nation* Marshall had urged tribal attorneys to bring a property rights case. Apparently anxious to assert that a personal liberty case was no less important, the Court now said that Worcester had no less an interest in Georgia's laws "than if they affected his property."[156] The Court accepted Worcester's appeal, and the Cherokee Nation and the state of Georgia squared off, with Georgia, however, as in *Cherokee Nation*, refusing to appear through counsel.

In *Worcester* the Court held that the missionaries were "apprehended, tried, and condemned, under colour of a law which has been shown to be repugnant to the constitution, laws, and treaties of the United States."[157] The Court did not confine itself to a narrow examination of Georgia's statute.[158] Rather, the Court outlined the clearest, and most pro-Indian, principles embodied in a Court opinion of the time, considerably refining principles announced in earlier Supreme Court opinions.

Worcester has been called the Supreme Court's declaration of "Indian independence."[159] Despite continued support for the preemptive rights of the discoverer, *Worcester* sharply defended the unchanged nature of tribal hegemony and property rights against state jurisdictional challenges.[160] Relying heavily upon interpretation of colonial charters, treaties between England, the United States, and Native American governments, and rethinking the fundamental premises of discovery-conquest doctrine, the Court now underscored the sovereign national status of tribal governments as recognized in United States law.[161]

The refinements of the opinion addressed the ambiguities and illogic of earlier Court text on federal Indian law, specifically the language of "guardianship" and "domestic dependent nation" contained in *Cherokee Nation* and the assertion of conquest and ambiguity about Indian consent found in *Johnson*.[162] The possible encouragement of its earlier conquest language upon political events in Georgia appears to have been very much on the Court's mind in the *Worcester* opinion.[163] In a long discussion of history and treaties, Chief Justice Marshall veered away from the suggestion of conquest so prominent in *Johnson*, writing rather that "[i]t is difficult to comprehend . . . that the discovery . . . should give the discoverer rights in the country discovered, which annulled the pre-existing rights of its ancient possessors."[164] The opinion described as "extravagant and absurd" the idea that European discovery and settlement constituted conquest or yielded property title under the common law of Europe.[165] Rather, the preexisting rights of the ancient possessors coupled with European law of discovery granted no more to the settler than the exclusive right to purchase title should tribal governments consent to sell.[166] Underscoring the importance of Indian consent, Marshall described European colonial charters as "grants assert[ing] a title against Europeans only . . . [that] were considered as blank paper so far as the rights of the natives were concerned."[167] Warning land hungry Americans, a stern Court admonished that "[t]he power of war is given only for defense, not for conquest,"[168] and that extinguishment of property title resulting from aggression would not be recognized.[169] Without explicitly citing *Johnson*, the Court had turned its back on that opinion's tough and incorrect assertion of European conquest of North American tribes.[170]

In *Worcester* the Court also elaborated on its description of tribes as "domestic dependent nations": "The Indian nations ha[ve] always been considered as distinct, independent political communities, retaining their original natural rights, as the undisputed possessors of the soil."[171] Analyzing the specific legal position of the Cherokee Nation, the Court stated that relevant treaties, such as the Treaty of Holston and the Treaty of Hopewell, recognized explicitly the national character of the Cherokees as well as their right to self-government, guaranteed their lands, and imposed on the federal government the duty of protecting these rights.[172] Still, the guardianship or trust language from *Cherokee Nation* seemingly burdened *Worcester*'s characterization of Native American governments as fully sovereign and national in form. Drawing directly upon Vattel to provide the necessary correctives, the Court now wrote:

> [T]he settled doctrine of the law of nations is, that a weaker power does not surrender its independence – its right to self-government, by associating with a stronger, and taking its protection. A weak state, in order to provide for its safety, may place itself under the protection of one more powerful, without stripping itself of the right of government, and ceasing to be a state.[173]

"Protection," stated the chief justice, "does not imply the destruction of the protected."[174]

Consistent with *Johnson* and *Cherokee Nation*, tribal governments are not conceded in *Wocester* to be in complete control of their foreign relations; in particular, they lack the right to cede tribal land to any sovereign other than the discovering nation.[175] The tribe is, thus, meaningfully described as a "nation like any other nation" with the power of internal self-government, but it is significantly delimited in certain external dealings so that the discoverer nation may protect its preemptive rights. Interpreting treaty text acknowledging the United States to have "the sole and exclusive right of regulating the trade with the Indians, and *managing all their affairs*," the Court also underscored its interpretation of the relationship with Native American nations as spelled out in documents of foreign relations: "To construe the expression . . . into a surrender of self-government, would be, we think, a perversion of their necessary meaning, and a departure from the construction which has been uniformly put on them. . . . It is . . . inconceivable that they could have supposed themselves, by a phrase thus slipped into an article, on another and most interesting subject [trade], to have divested themselves of the right of self-government on subjects not connected with trade."[176] Drawing upon the Northwest Ordinance and the commerce clause, Marshall argued that the proper construction of these phases expressed a charge to the United States government, not individual states, to carry on trade and intercourse with tribal nations and to do so according to tribal consent.[177] The laws of Georgia could have no force within the Cherokee Nation.

Contemporary with the passage of the Removal Act and Georgia's aggrandizing conduct, the Court's message was unequivocal. In the face of considerable animus from its own government, the majority reached out in a conciliatory manner to Native American governments finding not only that a non-Indian, Samuel Worcester, had been condemned under a law "shown to be repugnant to the constitution, laws, and treaties of the United States," but also that tribal nations held significant national political, and property, rights owed the highest respect by the United States.[178] Although not direct parties in this round of litigation, the Cherokee Nation had finally won its case. Marshall, usually a pragmatic statesman and jurist, seemingly abandoned a calculus of self-serving judicial politics, putting the rights of tribal nations squarely on the line against the announced positions of the political branches of the federal government and the ardent advocates of states' rights.[179]

The limits of the law, however, are amply demonstrated by *Worcester*. Victory for both the missionaries and the Indians depended upon enforcement of the Supreme Court's decision. Here they both lost – the Cherokee with devasting results. Georgia refused to release the missionaries. They languished in prison for several months while negotiations to free them proceeded.[180] Meanwhile, rapidly changing political events resulting from South Carolina's Nullification Ordinance altered the political climate in the United States and further diminished the ability of the Cherokee Nation to use the *Worcester* opinion to invoke the protection of the United States government against Georgia.[181] The danger of civil war over the nullification issue – real or imagined – caused many of President Jackson's former opponents to rally now to his support.

At this point the Cherokee government had no influence over the course of events affecting it. To the extent that political support for the tribe's cause had been directly related to anti-Jackson sentiment and rejection of his states's rights position, change in the president's policies as a result of South Carolina's rebellious act brought about a regrouping of the Indians' friends and allies. Jackson's nationalistic proclamation against South Carolina's nullification and the desire to protect the Constitution and the Union required that the fight on behalf of the Cherokee cease and the Jackson administration be supported.[182] As only indirect parties to Worcester's case, the Cherokee were unable to pursue further legal action in this case. Pawns in the political game of men like Webster, Wirt, and Sergeant, the tribe had no legal recourse when the missionaries accepted a pardon early in 1833. Cherokee leadership continued a strategy of litigation for two years more but ultimately faced involuntary removal west over the "trail of tears."[183]

The Early Test: Mid-Nineteenth Century Challenges to Original Principles

The removal of the Cherokee after the *Worcester* decision demonstrated the limits of the judiciary's ability to reconcile basic conflict. In the 1830s the legal victories of *Worcester* could not be translated into political guarantees. Moreover, while later courts found continuing authority for Indian sovereignty and property rights in the language and conclusions of *Worcester*,[184] in the decades immediately following, courts also tortured the meaning of the *Worcester* decision or ignored it, usually in favor of *Johnson's* less supportive language of Indian rights.[185]

United States federal Indian policy vacillated considerably in the midnineteenth century: Indian nations were urged, and made, to move; isolated reservations were created to protect them; the military was sent after them. They were believed to be a vanishing race and, in the 1880s, became the object of land allotment legislation designed to reverse the earlier policy of isolation, to "Americanize" them, and to end tribal society and government.[186] Supreme Court decisions in the nineteenth century after *Worcester* heeded the principles of that "declaration of Indian independence," but increasingly, as the century progressed, the Court yielded to a more expansive view of the guardian-ward relationship and a more restrictive posture concerning Indian occupancy title and tribal right to govern. A pattern was established in which *Worcester* became a precedent followed often in name rather than substance as the Court sought to reconcile *Worcester*'s principles with public opinion and public policy.

In 1835 the Supreme Court had its first post-*Worcester* opportunity to discuss Indian title. That decision, *Mitchel v. United States*, held general faith with *Worcester* but was an early example of the use of *Johnson* as authority.[187] Justice Baldwin, who supported the extensive power of the United States over Indian nations, nonetheless asserted in his opinion for the Court that Indian occupancy title was "as sacred as the fee simple of the whites"[188] and, critically, that "Indian possession or occupation was considered with reference to their habits and modes of life; their hunting grounds were as much in their actual possession as the cleared fields of the whites."[189] The specific nature of the dispute in *Mitchel* permitted Baldwin to clarify what had been conceded only in dicta in *Johnson v. M'Intosh*, namely, that Indian title included the power to transfer as well as to occupy.[190] This conclusion, along with continuing support for the requirement that tribal consent be obtained to extinguish title, and the Court's explicit statement that culturally diverse lifestyles were not a bar to possession[191] suggest that the Court had not been daunted by political events subsequent to its *Worcester* decision. At the same time, however, the Court maintained its commitment to discovery theory and the dual, or split, nature of Indian land title.[192] If this Court was willing to support *Worcester* in the most general way, it was not inclined to expand upon that decision in ways that would undermine the ultimate real estate, or governing, interests of the United States.

Mitchel was immediately followed by several decisions similarly affirming Indian occupancy title.[193] But the tone and direction of Justice Taney's opinion in *United States v. Rogers*, an 1846 criminal jurisdiction case, spoke of a new era of judicial interpretation concerning the breadth of the doctrine of discovery and the nature of tribal sovereignty.[194] Describing Native Americans as an "unfortunate race" who have "never been acknowledged or treated as independent nations by the European governments, nor regarded as the owners of the territories they respectively occupied,"[195] the Court held that a white man, although he has married into and become an acknowledged citizen of an Indian tribe, "is not an Indian" and may not "throw off all responsibility to the laws of the United States."[196] According to the Court, although the murder of one white, adopted by the Cherokee Nation, by another white occurred within the territory of the Cherokee Nation, the United States did not relinquish jurisdiction over the crime because the Trade and Intercourse Act of 1834 concerned with criminal acts in Indian territory only extended the right of jurisdiction to tribes in cases of Indians born Indians.[197]

To support this conclusion, the Court rejected the view of some members of the lower court and of the accused, Rogers, that the Cherokee Nation "as a separate and distinct government . . . possessing political rights and powers [could] receive and adopt, as members of their state, the subjects . . . of the United States . . . and to naturalize such subjects . . . and make them exclusively . . . citizens of the said Indian tribe, with regard to civil and political rights and obligations."[198] Rather, in the Supreme Court's view, a tribe could make a white man a member of the tribe, but not a member of the Indian race, and by its interpretation the right described in the 1834 legislation applied to race not political citizenship.[199] Reinterpreting the doctrine of discovery, the Supreme Court now read into that doctrine the right to interfere in internal tribal affairs and to govern Indians.[200] The Court's opinion further diminished the tribal sovereignty acknowledged in the earlier Cherokee cases by asserting for the first time that the power of the United States over tribes "need not be tied to treatymaking and execution, or regulation, of commerce between Indians and outsiders."[201]

Rogers initiated an era of broad interpretation by federal courts of congressional power to regulate commerce with Indian tribes.[202] The 1834 statute challenged in the *Rogers* case was one of several laws based upon the commerce clause that, however, had "little or no relation to commerce, such as travel, crimes by whites against Indians or Indians against whites."[203] In the decades following *Rogers*, combining commerce and property clause authority[204] with a broad view of the guardianship authority asserted in *Cherokee Nation*, the Court on the one hand encouraged the political branches to uphold their responsibilities to tribes in foreign relations, while at the same time the justices increasingly approved federal regulation of domestic tribal concerns. The result mid-century was a legal contradiction in which the Court usually characterized tribes as nations in name and function and did not overturn *Worcester*, but, in fact, permitted the encroachment of the United States government into domestic tribal policy.

In the second half of the nineteenth century this new posture was expressed, for example, in important cases involving the regulation of Native American access to liquor. In *United States v. Holliday* the Supreme Court upheld the use of sweeping congressional power to forbid the sale of liquor to an "Indian under charge of an Indian agent," although the Indian was living off the reservation and in one of the states of the United States.[205] In *United States v. Forty Three Gallons of Whiskey,* the Court concluded that the power to regulate commerce with Indian tribes was "as broad and free from restrictions as that to regulate commerce with foreign nations." [206] The Court's decision in *Forty Three Gallons of Whiskey*, like *Holliday*, restricted the jurisdiction of state governments over Indians,[207] but also restricted the right of Indians to be free from United States' liquor regulations specific to Indians even where they lived beyond the borders of a reservation.[208] This authority to regulate the Indians themselves, and not merely the land occupied by tribes, eventually meant that federal liquor prohibitions were applied to Indians even when they "had assumed the responsibilities of state citizenship and . . . held fee simple title to the land they occupied."[209]

The meaning of wardship invoked in the 1830s *Cherokee* cases – that of a more powerful nation protecting a weaker one from foreign intrusions – shifted decisively in these 1860s and 1870s decisions toward the position announced by Congress in the 1830s. In a House report accompanying the Trade and Intercourse Act of 1834,[210] members of the Committee on Indian Affairs had argued that the liquor prohibition provisos were "to enable administrative officials to prevent the manufacture of whiskey by Indians, who believed that they had the right to do as they pleased in their own country, and acknowledged no restraint beyond the laws of their own tribe."[211] The liquor cases suggest that the Court had become comfortable with this expansive view of federal guardian power in the long-troubling matter of commerce in drink. But contemporary court decisions in land sales, and yet other matters, demonstrate that the justices increasingly found the broad powers of guardianship an appealing basis for rationalizing United States power over Indians in the late nineteenth century.[212]

In these same confusing years the Supreme Court continued to recognize the "national character" of tribes despite its earlier language in *Rogers*.[213] The Court also acknowledged the validity of binding treaties with tribal nations and the obligations undertaken by the federal government in those treaties.[214] In *The Cherokee Tobacco*, however, the Supreme Court agreed that an act of Congress might supersede a prior treaty with a tribe.[215] Invoking judicial restraint, the *Cherokee Tobacco* majority determined that the imposition of a federal tax on liquor and tobacco, despite prior treaty agreement prohibiting the levy of such taxes upon tribes, was acceptable. The Court reasoned: "The burden must rest somewhere. Revenue is indispensable to meet the public necessities. Is it unreasonable that this small portion of it shall rest upon these Indians?"[216] Certainly there is irony in the Court's approving the reasonableness of taxing a people often described by them as wards in a "state of pupilage."[217] In their dissent, Justices Bradley and Davis argued that Congress had not intended to tax in the Indian Territory and that Congress considered Indian populations "autonomies invested with the power to make and execute all laws for their domestic government."[218]

Continuing the uncertain pattern, two years after this repudiation of treaty rights and diminution of tribal sovereignty in *Cherokee Tobacco*, the Court rejected, for the third time since *Worcester*, the contention that land grants from the discoverer superseded title based upon Indian treaty.[219] In *Holden v. Joy*, the Court not only upheld the sanctity of treaties after the earlier aberration, *Cherokee Tobacco*, but cited the tribal consent requirement with approval.[220] One year after the *Holden* decision, however, the Court imposed a narrow reading of the occupancy and use principle, with significant effect for tribal property interests, in *United States v. Cook*.[221]

In *Cook*, Chief Justice Chase wrote that although the right of use and occupancy is unlimited, "[t]he land cannot be sold by the Indians, and consequently the timber, until rightfully severed, cannot be."[222] According to the Court, the cutting of timber had to be related to the improvement of the land and could not simply be taken to make a sale.[223]

The *Cook* decision contains two opposing principles. On the one hand, the Court described Indian occupancy and use as of unlimited duration.[224] On the other hand, Justice Chase analogized Indian title in *Cook* to that of the tenant for life: "What a tenant for life may do upon the lands of a remainder-man the Indians may do upon their reservation, but no more."[225] Thus, to improve agriculture, the tribe might legally cut timber, but even dead wood could not be sold as a purely entrepreneurial effort.[226] *Cook* thus limited the ability of tribes to enter into, and compete in, the capitalist – cash – economy of North America.[227]

Conclusion

In the renaissance of tribal rights litigation in the 1970s, the principles of the 1832 *Worcester* opinion were cited as "direct authority " to validate claims.[228] Inasmuch as the decision has never been overturned, it contains legal principles of continuing authority. Yet much has changed in United States-Native American relations in these 150 years. Both the letter and the spirit of the principles articulated in *Worcester* have been severely tested: the opinion has been ignored in favor of the earlier *Johnson* decision.[229] The premises of tribal sovereignty and property rights contained in *Worcester* have been rewritten, yielding significantly narrower and weaker tribal prerogatives.

The Marshall Court had a rich body of international law and considerable political relations from which to build a doctrine of federal Indian law. Initially, the Court addressed the question of Indian title as it designed a law of real property for the Republic. It granted no absolute title to tribal land, but rather various rights to different parties. In order to clarify questions of foreign relations with Native American governments and issues of United States federalism as they affected interactions with tribes, the Court also affirmed the national character of Indian governments.

Increasingly, however, the work of the Supreme Court detoured this law from original intentions, especially as expressed in *Worcester*. The political branches of the United States government vacillated in their federal Indian policy from the 1830s through the 1870s; so did the Court. Without abandoning a framework of law, the United States sought a social, political, and economic order that would minimize the presence and power of Native Americans. In the legal opinions of the Supreme Court in the mid and late nineteenth century, there was confusion as jurists clung to the ideal of a nation of laws, while trying to accommodate expansionist nationalist interests. As the Court wavered in its commitment to original federal Indian law doctrine, it became facile to use *Worcester* as the proper legal vessel, to be filled, however, with reworked principles. In time, this evolutionary process made possible a body of late nineteenth- and early twentieth-century law that recast the status of Native Americans and United States power over them. In developing federal Indian case law consonant with American political and economic goals, the Supreme Court deferred to what it described as the plenary power of Congress in Indian affairs and elevated, indeed transformed, guardianship into a fiduciary power of sweeping proportions – sheltering certain Native American interests while broadly asserting the prerogatives of an expansionist American state.[230]

Notes

1. L. Carroll, *The Annotated Alice: Alice's Adventures in Wonderland and Through the Looking-Glass* 95 (Hardmondsworth, Middlesex England, 1965).
2. G. Lester, "The Territorial Rights of the Inuit of the Canadian Northwest: A Legal Argument" 175 (unpublished diss., York University, 1981).
3. *Worcester v. Georgia*, 31 U.S. (6 Pet.) 515 (1832); *Cherokee Nation v. Georgia*, 30 U.S. (5 Pet.) 1 (1831); *Johnson v. M'Intosh*, 21 U.S (8 Wheat.) 543 (1823); *Fletcher v. Peck*, 10 U.S. (6 Cranch) 87 (1810). Perhaps because John Marshall authored all four opinions for the Court, many authors present the sequence of cases as a self-contained unit of early federal Indian law. See, e.g., Burke, "The Cherokee Cases: A Study in Law, Politics, and Morality," 21 *Stan. L. Rev.* 500, 500–502 (1969). Marshall, however, also penned the decision in a case touching upon tribal sovereignty, *New Jersey v. Wilson*, which is discussed less often. See *New Jersey v. Wilson*, 11 U.S. (7 Cranch) 164 (1812). The Court had also accepted the appeal of Corn Tassel, a Cherokee accused of murder, in 1830, but Georgia defied federal judicial power and executed him before the Court could rule on the case. The frequent use of *Worcester* as a capstone case has been encouraged by its fine tuning of earlier points of law concerning tribal sovereignty and property rights.
4. See generally Newton, "Federal Power over Indians: Its Sources, Scope, and Limitations," 132 *U. Pa. L. Rev.* 195 (1984) (analyzing subsequent Supreme Court opinions that undercut the view of federal power and Indian sovereignty developed in *Johnson* and *Worcester*). See also Deloria, "Laws Founded in Justice and Humanity: Reflections on the Content and Character of Federal Indian Law," 31 *Ariz. L. Rev.* 203 (1989) (questioning our ability to understand the doctrines that have come to be called federal Indian law when that understanding is not grounded in an historical context).

5. *Beecher v. Wetherby*, 95 U.S (5 Otto) 517, 525 (1877).

6. *Mitchel v. United States*, 34 (9 Pet.) 711 (1835).

7. The most important legislation of this era was the General Allotment (Dawes) Act, ch. 119, 24 Stat. 388 (1887) (codified as amended as 25 U.S.C. §§ 331–58 (1976). This legislation, supplemented by other statutes, provided for the allotment of communal tribal land as private property to individual Indian households. These allotments, however, were limited to 160 acres per family, and the excess tribal land was declared "surplus" by the United States and opened to white settlement. During the allotment period, 1887 to 1934, whose ostensible purpose was assimilation of the Native American into white society, tribal land holding was reduced from 138 million acres to 48 million acres. See chapter 2.

8. S. Morison, *The Oxford History of the American People* 17–33 (New York, 1965). In the early years during their search for valuable minerals, the Spanish often attempted to enslave indigenous people, imposing the system known as *encomienda*; settlement was generally not a primary goal but religious conversion was. L. Hanke, *The Spanish Struggle for Justice in the Conquest of America* 19–20, 23–25 (Boston, 1965). In contrast, Englishmen came as permanent settlers, the French as traders, missionaries, and sometimes settlers, but neither made Native Americans subject people in the early years of settlement. The Spanish Crown established a highly centralized law to govern Spanish America. The British Crown, however, was far more lackadaisical in the concern paid to centralized control of colonial-Native American interactions.

9. Williams, "Documents of Barbarism: The Contemporary Legacy of European Racism and Colonialism in the Narrative Traditions in Federal Indian Law," 31 *Ariz. L. Rev.* 237 (1989); Williams, "The Medieval and Renaissance Origins of the Status of the American Indian in Western Legal Thought," 57 *S. Cal. L. Rev.* 1 (1983–84) (hereinafter cited as Williams, "Medieval"); Williams, "The Algebra of Federal Indian Law: The Hard Trail of Decolonizing and Americanizing the White Man's Indian Jurisprudence," 1986 *Wisconsin L. Rev.* 219 (1986) (hereinafter cited as Williams, "Algebra"); W. Washburn, *Red Man's Land/White Man's Law* 3 (New York, 1971).

10. W. Washburn, *supra* note 9, at 4–6. American Indian Policy Review Commission, *Task Force One: Trust Responsibilities and the Federal-Indian Relationship* 88–90 (Washington, D.C, 1976) (hereinafter *The Federal-Indian Relationship*). This theological law was influential only among certain Catholic heads of state. *Id.* at 89. Anti-Catholic bias led governments as well as jurists to disclaim the influence of the Spanish and the Catholic Church in the development of law as it applied to the treatment of indigenous people. *Id.* at 89.

11. W. Washburn, *supra* note 9, at 5; L. Hanke, *supra* note 8, at 25.

12. F. de Victoria, *De Indis Et De Ivre Belli Relectiones* 120, 143 (E. Nys ed.) (Washington, D.C., 1917); L. Hanke, *supra* note 8, at 25–26.
13. L. Hanke, *supra* note 8, at 11. Gonzalo Fernandez de Oviedo was among the school that believed Indians were inferior to whites, as evidenced by his statement:

> [The Indians are] naturally lazy and vicious, melancholic, cowardly, and in general a lying, shiftless people. Their marriages are not a sacrament but a sacrilege. They are idolatrous, libidinous and commit sodomy. Their chief desire is to eat, drink, worship heathen idols, and commit bestial obscenities. What could one expect from a people whose skulls are so thick and hard that the Spaniards had to take care in fighting not to strike on the head least their swords be blunted?

Id.
14. *Id.* Bartolome de Las Casas was among the "noble Indian" group, as evidenced by this statement:

> God created these simple people without evil and without guile. They are most obedient and faithful to their natural lords and to the Christians whom they serve. They are most submissive, patient, peaceful and virtuous. Nor are they quarrelsome, rancorous, querulous or vengeful. Moreover, they are more delicate than princes and die easily from work or illness. They neither possess nor desire to possess worldly wealth. Surely these people would be the most blessed in the world if only they worshipped the true God.

Id.
15. F. de Victoria, *supra* note 12, at 128.
16. *Id.* at 134.
17. *Id.* at 139; Williams, "Medieval," *supra* note 9, at 79–86.
18. F. de Victoria, *supra* note 12, at 143–44.
19. Williams, "Medieval," *supra* note 9, 92–99. Victoria's theories also received support in the papal bull of 1537 and later in the Spanish Laws of the Indies (1594), which, in turn, are part of a body of law that comes to have importance as moral force and, specifically, as provisions in treaties. See *The Federal-Indian Relationship, supra* note 10, at 90. United States federal Indian law, in turn, was influenced by this body of thought and law. *Id.* A United States Task Force has stated:

> The Spanish law and Catholic doctrines do have fundamental importance to the questions of Indian Affairs . . . partly because of

their past presence in territories which ultimately were to become part of the United States; . . . because their prior laws have relevance to rights succeeding their departure or land cessions to other nations; and because of the provisions of treaties between the various nations affecting the rights of Indian people.

Id. Cohen argued that Victoria's declaration of human rights is restated in the Northwest Ordinance. *Id.* He also writes that while Victoria was not directly cited in early opinions of the United States Supreme Court, opinions dealing with Native American property rights and sovereignty often refer to the writings of Grotius and Vattel "that are either copied or adapted from the words of Victoria." F. Cohen, *The Legal Conscience: Selected Papers of Felix S. Cohen* 248 (L. Cohen ed.) (New Haven, 1960).

20. F. Cohen, *Handbook of Federal Indian Law* 47 (Washington D.C., 1942).
21. *Id.*
22. Washburn, "The Moral and Legal Justifications for Dispossessing the Indians," in *Seventeenth-Century America* 15, 25 (J. Smith ed. Chapel Hill,1959). As early as 1684, colonial New York required approval by the governor of individual land purchases from tribal governments. Clinton & Hotopp, "Judicial Enforcement of the Federal Restraints on Alienation of Indian Land: The Origins of the Eastern Land Claims," 31 *Me. L. Rev.* 17, 21 (1979).
23. Some land deals with Native Americans who did not know the language and terms of land agreements were characterized by fraud. Competition among colonists and lack of centralized control by the Crown also resulted in overlapping claims. Government and speculators, for example, would sell land to immigrants. F. Cohen, *supra* note 20, at 47; G. Nammack, *Fraud, Politics, and the Dispossession of the Indians: The Iroquois Land Frontier in the Colonial Period* 17–18 (Norman, Okla., 1969); F. Prucha, *American Indian Policy in the Formative Years* 6 (Cambridge, Mass., 1962); W. Washburn, *supra* note 9, at 41.
24. R. Barsh & J. Henderson, *The Road: Indian Tribes and Political Liberty* 37 (Berkeley, 1980). In 1753 the Board of Trade in London began instructing certain colonial governors that they should bar future purchases of Indian land by private individuals. 1 F. Prucha, *The Great Father* 22 (Lincoln, Nebr., 1984). This order was generalized in 1761. *Id.* Preliminary steps were taken in 1755 to remove Indian affairs from the colonial governments and to centralize political control in the imperial government. *Id.* at 21. In a major effort to establish central policy for the management of Indian affairs, George III announced in 1763 a formal boundary between the British colonies and the Indian nations to the West and ordered that no warrants for

survey or patents for lands be issued beyond this line. *Id.* at 23. A year later the Board of Trade proposed a plan for the licensing of trade with the Indian nations, but the plan was never formally adopted. *Id.* at 26. See also Clinton, "The Proclamation of 1763: Colonial Prelude to Two Centuries of Federal-State Conflict over the Management of Indian Affairs," 69 *B.U. L. Rev.* 329 (1989).

25. G. Nammack, *supra* note 23, at 17. The European crowns-of-state who sought to establish colonial empires in the New World understood the potential political and military weight of the Indian nations. See G. Beer, *British Colonial Policy* 252 (New York, 1907). In the war of the French and British in 1754 and in our own revolutionary war, Indian nations were wooed by both sides as allies who could make a difference in the outcome of war.

26. Native Americans shared neither the Europeans' feudal nor common-law traditions regarding sovereignty and property. Nor had they been permitted to contribute to the development of the so-called international law of nations. The indigenous tribes had no knowledge of Victoria, Vattel, Blackstone, or Locke. But they had, with variations, legal systems of their own. For the most part, these indigenous systems of law stressed communal use of land by related people and individual use of personal property. Systems of citizenship, decision making, and leadership varied: there were small and organizationally simple tribes like the Shoshone, aggressively competitive people like the Kwakiutl, and large supernations perhaps best represented by the Iroquois League. The European value of trading land as capital was alien to Native American tribes. See generally P. Farb, *Man's Rise to Civilization As Shown by the Indians of North America From Primeval Times to the Coming of the Industrial State* 3–9 (New York, 1968) (discussing the diversity of customs, laws, and beliefs among the various Indian tribes).

27. The Continental Congress, and subsequently the government of the United States, conducted nation-to-nation diplomacy with Native American governments. Alliances were sought with certain Indian governments in the war against Great Britain. Treaties became the primary mechanism of legal relations beginning with the 1778 treaty of alliance with the Delaware Nation. See Treaty with the Delawares, September 17, 1778, United States-Delaware Indians, 7 Stat. 13; see also F. Cohen, *supra* note 20, at 47–62 (discussing a history of Indian treaties).

28. F. Prucha, *supra* note 23, at 10, 26–28.

29. R. Barsh & J. Henderson, *supra* note 24, at 32. Prucha comments that in contrast to the land purchase and trade abuses of local colonists, the concerned record of imperial officials disposed the tribes to the Crown rather than to the Continental Congress. F. Prucha, *supra* note 24, at 39–40.

30. Treaty with the Delawares, September 17, 1778, United States-Delaware Nation, 7 Stat. 13.
31. Proclamation of the Continental Congress, Sept. 22, 1783, *Journals of the Continental Congress* 24:264 and 25:602 (1922).
32. Northwest Ordinance, July 13, 1787, ch. 8, 1 Stat. 50. Specifically, article III of the Northwest Ordinance declared Indian property, rights, and liberty to be inviolate:

> The utmost good faith shall always be observed towards the Indians, their lands and property shall never be taken from them without their consent; and in their property, rights and liberty, they never shall be invaded or disturbed, unless in just and lawful wars authorised by Congress; but laws founded in justice and humanity shall from time to time be made, for preventing wrongs being done to them, and for preserving peace and friendship with them.

Id. at 52. Men like Washington, Knox, and Jefferson were instrumental in the develoment of these policies. F. Prucha, *Documents of United States Indian Policy* 1 (Lincoln, Nebr., 1975). Washington, for example, wrote to James Duane, on September 7, 1783: "I am clear in my opinion, that policy and economy point very strongly to the expediency of being upon good terms with the Indians, and the propriety of purchasing their Lands in preference to attempting to drive them by force of arms out of their Country . . . In a word there is nothing to be obtained by an Indian War but the Soil they live on and this can be had by purchase at less expence [sic], and without that bloodshed." *Id.* at 2.

33. *Federal-Indian Relationship*, *supra* note 10, at 81.
34. *Id.* at 90. Dominican Bernardino de Minaya traveled from Peru to Rome seeking Pope Paul III's support of a policy prohibiting exploitation of the Indians of the New World. W. Washburn, *supra* note 9, at 13. After Minaya's audience with the pope, the pope issued a papal bull, *Sublimis Deus*, on June 9, 1537, providing in part:

> [T]he said Indians and all other people who may later be discovered by Christians, are by no means to be deprived of their liberty or the possession of their property, even though they be outside the faith of Jesus Christ . . . nor should they be in any way enslaved; should the contrary happen it shall be null and of no effect.

Id.

35. U.S. Const., art. I, sec. 8, cl. 3.
36. Articles of Confederation, art. IX, para. 4 (1777). Article IX, paragraph 4 of the Articles of Confederation provided, in relevant part:

"The United States, in Congress assembled, shall also have the sole and exclusive right and power of regulating the . . . trade and managing all affairs with the Indians, not members of any of the States; provided that the legislative right of any State, within its own limits, be not infringed or violated."

Id. The Articles of Confederation were not ratified and in force until 1781 because Maryland had refused to ratify. F. Prucha, *supra* note 23, at 31. For importance to contemporary land claims litigation, see *Oneida v. New York*, 860 F.2d 1145 (2d Cir. 1988). (Articles of Confederation empowered New York State to make purchase of lands from the tribe without the consent of Congress.)

37. U.S. Const. art. I, sec. 8, cl. 3 and art. II, sec. 2, cl. 2.
38. Indian Trade and Intercourse Act, July 22, 1790, ch. 33, 1 Stat. 137 (codified as amended at 25 U.S.C. § 177 (1982)).
39. *Id.* at 137.
40. *Clark v. Smith*, 38 U.S. (13 Pet.) 195, 201 (1839).
41. 10 U.S. (6 Cranch) 87 (1810).
42. C. Magrath, *Yazoo – Law and Politics in the New Republic: The Case of Fletcher v. Peck* 14 (New York, 1966).
43. 1 *Democracy in America* 368–69 (New York, 1945).
44. *Fletcher v. Peck*, 10 U.S. (6 Cranch) 87, 142 (1810). For a full discussion of the history and politics of *Fletcher*, see C. Magrath, *supra* note 42, at 14.
45. C. Magrath, *supra* note 42, at 54–55. To test often complex land title, Americans had further developed the British practice of actions of ejectment with fictional adversaries. See L. Friedman, *A History of American Law* 22–23, 64–65 (2d ed. New York, 1985). These pleas were widespread in use and reflected no disrepute on the character of the parties. *Id.*
46. *Fletcher*, 10 U.S. (6 Cranch) at 127–29.
47. C. Magrath, *supra* note 42, at 53–54; see *Fletcher*, 10 U.S. (6 Cranch) at 128.
48. C. Magrath, *supra* note 42, at 53–54.
49. *Fletcher*, 10 U.S. (6 Cranch) at 139.
50. *Id.* at 139–43.
51. *Id.* at 142.
52. *Id.* at 142–43.
53. Cohen, "Original Indian Title," 32 *Minn. L. Rev.* 28, 39–40 (1947). For language of the Northwest Ordinance concerning consent, see *supra* note 32.
54. *Fletcher*, 10 U.S. (6 Cranch) at 142.
55. *Id.* at 142–43. See also Berman, "The Concept of Aboriginal Rights in the Early Legal History of the United States," 27 *Buffalo L. Rev.* 637, 649 (1978) whose careful reading of the judicial texts rejects a hierarchical ordering of the terms "absolute title" and "occupancy rights."

56. United States Comm'n on Civil Rights, *Indian Tribes: A Continuing Quest for Survival* 16 (1981) (hereinafter cited as *Indian Tribes*).
57. *Id.* Pursuant to the doctrine of discovery, unoccupied land included land not occupied by Europeans.
58. *Id.* at 16–17; see 1 W. Blackstone, *Commentaries* 107–8 (Chicago, 1979); B. De Montesquieu, *The Spirit of Laws* 281–84 (D. Carrithers ed. and trans.) (Berkeley, 1977); E. Vattel, *The Law of Nations* 98–101, 170–71 (J. Chitty ed. Philadelphia, 1883); F. De Victoria, *supra* note 12, at 120. See also Bennett, "Aboriginal Title in the Common Law: A Stony Path through Feudal Doctrine," 27 *Buffalo L. Rev.* 617, 627–34 (1978) (discussing Blackstone's interpretation of the discovery doctrine).
59. *Indian Tribes, supra* note 56, at 16.
60. *Fletcher,* 10 U.S. (6 Cranch) at 142. The Court in *Fletcher* stated, "It is the opinion of the court, that the particular land stated in the declaration appears . . . to lie within the state of Georgia, and that the state of Georgia had power to grant it." *Id.*
61. Berman, "Aboriginal Rights," *supra* note 55, at 642.
62. *Fletcher,* 10 U.S. (6 Cranch) at 142.
63. *Id.*
64. *Id.* at 142–43.
65. One hundred and fifty years after the *Fletcher* decision, a United States Task Force commented upon a central difficulty with the majority's solution:

> By *Fletcher* . . . the national government was encouraged to pursue its methods of extinguishing Indian title to lands by the process of public treaties. Georgia, on the other hand, was encouraged to regard Indian rights and property claims as being very tenuous in nature; or insufficient in force to prevent the succeeding legislative assault against them by that State in its famed controversies with the Cherokee Nation.

The Federal-Indian Relationship, supra note 10, at 75.
66. *Fletcher,* 10 U.S. (6 Cranch) at 146 (Johnson, J., dissenting).
67. *Id.* at 146.
68. *Id.* at 146–47.
69. *Id.* at 147.
70. *Fletcher,* 10 U.S. (6 Cranch) at 147 (Johnson, J., dissenting).
71. *Id.*
72. 11 U.S. (7 Cranch) 164 (1812).
73. *New Jersey v. Wilson,* 11 U.S. (7 Cranch) 164–66 (1812). The New Jersey Supreme Court determined that the act repealing tax exemption was valid and declared the land liable to taxation.
74. *Id.* at 166.

75. R. Barsh & J. Henderson, *supra* note 24, at 39.
76. 21 U.S. (8 Wheat.) 543 (1823).
77. Berman, *supra* note 55, at 655.
78. *Id.* at 650. The speeches and literature of European and early citizens of the United States were rife with expressions of racial and cultural superiority. The language of justification for the taking of Native American land drew upon Vattel and others who stressed the supremacy of the pastoral-agricultural life over that of the hunter-gatherer and who usually misunderstood or did not mention the Native Americans who created towns. See E. Vattel, *supra* note 58, at 100–01. Moreover, the Indian was portrayed as an animal and a savage. *Id.* Authors varied as to whether the Indian could be civilized. See R. Drinnon, *Facing West: The Metaphysics of Indian-Hating and Empire Building* 126–27 (Minneapolis, 1980) (referring to Indians as varmints); Brackenridge, "The Animals, Vulgarly Called Indians," in *The Indian and the White Man* 116 (W. Washburn ed. New York, 1964) (stating that the torturing Indians do to their bodies justifies their extermination); see generally R. Berkhofer, *The White Man's Indian* (New York, 1979) (discussing the various conceptions by whites of Native Americans).
79. Berman, *supra* note 55, at 643. Professor Berman argues that *Johnson* was part of an early effort to free the law of real property from the restrictions of status relationships grounded in European concepts of feudal tenures. *Id.* at 643 n. 31. Berman states: "By qualifying the issues raised in cases concerning land acquisition from Indian nations in real property terms, Marshall was able to create a law of real property that arose directly from territorial claims within the United States, which could be interpreted according to principles derived from the 'natural law' philosophy of John Locke." *Id.*
80. *Johnson*, 21 U.S. (8 Wheat.) at 550–60.
81. *Id.* at 555–58, 572.
82. *Fletcher*, 10 U.S. (6 Cranch) 87, 139–40.
83. *Johnson*, 21 U.S. (8 Wheat.) at 584.
84. *Id.* at 574.
85. *Id.* at 604–5. The plaintiffs failed in their appeal, with the Supreme Court determining that title, having been obtained by individuals without the approval of the federal government, could not be sustained in federal court.
86. *Id.* at 574.
87. Newton, "At the Whim of the Sovereign: Aboriginal Title Reconsidered," 31 *Hastings L.J.* 1215, 1223 (1980).
88. Berman, *supra* note 55, at 643.
89. *Id.* at 646. Berman argues that Marshall deliberately chose discovery doctrine over other available legal theories upon which to rest this

new law of property and diminished tribal sovereignty. He states that "[a]n extensive literature on the law of nations existed concerning the rights of non-European peoples . . . Vattel, Grotius, Puffendorf . . . [and] w[as] introduced in the pleadings of *Fletcher v. Peck* and *Johnson v. M'Intosh* to argue the validity of Indian sovereignty." *Id.*

90. W. Veeder, *Suppression of Indian Tribal Sovereignty* 14 (1973) (unpublished manuscript).

91. *Johnson*, 21 U.S. (8 Wheat.) at 574.

92. *Id.* at 592.

93. Numerous international political events as they affected the New World must have weighed on the Court as it wrote an American law of real property: the birth of several new republics in South America had caused concern about intervention in Latin America by the European Holy Alliance; French invasion of Spain in 1823 gave it access to Spain's colonial empire; the United States had only recently obtained all of Spain's holdings east of the Mississippi together with her claim to Oregon country; and Russia was pushing her trading posts from Alaska toward San Francisco Bay. S. Morison & H. Commager, 1 *The Growth of the American Republic* 452–57 (New York, 1962).

94. *Fletcher*, 10 U.S. (6 Cranch) at 142– 43; *Johnson*, 21 U.S. (8 Wheat.) at 596.

95. *Johnson*, 21 U.S. (8 Wheat.) at 587–90. Marshall wrote:

> [C]onquest gives a title which the Courts of the conqueror cannot deny . . . [the] Indians inhabiting this country were fierce savages, whose occupation was war . . . [T]o leave them in possession of their country, was to leave the country a wilderness; to govern them as a distinct people, was impossible, because . . . they were . . . ready to repel by arms every attempt on their independence. What was the consequence . . . ? The Europeans were under the necessity either of abandoning the country, . . . or of enforcing those claims by the sword.

Id. J. Youngblood Henderson argues that Marshall was, in fact, only referring to the conquest of European competitors. Henderson, "Unravelling the Riddle of Aboriginal Title," 5 *Am. Ind. L. Rev.* 75, 92 (1977).

96. Berman, *supra* note 55, at 648. Professor Jean Zorn further suggests that because it was believed that some Indian lands had been taken by conquest, Marshall did not want to imply by omission that these takings were unlawful. Communication, Jean Zorn to Jill Norgren (August 13, 1987).

97. The Monroe Doctrine, December 2, 1823. This United States proclamation occurred after months of discussion with England on the

possibility of joint action concerning instability in the New World following rapidly changing political events in France, Spain, and Portugal. The doctrine, issued only by the United States, asserted that the hemisphere was henceforth not to be newly colonized by European powers, although existing colonies of the European powers would not suffer intervention by the United States. The proclamation provided that any violation of this principle by European powers would be perceived as a danger to the peace and safety of the United States.

98. Veeder, *supra* note 90, at 17.
99. Berman, *supra* note 55, at 649. Berman, however, appears to contradict himself by an earlier statement: "[T]he reasoning of the case created a theory of conquest that stands as a *centerpiece for the judicial diminution* of native rights." *Id.* at 644 (emphasis added).
100. *Id.* at 647–49.
101. *Fletcher v. Peck*, 10 U.S. (6 Cranch) 87, 142–43; *Johnson*, 21 U.S. (8 Wheat.) at 596.
102. G. Lester, *supra* note 2, at 193, 199.
103. Berman, *supra* note 55, at 644, 647.
104. As a result of 150 years of land deals, by the beginning of the nineteenth century many of the Indian nations had moved inland and were not "visible" to the new Americans. Discussions of a new federal policy of removal of Indian nations to western lands also began in the early nineteenth century. See Monroe, First Annual Message, December 2, 1817, in 2 *A Compilation of the Messages and Papers of the Presidents* 17 (J. Richardson ed. 1897); Adams, Fourth Annual Message, December 2, 1828, *Id.* at 415–16. The national government also specifically encouraged the belief that the Indian would soon be gone from eastern lands by entering into agreements to remove tribes. In 1802, for example, the United States and Georgia signed an agreement by which Georgia would cede land for the incorporation of the states of Alabama and Mississippi in return for the promise that the United States would, at its expense, extinguish existing Indian title to land within the boundaries of Georgia as soon as it could be done on peaceful and reasonable terms. Georgia Cession, April 26, 1802, in 1 *American State Papers: Public Lands* 126 (Washington, D.C., 1832). In 1830 Congress further committed itself to a formal policy of removal passing the Indian Removal Act. See Removal Act, ch. 148, 4 Stat. 411 (1830) (codified as amended at 25 U.S.C. § 174 (1982)). The first treaty of removal followed immediately. See Treaty of Dancing Rabbit Creek, September 27, 1830, United States-Choctaw Nation, 7 Stat. 333 (1830).
105. Treaty of Holston, July 2, 1791, United States-Cherokee Indians, 7 Stat. 39.
106. Georgia Cession, April 26, 1802, in *American State Papers: Public*

Lands 126 (Washington, D.C., 1832). By this agreement Georgia ceded land for the incorporation of the states of Alabama and Mississippi. *Id.*

107. Letter from the Cherokee Council to the U.S. Treaty Commissioners, October 20, 1823 (emphasis in text). After four decades of having made "cession after cession . . . to gratify the wishes of [their] neighboring brethren," the Indians had learned that it would be "unreasonable to presume that a small cession at any time would ever satisfy" their neighbors' hunger for land. Once they fully understood that white pressure for trade or cession of their land would never end, the Indians drew the inescapable conclusion that giving in to yet another request for land would be their undoing: "Our brethren of Georgia," they told the President's treaty commission, "cannot or ought not, to desire us to destroy ourselves." M. Price, *Law and the American Indian*, 389–405 (Indianapolis, 1973). See also, 1 *The Papers of Chief John Ross*, 49–55 (G. Moulton ed. Norman, Okla., 1985).

108. See G. Woodward, *The Cherokees* 158 (Norman,Okla., 1963).

109. H. Malone, *Cherokees of the Old South* 172–73 (Athens, Ga., 1956). Act of December 20, 1828, *Acts of the General Assembly of the State of Georgia* (1829), pp. 88–89.

110. H. Malone, *supra* note 109, at 172.

111. Removal Act, ch. 148, 4 Stat. 411 (1830) (codified as amended at 25 U.S.C. § 174 (1982)).

112. F. Prucha, *supra* note 24, at 183–84. The acquisition of the vast Louisiana Purchase created space, in the minds of whites, for the removal of Indian nations east of the Mississippi. Jefferson believed Indians were genetically equal to whites but that they were what, today, would be labeled culturally deprived. C. Chinard, *Thomas Jefferson: The Apostle of Americanism* 425–27 (Ann Arbor, 1962). He favored their assimilation into Western culture: this would mean their taking up farming, which required less land than hunting and gathering. *Id.*

113. Troops were sent in June of 1830 following the proclamation by Governor Gilmer of Georgia that the state owned all Cherokee land including their gold mines. G. Foreman, *Indian Removal: The Emigration of the Five Civilized Tribes* 229–30 (Norman, Okla., 1972).

114. 7 *Cong. Deb.* app. x (1830).

115. House Comm. on Indian Affairs, *H.R. Rep. No. 227*, at 11 (1830).

116. 6 *Cong. Deb.* 1007–8 (1830).

117. *Id.* at 1008.

118. *Id.* at 1010.

119. R. Satz, *American Indian Policy in the Jacksonian Era* 40–41 (Lincoln, Nebr., 1974); Burke, "The Cherokee Cases: A Study in Law, Politics, and Morality," 21 *Stan. L. Rev.* 507–8 (1969). Most of the men

who opposed Jackson and the policy of removal were Easterners. Henry Clay from Kentucky, however, was a Westerner and leader of the Adams-Clay political faction that opposed the Democratic party led by Jackson and Calhoun. See S. Morison, *supra* note 8, at 421. Critically, the removal debate begins in the decade of the 1820s when the Jeffersonian Republican party was breaking up and men like Jackson, Clay, Webster and others competed to establish the new political parties, and vision, for the Union. See *Id.* at 422–23. Removal policy became a pawn in a discourse that is somewhat facilely characterized as the nationalist Whigs against the states' rights Democrats. *Id.* at 423–24.

120. Removal Act, ch. 148, 4 Stat. 411, 411–12 (1830) (codified as amended at 25 U.S.C. § 174 (1982)). The legislation empowered the president to create suitable districts for:

> the reception of such tribes or nations of Indians as may choose to exchange the lands where they now reside, and removal there . . . [to] forever secure and guaranty to them, and their heirs or successors, the country so exchanged with them; and if they prefer it, that the United States will cause a patent or grant to be made and executed to them for the same.

Id. The act also directed that "nothing in this act . . . shall be construed as authorizing or directing the violation of any existing treaty between the United States and any of the Indian tribes. *Id.* at 412.

121. *Id.* at 411–12. The Removal Act prescribed that land west of the Mississippi River could be designated "for the reception of such tribes or nations of Indians as may choose to exchange lands where they now reside and remove there." *Id.* at 412. The act provided that the president could authorize aid and assistance to the Indians as was necessary to enable the Indians to remove to the exchanged land and as was necessary for their support and subsistence for the first year after removal. Five hundred thousand dollars was appropriated to carry out the provisions of the act. *Id.*

122. W. Kennedy, 2 *Memoirs of the Life of William Wirt* 289 (Philadelphia, 1849).

123. *Id.*; G. Moulton, *supra* note 107, at 189–90.

124. R. Satz, *supra* note 119, at 39.

125. T. Wilkins, *Cherokee Tragedy: The Story of the Ridge Family and the Decimation of a People* 208 (Norman, Okla., 1970).

126. *Id.* at 209.

127. *Id.*

128. *Cherokee Nation v. Georgia*, 30 U.S. (5 Pet.) 1, 15 (1831).

129. *Cherokee Nation*, 30 U.S. (5 Pet.) at 17.

130. *Id.* at 16.
131. *Id.* at 19.
132. *Id.* at 16.
133. *Id.* at 19.
134. *Id.* at 20; see U.S. Const. art. III, sec. 2 (describing the extent of judicial power).
135. *Cherokee Nation*, 30 U.S. (5 Pet.) at 17–18.
136. *Id.*
137. *Id.* at 16.
138. *Id.* at 17.
139. *Id.*
140. *Id.* at 16–17.
141. *Id.* at 17–18.
142. *Id.* at 17. Marshall stated that the Indians had an unquestionable right to the lands they occupied "until that right be extinguished by voluntary cession to our government. *Id.*
143. *Id.* at 20.
144. *Id.* at 15. Williams, "Algebra" *supra* note 9, argues that Marshall's opinion in *Cherokee Nation* ignored the fact that Native American tribes had been frequent litigants in colonial New England courts since the mid-seventeenth century and that land rights and titles were the most frequent cause of the numerous judicial disputes. *Id.*, note 134 and accompanying text.
145. C. Warren, *The Supreme Court in United States History*, 726, 736 (Boston, 1926); Judiciary Act of 1789, ch. 20, § 25, 1 Stat. 73, 85–87 (describing the court's appellate jurisdiction). The Whigs opposed the repeal of Section 25 and ultimately defeated legislation proposing the change. C. Warren, *supra* at 738, 741. States' rights advocates then suggested amending the Constitution so as to limit the term of federal judges. *Id.* at 743. This, too, failed.
146. *Cherokee Nation*, 30 U.S. (5 Pet.) at 20.
147. *Id.* See also concurring opinions by Justices Baldwin and Johnson. Baldwin flatly denied that Indian tribes constituted political communities and agreed with Georgia that she properly had jurisdiction over the Cherokee and fee simple title to Cherokee lands. *Id.* at 47–50. Justice Johnson was more conciliatory than Baldwin on the question of self-governance but stopped short of accepting Marshall's "domestic, dependent nation" language. *Id.* at 21–29.
148. *Id.* at 52–64. Justice Thompson argued that the Indian tribes constituted nations by virtue of the definition of nation. That is, nations consisted of people living together as a society and governing themselves as a sovereignty. Moreover, Thompson noted that the United States had always treated them as a sovereign and independent authority. Land had been purchased by the government through treaties; yet, all remaining land not so ceded had remained in the

governance of the Indian nation. *Id.* at 53. Thompson also emphasized that the Indian nations had never been "by conquest, reduced to the situation of subject to any conqueror." *Id.* at 54. As such, Thompson reasoned that "there is as full and complete recognition of their sovereignty, as if they were the absolute owners of the soil." *Id.* at 55.

149. *Id.* at 75.

150. *Id.* at 77.

151. *Id.* at 78. Thompson stated, "The complaint is not of a mere private trespass, admitting of a compensation of damages; but of injuries which go to the total destruction of the whole right of the complainants. The mischief threatened is great and irreparable." *Id.*

152. Act of December 22, 1830, *Acts of the General Assembly of the State of Georgia* (1831), pp. 114–17.

153. G. Foreman, *supra* note 113, at 234; see *Worcester*, 31 U.S. (6 Pet.) at 538.

154. *Worcester v. Georgia*, 31 U.S. (6 Pet.) 515, 541 (1832); see Judiciary Act of 1789, ch. 20, § 25, 1 Stat. 73. In *Worcester*, as in *Cherokee Nation*, the state of Georgia failed to appear through counsel (or in any other fashion).

155. *Worcester v. Georgia*, 31 U.S. (6 Pet.) at 541.

156. *Worcester*, 31 U.S. (6 Pet.) at 562.

157. *Id.* The Court concluded that the actions by the state of Georgia were violative of the Constitution of the United States after determining thus:

> The Cherokee nation, then, is a distinct community occupying its own territory, with boundaries accurately described, in which the laws of Georgia can have no force, and which the citizens of Georgia have no right to enter, but with the assent of the Cherokees themselves, or in conformity with treaties, and with the acts of congress. The whole intercourse between the United States and this nation, is, by our constitution and laws, vested in the government of the United States.

Id. at 561.

158. *Id.* at 562.

159. G. Lester, *supra* note 2, at 200.

160. *Worcester*, 31 U.S. (6 Pet.) at 560.

161. *Id.* at 548–63.

162. *Cherokee Nation v. Georgia*, 30 U.S. (5 Pet.) at 17 (1831); *Johnson*, 21 U.S. (8 Wheat.) at 587–90.

163. *Id.*; *Worcester*, 31 U.S. (6 Pet.) at 543.

164. *Worcester*, 31 U.S. (6 Pet.) at 543. Compare *Worcester*, 31 U.S. (6 Pet.) at 543 (Court disaffirmed the discovery doctrine's independent con-

veyance of rights) with *Johnson*, 21 U.S. (8 Wheat.) at 574 (Court stated that discovery gave the discoverer the exclusive right to appropriate lands that the Indians occupied and that Indian rights in such lands were necessarily diminished by the discovery doctrine).

165. *Worcester*, 31 U.S. (6 Pet.) at 544–45.

166. *Id.* at 545.

167. *Id.* at 546.

168. *Id.*

169. *Id.* at 545–56.

170. *Id.*; *Johnson*, 21 U.S. (8 Wheat.) at 574.

171. *Worcester*, 31 U.S. (6 Pet.) at 559.

172. Treaty of Holston, July 2, 1791, United States-Cherokee Indians, 7 Stat. 39; Treaty of Hopewell, November 28, 1785, United States-Cherokee Indians, 7 Stat. 18; *Worcester*, 31 U.S. (6 Pet.) at 551–56.

173. 31 U.S. (6 Pet.) at 561.

174. *Id.* at 552.

175. *Id.*; see *Cherokee Nation*, 30 U.S. (5 Pet.) at 17; *Johnson*, 21 U.S. (8 Wheat.) at 574.

176. *Id.* at 553–54.

177. *Id.* at 554, 557. In *Worcester* the chief justice cautions the reader that documents of diplomacy between Native American governments and the United States, written in English, were ultimately controlled by whites and, thus, subject to the mischief of translation and translators. *Id.* at 547, 554, 555, 559–60.

Specifically, Marshall points out that "the words nation [and] treaty are words of our language . . . having definite and well understood meaning. We have applied them to Indians, as we have applied them to the other nations of the earth. They are applied to all in the same sense." *Id.* at 559–60.

178. *Id.* at 562.

179. *Id.* The extent to which judicial power was put on the line is reflected in the famous, perhaps apocryphal, comment by President Jackson following the reading of the opinion: "John Marshall has made his decision, now let him enforce it!" C. Warren, *supra* note 145, at 754. On the other hand, it is possible to argue that the broad, forthright support of Indian sovereignty expressed in *Worcester* was abstract and occurred because white men's rights and liberties were directly at issue. For a discussion of politics subsequent to the decision, see Norgren & Shattuck, "Limits of Legal Action: The Cherokee Cases," 2 *Am. Ind. Culture and Research J.* 20–23 (1978).

180. G. Foreman, *supra* note 113, at 235.

181. South Carolina Nullification Ordinance (November 23, 1832). South Carolina, on the sixth day of a state convention called to consider the question of what it deemed an unconstitutional federal tariff, declared the tariff null and void in that state. D. Houston, *A Critical Study of*

Nullification in South Carolina 110 (Gloucester, Mass., 1968). State officials began organizing an army to enforce the order that tariffs not be collected within its borders and threatened secession if the federal government attempted to use force. *Id.* at 113. Compromise was achieved in the spring of 1833: the tariff was reduced while, at the same time, the president was authorized to use force to collect duties. South Carolina then repealed its ordinance. *Id.* at 129–133.

182. D Houston, *supra* note 181, at 118–9 and 128–9. Burke, *supra* note 119, at 530– 31.

183. See Jill Norgren, "Lawyers for the Cherokee Nation, 1828–1835" (forthcoming).

184. See, e.g., *Mitchel v. United States*, 34 U.S. (9 Pet.) 711, 746 (1835) (concluding that Indian title was as sacred as that of the whites).

185. See, e.g., *United States v. Rogers*, 45 U.S. (4 How.) 567, 572 (1846) (stating that the native tribes had never been treated as independent nations nor regarded as owners of the territories they occupied). Sid Harring also points out that Justice McLean, who had written a concurring opinion as part of the *Worcester* majority, wrote two subsequent circuit court decisions that undermined the *Worcester* decision. S. Harring, *Crow Dog's Case: American Indian Sovereignty, Tribal Law, and American Law in the Nineteenth Century* (forthcoming).

186. Welsh, "The Needs of the Time," in *Americanizing the American Indians* 96, 96–99 (F. Prucha ed. Cambridge, Mass., 1973).

187. 34 U.S. (9 Pet.) 711, 746 (1835).

188. *Mitchel*, 34 U.S. (9 Pet.) at 746 (citing *Cherokee Nation v. Georgia*, 30 U.S. (5 Pet.) 1, 48 (1831)).

189. *Id.* In *Mitchel*, the petitioners asserted title to lands in Florida pursuant to grants from various Indian tribes of the Creek confederacy, and which grants were confirmed by Spain prior to the cession of Florida to the United States. *Id.* at 725. The Supreme Court, reversing the decision of the Superior Court of Middle Florida, confirmed Mitchel's title. *Id.* at 761–63.

190. Cohen, *supra* note 53, at 50; see Mitchel, 34 U.S. (9 Pet.) at 758–59; *Johnson*, 21 U.S. (8 Wheat.) at 588.

191. *Mitchel*, 34 U.S. (9 Pet.) at 746.

192. *Id.* at 745–46.

193. See, e.g., *Lattimer v. Poteet*, 39 U.S. (14 Pet.) 4, 14 (1840) (ultimate title in Indian land is encumbered with the right of tribal occupancy); *Clark v. Smith*, 38 U.S. (13 Pet.) 195, 201 (1839) (same).

194. *Rogers*, 45 U.S. (4 How.) at 571–72. William S. Rogers, a white man, was charged with the murder of Jacob Nicholson, also a white man, which murder was alleged to have occurred in territory occupied by Cherokee Indians. *Id.* at 571. Rogers asserted that both he and Nicholson had, prior to Nicholson's death, become citizens of the

Cherokee Nation and therefore, the United States court had no jurisdiction in the matter. *Id.* Taney's majority decision drew upon Justice Johnson's concurring opinion in *Cherokee Nation v. Georgia.*

195. *Id.* at 572.

196. *Id.* at 572–73; see Indian Trade and Intercourse Act, ch. 161, § 25, 4 Stat. 729, 733 (1834) (codified as amended at 18 U.S.C. § 1152 (1976)). The act provides, in relevant part: "[S]o much of the laws of the United States as provides for the punishment of crimes committed within any place within the sole and exclusive jurisdiction of the United States, shall be in force in the Indian country: *Provided*, the same shall not extend to crimes committed by one Indian against the person or property of another Indian."
Id. (emphasis in original). The *Rogers* court explicitly approved, for the first time, the racial implications of the Act. See Rogers, 45 U.S. (4 How.) at 573. For a discussion of federal criminal jurisdiction in Indian territory, see V. Deloria & C. Lytle, *American Indians, American Justice* 161–92 (Austin, 1983) and Clinton, "Development of Criminal Jurisdiction Over Indian Lands: The Historical Perspective," 17 *Ariz. L. Rev.* 951 (1975).

197. *Rogers*, 45 U.S. (4 How.) at 572–73.

198. *Id.* at 570.

199. *Id.* at 572–73. The Court asserted the right to establish criminal jurisdiction within Indian nations:

> [W]e think it too firmly and clearly established to admit of dispute, that the Indian tribes residing within the territorial limits of the United States are subject to their authority, and where the country occupied by them is not within the limits of one of the states, Congress may by law punish any offence committed there, no matter whether the offender be a white man or an Indian.

Id. at 572. The Court further stated that while the treaty of the United States with the Cherokees guaranteed that nation the right to make laws for its people, these laws "shall not be inconsistent with the Constitution of the United States [or] acts of Congress . . . regulating trade and intercourse with the Indians." *Id.* at 573.

200. *Rogers*, 45 U.S. (4 How.) at 573.

201. Newton, *supra* note 4, at 211; *Rogers* 45 U.S. (4 How.) at 573. Harring states that *Rogers* "did not impair the sovereignty of Indian tribes by forbidding such adoptions. Rather they held concurrent jurisdiction: the United States did not give up its jurisdiction over its citizens when they chose to become adopted into an Indian tribe." S. Harring, *supra* note 185, at 82. To the extent that Harring's interpretation does not understand *Rogers* as a significant judicial attempt to undercut the tribal sovereignty sanctioned in the Cherokee

cases, it is at odds with Newton's.

202. *Rogers*, 45 U.S. (4 How.) at 573. The Court invoked political question doctrine as a barrier to judicial examination of the federal government's assertion of sovereignty over tribal governments, stating that the sovereignty question is one "for the law-making and political department of the government, and not for the judicial." *Id.* at 572. In federal Indian law, the weak sovereignty line of cases [from *U.S. v. Kagama* 118 U.S. 375 (1886) to *Oliphant v. Suquamish Indian Tribe* 435 U.S. 191 (1978), and beyond] is generally observed to work from *Rogers*.

203. F. Cohen, *supra* note 20, at 92. U.S. Const. art. I, sec. 8.

204. U.S. Const. art IV, sec. 3, cl. 2.

205. 70 U.S. (3 Wall.) 407, 416 (1865). *Holliday* involved a challenge to United States's interpretation of commerce power, as applied in the Trade and Intercourse Act, that included the right to regulate the sale of liquor to individual Indians, off the reservation as well as on it. *Id.*; Indian Trade and Intercourse Act, ch. 161, § 4 Stat. 729, 729, 732, 733 (1834).

206. 93 U.S. 188, 194 (1876). In this case the United States sought a declaration of forfeiture for spirituous liquor introduced into Chippewa Indian territory in violation of Section 20 of the Indian Trade and Intercourse Act of 1864. *Id.* at 189; see Indian Trade and Intercourse Act, ch. 161, § 20, 4 Stat. 29, 29 (1864) (imposing penalty for disposing of liquors to Indians).

207. *Forty Three Gallons of Whiskey*, 93 U.S. at 195; *Holliday*, 70 U.S. (3 Wall.) at 418.

208. *Forty Three Gallons of Whiskey*, 93 U.S. at 195.

209. D. Getches, D. Rosenfelt, & C. Wilkinson, *Cases and Materials on Federal Indian Law* 183 (St. Paul, 1979).

210. See Indian Trade and Intercourse Act, ch. 161, 4 Stat. 729 (1834) (regulating trade with Indian tribes).

211. F. Cohen, *supra* note 20, at 91 (citing *H. R. Rep. No. 474*, 23rd C. 1st Sess. 103 (1834) (report from the committee of Indian Affairs)).

212. 77 U.S. (10 Wall.) 321, 326 (1870) (Congress was entitled to "safeguard [Indian reserves] against their own improvidence," a power that included the imposition of a restriction on the individual Indian's right of alienation).

213. See, e.g., *The Kansas Indians*, 72 U.S. (5 Wall.) 737, 757 (1866) (determining that Indians are under the protection of treaties and the laws of Congress and that Indian property is withdrawn from the operation of state laws); *Rogers*, 45 U.S. (4 How.) at 572 (stating that Indians had never been acknowledged or treated as independent nations, nor regarded as owners of territory they occupied).

214. See, e.g., *Kansas Indians*, 72 U.S. (5 Wall.) at 757 (determining that Indians are protected by the treaties and laws of Congress); *Fellows v.*

Blacksmith, 60 U.S. (19 How.) 366, 371–72 (1856) (same).

215. 78 U.S. (11 Wall.) 616, 621 (1870). In *Cherokee Tobacco*, the Court addressed the issue of whether Congress had the intent and power, pursuant to the Internal Revenue Act of 1868, to tax tobacco and tobacco products manufactured by citizens of the Cherokee Nation and sold within its boundaries, in the face of a 1866 treaty between the United States and the Cherokee Nation agreeing that such tobacco should be exempt from taxation; and whether, therefore, the seizure of defendants' tobacco in lieu of payment of taxes was legal. *Id.*

216. *Id.*

217. *Id.*; *Cherokee Nation*, 30 U.S. (5 Pet.) at 17.

218. *Cherokee Tobacco*, at 622 (Brady & Davis, J.J., dissenting). In the same period, the Court continued to reject the encroachment of state power upon Native American tribes. See, e.g., *The Kansas Indians*, 72 U.S. (5 Wall.) at 756, 759–61 (rejecting, as prohibited by treaty, efforts by the state of Kansas to tax tribes, while at the same time ruling that the federal taxing of Indians was approved).

219. See *Holden v. Joy*, 84 U.S. (17 Wall.) 211, 252–53 (1872) (rejecting the contention that land grants from the United States superseded title based upon Indian treaty); *Chouteau v. Molony*, 57 U.S. (16 How.) 203, 239 (1853) (same); *Mitchel*, 34 U.S. (9 Pet.) at 746–47 (same). In *Chouteau*, an ejectment action was brought by Chouteau, a Missouri citizen, to recover a large tract of land including the city of Dubuque, title of which he claimed traced back to grants from the Fox Indians. *Chouteau*, 57 U.S. (16 How.) at 221. Molony claimed the land under a patent from the United States. *Id.*

220. 84 U.S. (17 Wall.) 211, 244 (1872). *Holden* involved a challenge to the validity of a land grant pursuant to treaty to Joy, a Cherokee Indian. *Id.* at 221–22.

221. See *United States v. Cook*, 86 U.S. (19 Wall.) 591, 594 (1873). In *Cook* an action of replevin by the United States against the non-Indian, Cook, to recover possession of logs sold to Cook by reservation Indians was challenged on the grounds that tribal right to occupancy includes the right to sell as well as to make incidental use of land's resources. *Id.* at 592.

222. *Id.* at 593.

223. *Id.*

224. *Id.*; see *Mitchel v. United States*, 34 U.S. (9 Pet.) 711, 745 (1835) (stating that "Indians were protected in the possession of the lands they occupied, and were considered as owning them by a perpetual right of possession . . . from generation to generation, not as the right of individuals located on particular spots.")

225. *Cook*, 86 U.S. (19 Wall.) at 594.

226. *Id.* In 1889, Congress enacted legislation authorizing the sale of dead wood on Indian reservations, by the members of the tribe, when

approved by the president. Act approved February 16, 1889, ch. 172, 25 Stat. 673 (codified as amended at 25 U.S.C. § 196 (1982)).

227. See *Cook*, 86 U.S. (19 Wall.) at 594. *Cook* left several questions unsettled, including whether, in recovering the timber or its money value, the United States was to hold such capital in trust for the Indian tribe concerned or whether it rightfully accrued to the general treasury of the United States. F. Cohen, *supra* note 20, at 314. Only in 1911 did an opinion of the attorney general determine that occupants of executive order reservations were entitled to the proceeds of timber sales. *Id.*; 29 *Op. Att'y Gen.* 239, 240, 244 (1911).

228. See, e.g., *Oliphant v. Suquamish Indian Tribe*, 435 U.S. 191, 207 (1978) (citing *Worcester v. Georgia*, 31 U.S. (6 Pet.) 515, 555 (1832), for the principle that Indian nations are necessarily dependent on the United States for protection from lawless and injurious intrusions into their territory).

229. See, e.g., *Tee-Hit-Ton Indians v. United States*, 348 U.S. 272, 279–80 (1955) (citing *Johnson v. M'Intosh*, 21 U.S. (8 Wheat.) 543 (1823) for the principle that the United States by discovery and conquest had sovereignty over and ownership of Indian lands). Not only the same court, but the same justice, wrote the opinions in *Worcester* and *Johnson* yielding these original principles of federal Indian law. See *Worcester v. Georgia*, 31 U.S. (6 Pet.) 515 (1832); *Johnson v. M'Intosh*, 21 U.S. (8 Wheat.) 543 (1823). It can be argued, therefore, that when the same issues of Indian sovereignty or Indian title are addressed, the discussion in the last opinion, *Worcester*, should be authoritative. This is specifically supported by the significant modifications of *Johnson* in *Cherokee Nation* and, in particular, *Worcester*. See Berman, *supra* note 55, at 643.

230. See, e.g., *United States v. Kagama*, 118 U.S. 375, 384–85 (1886). In *Kagama*, tribal members challenged the constitutionality of extending United States jurisdiction to Indian nations in the case of a major crime. *Id.* at 375–76. The Court upheld the law, determining that tribes are only semi-independent and are not nations. The Court stated: "Indian tribes *are* wards of the nation. They are communities *dependent* on the United States [for protection from their weakness]." *Id.* at 383–84 (emphasis in original).

The right of Indian nations to self-government, including but not limited to criminal jurisdiction, can be abrogated by a higher sovereignty. *Lone Wolf v. Hitchcock*, 187 U.S. 553, 567–68 (1903) (articulating the Supreme Court's acceptance of the diminution of tribal rights in the name of guardianship: the plenary power of Congress is not subject to judicial review; Congress may abrogate treaties with tribes as their guardian). *Lone Wolf* involved a suit brought by the claimant to enjoin implementation of United States legislation transferring title to 2.5 million acres of "excess" Kiowa, Comanche, and

Apache land to itself. *Id.* at 560, 564. Lone Wolf argued that transfer could only occur, under terms of an 1867 treaty, with the consent of three-fourths of adult males of the tribe and that the failure to obtain this number violated the treaty's consent requirement and due process of law. *Id.* at 563–64. *Lone Wolf* has been called the Indians' *Dred Scott. Sioux Nation v. United States*, 601 F.2d 1157, 1173 (Ct. Cl. 1979) (Nichols, J., concurring), aff'd, 448 U.S. 371 (1980). See also, e.g., *Stephens v. Cherokee Nation*, 174 U.S. 445, 478 (1899) (affording the Supreme Court the opportunity to assert that the plenary power of Congress derived from the Indians' condition of dependency in a case involving an application for, and review of, Cherokee citizenship as part of an allotment proceeding by claimant whose parents were not Cherokee at the time of his birth; *McBratney v. United States*, 104 U.S. 621, 624 (1882) (upholding state jurisdiction over the murder of a non-Indian by a non-Indian within an Indian nation.)

2

Nineteenth-Century "Friends of the Indian" and the Rule of Law: Limits on the Use of Raw Power

The Spaniards pursued the Indians with bloodhounds, like wild beasts; they sacked the New World like a city taken by storm, with no discernment or compassion. . . . The conduct of the Americans of the United States towards the aborigines is characterized, on the other hand, by a singular attachment to the formalities of law. [They pursued Indian extinction and deprivation of rights] with a singular felicity, tranquilly, legally, philanthropically, without shedding blood, and without violating a single great principle of morality in the eyes of the world. It is impossible to destroy men with more respect for the laws of humanity.

Alexis de Tocqueville[1]

Introduction

The sharply contradictory results of federal Indian law reflect the lasting conflict of economic and political pressures to take Indian land, resources, and sovereignty against the struggle of Native Americans to protect the guarantees of original legal doctrine. At no time was this conflict sharper and more open than during the second half of the nineteenth century. By then Native Americans were portrayed as in most everybody's way, and they had lost much of the force they once had to resist the relentless pressure to give up what land remained theirs. As white civilization was spreading across the entire continent and "white men were crowding upon, surrounding and coveting Indian land," the most expedient mechanism for dealing with the "evils" of the Indian presence – "the crude and simple process of removing the Indian tribes to remote regions" – was no longer viable.[2] An anachronistic presence to most whites, Native Americans seemed destined to disappear.

For most citizens of the United States neither moral nor prudential arguments dictated the defense of the rights of this "vanishing race." To the contrary, scientific notions of the natural inferiority of the natives served to buttress arguments about the economic and political necessity of freeing the nation of a people so obstinately unfit to participate in progress. To a majority imbued with the mission of "manifest destiny," sure of its economic and social premises, and confident of its power, legal and moral arguments for the protection of Indian rights were implausible.

The argument for Indian rights was a compelling one, nevertheless, and it was made by the "friends of the American Indian," whose reform influence in the formulation – and reformulation – of Indian policy throughout the second half of the nineteenth century was far-reaching.[3] Against the driving forces of economic expansion and racial superiority, the argument against the wholesale abandonment of the protections of the law and human decency was made by law professors, leaders of the Bar, church leaders, and some members of Congress who prided themselves on their good deeds and attitudes toward their Indian friends. In this struggle, these men and women sought to maintain the autonomy and integrity of American legal and moral institutions. It was the argument of men like John Beeson, Episcopal bishop Henry Whipple, editor-minister Lyman Abbott, and of the Boston Citizenship Committee, the Philadelphia-based Indian Rights Committee, the Women's National Indian Association, the National Indian Defense Association, the Board of Indian Commissioners, and the Lake Mohonk Conference, among others, that linked adherence to principles of legal rationality and morality with the pragmatic needs of manifest destiny. Their debate proved a forceful and convincing counterpoint to the popular clamor for the abrogation of the legal and moral commitments of the past.

These reformers believed that upholding the principles of the rule of law, including principles of federal Indian law, would serve a larger political interest in the long run. Formal legal principles demanded independence of the law from crass and aggressive manipulation – without it the claim of law to universal validity would be undermined.[4] If powerful economic and political interests could openly prevail over legal principles guaranteeing the rights of weaker and smaller groups, the law's promise of justice and procedural fairness would be negated, its demand for obedience denied.

Legal autonomy was essential to the rapid extension of American jurisdiction over vast new geographic areas settled by an exploding

population of frontiersmen and farmers, fortune seekers and speculators, some of whom were recent immigrants, others Indians,
who had not yet been in contact with the United States.[5] Nothing
was more instrumental to the establishment of order and control
over a society in such flux than laws that could base their claim to
universal obedience on their demonstrated ability to withstand
special interests. A legal system openly catering to the needs of the
most powerful – or, conversely, openly permitting the dispossess-
sion of the least powerful – could not fulfill that vital function. And
such a system certainly would not convince the growing and
diverse population of the West – who were neither uniformly
accustomed to, nor convinced of, the benefits of obedience to law –
that law should be an indispensable part of the expansion and
establishment of American rule.[6]

From this perspective adherence to the original legal principles
defining Indian sovereignty and property rights and a growing
concern for individual Indian rights was an indispensable part of the
larger goal of guarding the legitimacy of American law, for it
demonstrated the adherence of the legal system to its own founding
principles and premises. It was this commitment – ideological and
programmatic – to legal norms and principles imbedded in the
Declaration of Independence and the Bill of Rights that imposed
limits on the political urge to proceed with the wholesale expropriation of Indian land and the destruction of Indian tribes. Where
much of the eighteenth century had been devoted to the military
and political work of becoming a republic, the nineteenth century
presented a crucible of another kind – one in which the people of
the United States sought to define, in terms more precise than those
written in their formal political documents, the working rules of
social relations.

It was a perspective also impelled by basic tenets of Protestantism
that stressed social commitment and reclamation. Two hundred
years of religious community in the New World complemented the
nineteenth-century reformers' faith in law and influenced their
work on behalf of the Indian. The earlier building of the Puritan's
earthly Holy Commonwealth rested upon a corporate spirit of
social contract and social ethics as well as individualism.[7] This
belief led to a calculus of conversion and incorporation of the
Indian. Even earlier than the foundation of rights and law established in the Declaration of Independence and the Constitution,
seventeenth-century Puritans built a moral house in which there
could be room for the native, albeit Christianized, American.

The twin strains of individual perfectability and social concern were brought forward into the eighteenth century, in particular, by the Quakers. In William Penn's famous colony, theological and worldly goals intertwined in optimistic belief that everything from personal behavior to national politics could be acted upon by the application of a perfectionist moral code. In New England, too, acculturation of Indians found expression in liberal Protestantism. Dartmouth College was chartered in 1769 "for civilizing, and Christianizing, and instructing the Indian natives of this land."[8] As the first half of the nineteenth century unfolded, Unitarians, Quakers, Transcendentalists, Evangelicals, and those identified with the "Second Great Awakening" in New England extended this vision of a more perfect America inclusive of Indians. Weaving concern for legal principles with theology, interdenominational and nondenominational organizations emerged that became influential advocates of Indian reform policy. It can be argued that this zeal for conversion and constitutionalism saved Native Americans from facing only policies of extinction. The drive across the continent, the reformers argued, had to be governed by the higher law of liberal constitutionalism and the higher purpose of a secular City on the Hill.

As the nineteenth century progressed, however, the reformers' argument for the protection of Indian rights turned increasingly into a legal and moral argument against the wholesale abrogation of original legal principles guaranteeing Indian sovereignty and land. What mattered was not the protection of Indian rights per se but the maintenance of the framework of legality. Large scale and systematic violation of legal principles had to be prevented not because it "wronged" the Indian – whose assimilation, they felt, would be promoted in any case by separating him from his communal landbase and tribal culture – but because it threatened the secular and religious prophecy of the United States as the model nation. This distinction was crucial for it permitted the satisfaction of the political and economic demands for Indian land as long as it could be done within the confines of the rule of law. It left room for a compromise between the conflicting needs of Indian policy – adherence to standards of legal and moral formalities and the demand for the dispossession of the Indian.

Providing "proper" rationalizations for the taking of Indian land in the second half of the nineteenth century was of more than ephemeral importance. For while it mattered little to the Indian whether tribal land was taken in the name of high-minded concern for welfare and progress or in open contempt of rights, the legality and morality of the United States's program of action mattered a great deal to the reformers. The moral and legal justification for policy was to set the reformers' civilizing program apart from what they considered merely greedy land grabbing at the frontier. The legality of the new course of American Indian policy was essential because otherwise the seizure of tribal land in violation of established law and treaty guarantees was no more than expropriation. Accepting this new policy transformed the taking of the land of the Sioux, the Comanche, the Ponca, or the Apache from a "lawless" deal to lawful real-estate transactions.[9]

The adaptation of original legal principles and moral perspectives to political needs in the last quarter of the nineteenth century accomplished the twin goals of transferring vast land areas – 100 million acres – from Indian to white possession and, importantly, of doing so, the reformers felt, without the direct abrogation of the founding principles of federal Indian law.[10] As described by de Tocqueville, tranquilly, legally, and philanthropically the work of the reformers, along with others, led to the loss of tribal land and the destruction of tribal government.

The Time Has Come for Them to Live among Us

The late nineteenth-century transformation of the original principles of federal Indian law occurred as part of a longstanding debate in the United States over the future of relations with Native Americans. Early in the nineteenth century national officials had been consumed with argument over the desirability and legality of an Indian removal policy. With the crush of whites at the frontier, a removal policy proved inadequate; midcentury the United States pressed a formal policy of reservations upon tribes. Reserves were to provide a means of isolating Indians from the base and violent elements of white society while "good people from Christian missions could teach an appreciation for agriculture, manufacture, and the English language."[11]

Quickly, however, officials and reformers realized these controlled environments could not withstand the pressures of manifest destiny. They were too much in the way of the "march of progress." Reluctantly, the reformers admitted the limitations of a reservation system. It was at this point, less than a decade after the American Civil War, that the reformers began to consider a more concrete program of Indian assimilation to be built upon a policy of allotment of tribal land into individually owned parcels.[12]

During the American Civil War questions of Indian rights remained in shadow. During these years, Beeson and Whipple, among others, wrote and spoke extensively about the negative effects of white contact on western tribes. They described chaos on the frontier and argued that it could be mitigated by giving Native Americans the advantages of law, by which they meant the extension of United States civil and criminal jurisdiction to Indian nations.[13] For most of the reformers, the issue was more complex and far-reaching than resolving disorder on the frontier. To these men and women, the absence of Anglo-American law meant Native Americans were without a fundamental value – gift – of western civilization. Lacking an understanding of, or respect for, indigenous systems of social control and conflict mediation, many reformers incorrectly depicted Native Americans as lawless people in their own cultures, who (despite treaties) also held an unprotected status with respect to the United States.

The reformers were sufficiently persuasive for their arguments to reach President Lincoln, who reportedly told Beeson: "I have heard your arguments time and again. I have said little but thought much, and you may rest assured that as soon as the pressing matters of this war is (sic) settled the Indians shall have my first care."[14] Assassinated within days of Lee's surrender, the president could not make good on his promise. Nevertheless, the ever-increasing contact between Indians and whites and the Fourteenth Amendment ratification debates made it possible for the reformers and members of the Bureau of Indian Affairs (BIA) to bring attention to what they termed the inchoate legal and political status of the Indian. They described, for example, custom and law barring Native Americans from making legally binding contracts with whites or from giving testimony and bringing lawsuits in federal courts.[15] They identified the extension of United States criminal jurisdiction to reservations as an imperative.

Central to this postwar discussion of formal legal status was the question of the Indian under the Fourteenth Amendment. To the friends of the American Indian fairness demanded that Native Americans be given the rights of political citizenship if they were to be brought under the laws of the United States. But the complexity of the initiative was quickly exposed after it was argued that the acceptance of citizenship by Native Americans would undercut rights and privileges flowing to tribes as sovereignties. Moreover, numerous Indian leaders opposed the extension of the Fourteenth Amendment to their people. They questioned white motives for the proposal, fearing the loss of inalienable tribal land rights and tribal annuities.[16] They also reminded Congress that Native

Americans were already citizens of their own nations.

Ignoring these objections, reformers pushed legislators to consider the amendment's application to Native Americans. The first of a number of Indian citizenship bills was introduced in Congress in 1873. Extensive disagreement over the conditions of citizenship, particularly whether Native Americans would have to give up tribal life, marked debate over these early initiatives. Acknowledging original principles of federal Indian law, some proposals would have granted citizenship to Native Americans while continuing tribal annuity payments and certifying inalienable land status. Opponents of this approach, however, successfully argued that a policy granting Native Americans United States citizenship *and* a special status was ill-conceived.

Throughout the 1870s, congressional debate continued on an Indian citizenship bill, along with land allotment legislation and laws that would extend United States criminal jurisdiction over Indians. For a variety of reasons, the proposals were premature and the legislature never completed action. Several publicized incidents of the late 1870s and early 1880s, however, permitted the BIA and the reformers to refocus attention on citizenship, land allotment, and jurisdiction policy. One of these incidents was the arrest, in 1879, of the Ponca chief Standing Bear.

The Trial of Chief Standing Bear

In 1865 the Ponca agreed by treaty to remove to land that the United States subsequently also signed over to the Sioux Nation.[17] Both the Ponca and the United States sought solutions to this American folly, but by 1875 a satisfactory policy continued to elude both governments. The United States, through the executive branch, then decided – without consulting the Ponca – that the tribe would do best to leave the Northern Plains altogether and to move south to Indian Territory. A year later Congress lent its approval by appropriating twenty-five thousand dollars for their removal and resettlement.[18] On the Ponca side there was no enthusiasm for the move, and in an effort to block forced removal, the Ponca countered by hiring local attorney Solomon Draper to assert Ponca treaty rights. Local whites also petitioned Washington to leave the peaceful and neighborly Ponca where they were. All efforts were rebuffed, however, with the firm statement that United States policy was fixed and that the Ponca must move south. Ignoring the provision requiring Ponca consent prior to removal, the United

States army was brought in to carry out the order.[19]

Ponca chief Standing Bear had been an outspoken opponent of the plan and had been imprisoned briefly by the army prior to the march south because of his criticism. The forced resettlement took place, however, followed almost immediately by a deadly outbreak of malaria. Standing Bear became convinced that his people would be crushed if they remained on the unwanted, inhospitable, malarial land. Despite the intention of the United States to keep the Ponca where they were, Standing Bear set off north with two dozen followers, journeying for ten weeks in brutal weather toward the territory of allies, the Omaha. The Omaha gave Standing Bear's band land, tools, and seed, and the survivors took up life, within the jurisdiction of the Omaha tribe, as farmers. But in March of 1879, in yet another show of strength, Secretary of the Interior Carl Schurz ordered that the "runaways" be taken into military custody at Fort Omaha and returned to Indian Territory by the army.

Shortly after the arrest of Standing Bear and his band, Omaha newspaperman Thomas Tibbles heard of the Ponca's troubles and traveled to the Fort Omaha brigade hoping for an interview.[20] His immediate involvement with the cause of the Ponca led him to devise a strategy of public appeals for their release. After five days, however, he decided that appeals alone would be insufficient and concluded that only through a test case in a court of law could it be determined whether Native Americans possessed rights of personal liberty that had to be respected by the United States.

Tibbles recruited two prominent Omaha attorneys, Andrew J. Poppleton and John L. Webster, to take on the Ponca's legal defense.[21] Why the attorneys agreed to act as counsel, with no promise of fees, is revealed in Webster's communications to Tibbles: "This is a question of vast importance. A petition for such a writ [habeas corpus] must be based upon broad constitutional grounds, and the questions involved in it underlie all personal liberty. It is a question of the natural rights of men, such as was discussed by the fathers and founders of this government. I am not convinced that a writ would hold, on account of the peculiar relation of Indians to the government. They have always been treated as 'wards,' as incapable of making contracts, etc., but it will do no harm to try." Reflecting upon his hopes for a court free from political influence, Webster concluded by telling Tibbles that "there ought to be power somewhere to stop this inhuman cruelty, and if it does not reside in the courts where shall we find it?"[22]

Poppleton, a lawyer for the railroads, thought the Ponca had a good case. At an early meeting with Tibbles, Poppleton argued that "we can make the writ hold. It is true that the Indians have been held by the courts as 'wards of the nation,' . . . but it does not follow from that, that the guardian can imprison, starve or practice inhuman cruelty upon the ward. The courts always have, and always will interfere in such cases."[23] On April 4, 1879, the lawyers filed an application for a writ of habeas corpus on behalf of Standing Bear and the twenty-five other Ponca, arguing that the Indians had been illegally "imprisoned . . . and restrained of their liberty."[24]

Prior to the arrest of the Ponca, it was an unsettled question whether Native Americans were *persons* under federal law entitled to bring suit in courts of the United States. Such was the anomolous legal status of the Indian. As a result, lawyers could not say if, for *these* people, an American court would even entertain a petition for that most basic of Anglo-American rights: habeas corpus. For the nineteenth-century reformers so wedded to norms of formal legality and convinced that being "civilized" relied upon holding the rights and obligations of Anglo-American law, no issue could have been more basic to their cause, no legal case better suited to their growing campaign to "bring law to the Indian." Whipped up by Tibbles, the case of the imprisoned Ponca excited and mobilized them: In a court of law a wrong against the Indian could be righted. The Ponca could win their freedom from the army. But more important, there was an opportunity to establish binding legal precedents establishing the authority of liberal legal standards where Indians were concerned.

Federal district court judge Elmer Dundy scheduled the case for April 30, 1879. The atmosphere of the trial court was charged. Tibbles had created extensive publicity through his newspaper articles, notice that included the aggressive stance to be taken by the district attorney, Genio Lamberton. At the start of proceedings Lambertson showed his hand by attempting to block the testimony of Chief Standing Bear: "Does this court think an Indian is a competent witness?"[25] Judge Dundy did. He went on to rule that the Ponca were persons under federal law and ordered their release.[26] Considered by physical result, *United States ex. rel Standing Bear v. Crook* represented a resounding victory for the Indians and a significant clarification of Indian legal status: the Ponca were free; habeas corpus was a right Native Americans could claim under United States law. Nevertheless, much of the oral argument, as well as Judge Dundy's opinion, clearly supported extensive federal power over Indians by accepting the desirability of Native American assimilation and by dismissing the importance of Indian cultural autonomy or tribal sovereignty.

Standing Bear ordered that the army release the Ponca, but the decision also asserted the "almost unlimited power" of the executive branch over anyone in the Indian country without the authority of United States law. According to Judge Dundy, the United States could make laws "for the government of the Indian country including the power to restrict, with 'necessary force' by the military where required, access of whites and Indians to reservations."[27] Standing Bear had obtained his freedom, not because the court recognized the right of the Omaha Nation to have the Ponca in its country, but because Dundy found that procedural due process had been violated. While the army had correctly exercised powers in removing Standing Bear from the Omaha reservation, it had failed to turn him over to civil authorities.[28]

As with Dundy's opinion, the legal strategy adopted by Webster and Poppleton similarly suggests that the attorneys' priority centered upon an affirmation of the fundamental principles of Anglo-American law rather than the original guarantees of federal Indian law. Their concern was with liberal law and personal liberty, not tribal sovereignty. Although the cause of the conflict involved the Ponca nation's loss of its tribal land and the subsequent decision of one part of the tribe to join Chief Standing Bear in his rejection of the inadequate, malarial "homeland," Webster and Poppleton framed the appeal solely as one of individual rights. They emphasized rights owed to Standing Bear as a person who had "withdrawn from the tribe . . . completely severed tribal relations . . . and had adopted the general habits of whites."[29] During the trial, the lawyers went to extreme lengths, stretching Standing Bear's words, to draw the picture of a man committed to white teachings about agriculture, Christianity, and democratic authority.

Dundy's opinion accepts and works out of the structure set up by the Ponca's attorneys. The text of his opinion addresses questions of individual rights and liberties and avoids the issue of tribal prerogatives. Along with the lawyers, Dundy sidesteps discussion of Ponca nationality. He discusses treaties but describes the Ponca as wards rather than co-nationals and specifically calls them "natives of our own country."[30] Moreover, in order to order Standing Bear's release and also to support his right to leave the Indian country permanently, Judge Dundy asserts that Indians as well as whites hold the right of expatriation. Standing Bear could not be forced back to Indian Territory by the United States because "the individual Indian possesses the clear and God-given right to withdraw from his tribe and forever live away from it, as though it had no further existence."[31] For the record, Dundy represents Standing Bear's group as ready to disband and to "civilize," although the actual record – which Dundy acknowledged – showed them to have been traveling north on a "procession homeward" ready to "brave every peril to return and live and die where they had been reared."[32]

The fiction that Standing Bear wished to be an expatriot in the United States and repeated statements by Thomas Tibbles on behalf of the reform-focused Omaha Committee indicate support by the court and the reformers for policies of allotment and assimilation. Thus, while not openly advocating the violation of tribal sovereignty and occupancy rights, reformers associated with Tibbles did not believe in, or argue on behalf of, the viability of Indian sovereignty or the desirability of Indian culture and communal landholding. The legal norms argued by the Ponca's lawyers did not demand that all Indians end tribal relations or that all tribal organization cease. Yet the rights sought by, and granted to, Standing Bear center on the liberty of the individual. Consciously or not, by fighting to extend liberal law to Standing Bear, the Omaha Committee aided the move away from original principles guaranteeing tribal sovereignty and land rights. This lapse was difficult to see in the midst of the reformers' crusade for justice. Surely, at the end of the Ponca trial, few Americans knew or cared that given the nature of the Dundy decision, it was now legally uncertain whether Standing Bear – no longer a "tribal" Indian – could return to the Ponca reservation without being arrested by the United States for entering without a permit. Standing Bear had declared the law a "better way," but this was at the price of having his lawyers declare him acculturated and willing to live by American law. The trial of Chief Standing Bear was a watershed. While it satisfied the norm of law over power, liberty over capricious politics, the legal strategy employed in the case and Judge Dundy's opinion demonstrate that, increasingly, the price to Indians for being saved from injustice would be both the recognition that the United States government could exercise extensive power over tribes and acculturation.

They Must Have Law, But . . .

In the early 1880s, the work of the Indian friends increasingly impelled them toward doctrinal schizophrenia: they deplored the violation of tribal treaty rights but at the same time believed that the Indian could avoid extinction only by individual assimilation. As a result they argued that ways had to be found to alter binding legal commitments guaranteeing political and cultural autonomy so that the Indian could be "saved." Documents of leading reformist organizations demonstrate this thinking. Members of the Philadelphia-based Indian Rights Association, for example, reported that "regarding the question of legal protection . . . certain of the laws of the States and Territories, in which reservations exist, should be extended over such reservations, and . . . ultimately all laws of said States and Territories should be enforced upon these Indian reservations, so that the Indians finally should exist not as a separate and distinct people, but should become part of our own nationality." The reformers imagined these proposals to be the contribution of "good men and women throughout the country who believe in pure government, in equality of rights, in mercy towards the helpless, in individual responsibility, and in God."[33]

For the reformers, liberal law was linked critically to the success of a policy of land allotment in severalty and the cultural grafting of the Protestant work ethic. William J. Harsha, a writer favored by the eastern reformers, hammered at this theme in an 1882 *North American Review* article. Only the naive, Harsha argued, could fail to see that the Indians were discouraged from attempts at self-support by the lack of legal protection. As wards of the United States, the law forbade them from making contracts or collecting wages by suit at law. Policies meant to educate the Indian, to "teach them to work," and to allot tribal land were meaningless – indeed, invidious – if he were not also made a person before the law. Without legal rights, these programs were no more than "pretentious form," for "Big Snake or Two Crow could as easily be put off a quarter section as the tribe off a reservation." "So long as white depredation goes on unchecked by legal protection," Harsha concluded, "toil can surely never be 'profitable'."[34] In the most basic sense, protections of the law finally would mean protection of property.

Yet Harsha also believed in laws that would treat Native Americans unequally: "Granting to Indians the protection of law does not necessarily imply making them citizens at once . . . that they should immediately be endowed with full citizenship. They may have a part of this great privilege without the whole."[35] Part, without the whole – this was the position of most of the reformist community in the years immediately following the trial of Standing Bear. In light of reformist zeal for legal protection and the previous grant of voting rights to former slaves, it amounted to a rather curious position – one that advocated a period of tutelage for Indians quite different from the legal and political treatment of blacks. The theory of the Fourteenth and Fifteenth Amendments expressed an immediate and full incorporation of blacks into the American political community. Indeed, in 1883, only two decades after the Emancipation Proclamation, a smug Supreme Court argued that blacks must take "the rank of mere citizen" and cease "to be the special favorite of the laws."[36] And in the same period, it was not uncommon for white resident alien males to be granted voting rights although they were not yet citizens.[37]

Henry S. Pancoast of the Indian Rights Association (IRA) also opposed immediate citizenship asserting "the idea of declaring all Indians citizens at once, without warning or preparation, is crude and unpractical." He rationalized that the mistakes of two hundred years could not be cancelled by a "dozen lines upon a statute book."[38] General George Crook, commanding officer at the arrest of Standing Bear, in a letter to the IRA in support of an allotment policy, also wrote approvingly of delayed suffrage rights: " . . . at some time, as a matter of justice, we should place in his hands his best weapon of defense – the ballot."[39] The sentiment was echoed in the annual report of the IRA. After describing its efforts to "make the Indian in some way accountable under our law" by drafting a criminal jurisdiction act for reservations, association officers acknowledged that at some unspecified moment Indians "should be able to avail themselves of some law of naturalization."[40]

In fact, the Indian friends could not agree on the most salutary rate of acculturation or on the related question of whether to grant immediate citizenship and voter status. The reformers described the Indian as in transition: tribes breaking down in structure and function; individual Indians separated or in the process of separating from tribes. But thorny differences remained among the reformers as to the degree of that separation, as well as acceptable forms of legal wardship. Nowhere were these differences more intensely underscored than in the policy recommendations of Dr. Thomas A. Bland, who organized the National Indian Defense Association.

Bland's policies urged innovative and less paternalistic use of law. He anticipated the ultimate incorporation of Native Americans into the United States but argued that United States Indian policy had to distinguish the needs of current and future generations of Native Americans and the varying ability, and will, of different tribes to accommodate programs of acculturation and assimilation. Bland's association lobbied for greater Indian control of Indian affairs and minimal U.S. government involvement unless explicitly petitioned by a tribe. Acknowledging, for example, the history of friction between tribes and agents sent to represent the United States, Bland proposed having each tribe vote annually whether to keep or dismiss the existing U.S. agent.[41]

Bland's was a conscious policy of maintaining tribal relations and a tribal landbase. His approach found a few supporters, including George W. Manypenny, former commissioner of Indian affairs, who now considered his stewardship of mid-1850s assimilationist allotment policy to have resulted in "high crime[s]."[42] The majority of reformist organizations, however, opposed his proposals and sought to shut Bland out from interorganizational meetings and lobby efforts. By "defending the Indian's right to be an Indian" and by arguing for far less rapid change, Bland threatened the whole of the program presented by the other major Indian reform organizations.[43] Although Bland's ideas interested President Cleveland, the National Indian Defense Association ultimately proved ineffectual in defeating the combined lobby of settlers and assimilation-oriented reformers who came together to pass the Dawes land allotment act in 1887. Yet, the approach outlined by Bland indicates that a few whites had identified policy alternatives less destructive of original principles of federal Indian law.

Few American law journals existed in this period and few took up the question of Indian rights. George Canfield's 1881 *American Law Review* article was unique, as was his analysis. Wrestling with the dilemma of the "important Indian problem" in a "country like ours founded on the idea of the equality of men," Canfield first joined the chorus of reformers who concluded that the Indian "must live among us" but is not "yet competent to vote intelligently." Unwilling to leave the Indian without the protection of the law, however, in particular against the "unrestrained power of Congress," Canfield proposed a constitutional amendment. "Let it be clearly ascertained what protection the Indian needs, and then give him that protection by means of an amendment specially adapted to his case. It is best that special cases should be provided for by special laws . . . the vital spirit of a constitution may be obscured by a court straining it to meet cases which it was not intended to cover."[44]

Canfield's idea for a constitutional amendment – and respite for the court – aroused little interest. Rather, the Indian friends joined with the Bureau of Indian Affairs in drafting what they termed reform-minded criminal and civil law legislation for consideration by Congress. The Indian Rights Association, for example, had its Committee on Law prepare a jurisdiction bill that would alter dramatically the legal and political landscape of reservations, dividing each one up into judicial districts headed by a judge (appointed by the U.S. president) to "have cognizance of all cases, civil and criminal." Still, the reformers hesitated to recommend a full complement of rights. "(T)here shall be no jury," the report argued, until "it could be safely done."[45]

Law, Finally, Is Written

Despite the introduction of Indian legislation from the mid-1870s through 1884, the Bureau of Indian Affairs, reformers, and congressional supporters failed to win support for bills proposing the extension of American law to reservations, Indian land allotment in severalty, and Indian citizenship. But two Supreme Court decisions of the early 1880s, *Ex Parte Crow Dog* (1883) and *Elk v. Wilkins* (1884), each condemned by different Indian policy constituencies, and the determination of the U.S. Bureau of Indian Affairs to move ahead with a unilateral policy of Indian acculturation altered the pace of legislative activity.[46] In three years, and with the support of most Indian reformers, Congress enacted two major Indian bills: the Major Crimes Act (1885) and the Dawes (General Allotment) Act (1887).[47] With these two statutes, federal Indian policy turned abruptly and decisively away from the doctrine of tribal sovereignty recognized in United States treaties and affirmed in the *Worcester* doctrine. With this new legislation, and supporting post-1886 Supreme Court decisions, the remaining barriers to United States control of "its territory" could be removed under the guise of bringing the Indian both law and the opportunity to join the American melting pot.

Crow Dog and the Major Crimes Act. On August 5, 1881, Spotted Tail, the well-known chief of the Brule Sioux, was shot and killed as he was leaving the Rosebud Agency at the close of a tribal council. There was no issue that his attacker was Crow Dog, a fellow Brule. A council was called immediately following the death, Brule citizens meeting together with the victim's family to discuss how to restablish "harmony and fellowship." Crow Dog was ordered to give Spotted Tail's relatives considerable property and services to compensate their loss. Community was restored.[48]

Despite the immediate and clear working of Brule law, Crow Dog was arrested by agents of the Bureau of Indian Affairs and taken to Fort Niobrara. Why Crow Dog was brought in for a second judgment is a matter of debate. A long-time, facile explanation focused upon the "public outcry" of local whites against the insufficiency of a tribal (customary) law punishment. Recent scholarship, however, suggests that the Bureau of Indian Affairs wanted the extension of United States criminal jurisdiction to reservations, knowing it would be a powerful tool of forced assimilation.[49]

Crow Dog was brought to Deadwood, Dakota and tried in a territory court. Although his court-appointed attorney, A.J. Plowman, contended that the United States did not hold jurisdiction over crimes among the Brule Sioux and argued well on his client's behalf, the non-Indian jury found Crow Dog guilty. A week later Judge G.C. Moody sentenced him to hang. Crow Dog's lawyer immediately filed an appeal which, under the contemporary structure of federal courts, was also heard by Judge Moody. Losing this intermediate action as well, Plowman filed for a writ of habeas corpus at the United States Supreme Court. At issue was Crow Dog's life as well as continued legal recognition of tribal sovereignty. In an ironic twist of international politics, Congress was convinced to pay Crow Dog's lawyer one thousand dollars to pursue the High Court appeal.[50]

Who could judge and punish an offense by one Native American against another on Indian land? Based upon the Supreme Court's reading of federal statutes and U.S. treaties with the Sioux, and the Court's finding that tribes maintain their own legal systems as an attribute of sovereignty, the justices held criminal jurisdiction to be a prerogative of tribes alone. Justice Matthews's opinion in *Ex Parte Crow Dog* rejected the government's reading of the disputed Sioux treaties, arguing instead that Indian sovereignty, as described by Marshall in the 1830s Cherokee cases and as recognized by the United States when it entered into these treaties, was binding. There could be no repeal of a treaty right by implication, and any new criminal jurisdiction policy on the part of the United States government would require "a clear expression of the intention of Congress."[51]

Clear expression of congressional intent. These words gave explicit direction to the political activity of the BIA's bureaucrats, and to the reformers, who saw the Court's acknowledgment of tribal jurisdiction as a setback. Quickly, and successfully, they mobilized following *Ex Parte Crow Dog* finally to win passage of a bill extending the criminal jurisdiction of the United States over Indian tribes. The 1885 law, entitled the Major Crimes Act, by the unilateral action of the United States removed seven serious crimes (murder, manslaughter, rape, assault with intent to kill, arson, burglary, and larceny) from tribal jurisdiction.[52] This long-sought statutory imposition of United States jurisdiction and the Supreme Court case *U.S. v. Kagama*, upholding the legislation, took dead aim at tribal sovereignty.[53] Together the reformers and the executive branch who had lobbied for the legislation, the legislators who had enacted the statute, and the court which had upheld its legality in *Kagama* asserted the correctness of an encroaching legal and political power over Indians even as it frankly diminished long-guaranteed tribal autonomy.

The idea of extending criminal jurisdiction over Indians by statute had enjoyed popularity for a decade. *Crow Dog* proved to be the final and necessary stimulus. The reformers understood that if Justice Matthews's invitation to clarify congressional intent was not acted upon, his recognition of tribal sovereignty would curtail their work on behalf of the Americanization of the Indian. The BIA was anxious to have legal methods of controlling increasingly assertive reservation populations. Congress felt secure in approving the legislation. The imprimatur of the Court, after all, had been on the Major Crimes Act before it was even written. It only remained for the Supreme Court to find a legal theory to fit the congressional result. Justice Miller obliged. In *Kagama* he wrote that with the end of the treaty-making era (1871), Congress had gained plenary power over Indian tribes and could assert necessary power over these sovereignties now transformed by Miller's rhetoric into "wards of the nation . . . dependent largely for their daily food . . . dependent for their political rights."[54]

The Case of John Elk. The Major Crimes Act pleased the reformers but, simultaneously, presented them with a grave problem. Congress had considered, but eliminated, a provision in the act that would have extended civil as well as criminal law to the Indian country. Charges were leveled that in this legislation, as in the general reluctance to extend citizenship, the United States "sought to exact justice from the Indian while exhibiting no justice to him."[55] Reformist policy was premised upon bringing the Indian out of the age of status into the world of contract. Yet, enjoining the Indian to white norms of criminality and punishment while denying access to the civil law at the core of economic and social opportunity transparently violated the reformers' promises of equality and justice.

The debate over Indians, law, and double standards did not stop at questions of civil and criminal jurisdiction. A year before passage of the Major Crimes Act, the Supreme Court's decision in *Elk v. Wilkins* underscored the vulnerability of Native Americans with respect to political rights. The plaintiff, John Elk, had been born into a tribal community. As a young man he left the reservation and came to Omaha. In 1880, having severed all ties with his tribe for more than a year, Elk presented himself as a voter in the city elections. Charles Wilkins, however, refused to register him on the grounds that Elk was an Indian, not a citizen of the United States and not, therefore, entitled to vote.

John Elk appealed Wilkins's decision to the Supreme Court with the aid of the two attorneys who had earlier won freedom for Chief Standing Bear. Elk argued that he had surrendered himself to the jurisdiction of the United States by leaving his tribe and that, under the Fourteenth Amendment, he was a citizen of the United States entitled to the rights and privileges of citizens. The Supreme Court disagreed. Writing for the Court, Justice Gray asserted that the "alien and dependent condition of the members of the Indian tribes could not be put off at their own will, without the action or assent of the United States."[56] Gray further rejected the Fourteenth Amendment claim by arguing that "persons not . . . subject to the jurisdiction of the United States at the time of birth cannot become so afterwards, except by being naturalized, either individually . . . or collectively, as by the force of a treaty."[57]

Indians were also, according to the weight of the opinion, subject to the will of the United States as principal in the trust relationship: "The national legislation has tended more and more towards the education and civilization of the Indians, and fitting them to be citizens. But the question whether any Indian tribes, or any members thereof, have become so far advanced in civilization, that they should be let out of the state of pupilage, and admitted to the privileges and responsibilities of citizenship, is a question to be decided by the nation whose wards they are and whose citizens they seek to become, and not by each Indian for himself."[58] Again, the reformers were caught in the contradictions of an increasingly transformed federal Indian law. While not uncomfortable with Gray's discussion of wardship, the "friends," who through their persistent lobbying had helped to create this Pandora's box, were dismayed at the actual denial of suffrage for John Elk. To many of the reformers, the legal situation of the Native Americans appeared untenable as the courts and Congress whiplashed them between the imposition of obligations and the denial of rights.

The Supreme Court had stated in both *Crow Dog* and *Elk* that it recognized a congressional right to legislate broadly on Indian policy questions. The *Elk* decision greatly affected the Indian reform community. For years they had engaged in genteel parlor discussions about premature citizenship. The specter of Indians who had donned "citizen's dress" but were to be denied a citizen's life now represented a contradiction too great to be tolerated by most of the reformers. With talk of premature citizenship behind them following *Elk*, the reformers leveled their sights on federal legislation that would enact immediate Indian citizenship: Henry Pancoast now argued that the mistakes of two hundred years *could* be remedied by immediate citizenship. Participants at the 1886 Lake Mohonk Conference renounced earlier theories of social engineering and resolved that "the duties of citizenship are of such a nature that they can only be learned by example and practice . . . quicker and surer progress in industry, education and morality will be secured by giving citizenship first, than by making citizenship depend upon the attainment of any standard of education and conduct."[59]

The reformers wanted to move quickly on the question of Indian political rights, fearing that if Congress could not be convinced that it must act, Justice Harlan's dissent in *Elk* spelled out the inescapable conclusion:

> If [Elk] did not acquire national citizenship on abandoning his tribe and becoming, by residence in one of the States, subject to the complete jurisdiction of the United States, then the Fourteenth Amendment has wholly failed to accomplish, in respect of the Indian race, what, we think, was intended by it; and there is still in this country a despised and rejected class of persons, with no nationality whatever; who, born in our territory, owing no allegiance to any foreign power, and subject, as residents of the States, to all the burdens of government, are yet not members of any political community nor entitled to any of the rights, privileges, or immunities of citizens of the United States.[60]

The work of the "friends" at this time was especially compelled by the aggressive rhetoric of Lyman Abbott, C.C. Painter of the IRA, and Captain Richard Henry Pratt, head of the Carlisle Indian Industrial School. Pratt supported immediate and, if necessary, compulsory assimilation, and Abbott, later described as the chaplain of Theodore Roosevelt's progressivism, said any means could be defended that would help "progress." The willingness to disregard means in the pursuit of assimilation policy particularly characterized these three men. They advocated uprooting without delay the reservation system previously championed by the reformers. Pratt frequently voiced the social Darwinist opinion that the Indians must be turned out "into the mass of the white population to . . . sink or swim."[61] To accomplish compulsory acculturation and assimilation, these reformers accepted that it might be necessary to cut off rations as a means of making Indians take up "citizen's" work. They quoted St. Paul approvingly: "He who will not work shall not eat."[62]

Citizenship and the Dawes (General Allotment) Act

Opposition to immediate citizenship still arose from different quarters. Bland argued that the failure to delay citizenship and assimilation would be detrimental to tradition-minded Native Americans. Senator Teller criticized legislation that ignored the diversity of tribes and charged that land allotment policy tied to citizenship did not have support within Indian communities. Genio Lambertson, United States district attorney in the *Standing Bear* and *Elk* litigation, wrote disparagingly of citizenship for a people he called "idlers" who had made "the tomahawk the arbiter of their wrongs." He argued that having absorbed the "undesirable classes driven out of Europe, it requires great faith in our robust virtues and saving efficacy of republican institutions to believe we can with safety absorb the Indians into our population and make them partners in the political functions of government."[63] L.Q.C. Lamar, secretary of the interior and later Supreme Court justice, also doubted the possibility of rapid assimilation. But these voices were overpowered as Congress was pushed to act on a joint citizenship and land allotment bill.

To squelch this opposition, the reformers had turned to supportive members of Congress, among them Senator Henry Dawes. A lawyer, Dawes had spent thirty-six years in Congress. He represented Massachusetts, a state where support for the Indian reform cause ran strong. In the post-*Elk* era, Dawes chaired the Senate Indian Affairs Committee. Dawes was not immediately won over by the reformers. He was nagged by conflicting assessments of their plans, particularly their newly acquired unwillingness to acknowledge the sanctity of Indian treaties and title deeds.

97

Dawes accepted invitations to the reformers' meetings in Washington and Lake Mohonk, New York but remained undecided about the next phase of federal Indian policy until the mid-1880s. Then in an 1886 speech recounting his findings from a recent visit to the Cherokee Nation in the Indian Territory, Dawes announced his support for a policy of land allotment in severalty and Indian citizenship. Dawes's paradoxical text described the economic and political stability of the Cherokee Nation and gave a glowing account of the Nation's schools, hospitals, and lack of a national debt. But in his conclusion Dawes pronounced: "They have got as far as they can go, because they own their land in common. It is Henry George's system, and under that there is no enterprise to make your home any better than that of your neighbor's. There is no selfishness, which is at the bottom of civilization. Till this people will consent to give up their lands, and divide them among their citizens so that each can own the land he cultivates, they will not make much more progress."[64] The talk demonstrated graphically how the senator had bought in to the reformers' insistence that the Indian must be "Americanized" – even where a healthy community already existed.

Henry Dawes was now ready to pick up and salvage the citizenship and general land allotment legislation designed to free the "unfortunate" natives from the debilitating restraints of tribal society that had first been introduced in the 1870s. Backed by the now relentless reformist lobby and the BIA, the Dawes [General Allotment] Act became law in February of 1887.[65] The bill called for most Indian reservations to be surveyed and the land allotted to individual Indians in severalty (in general, 160 acres to the head of a family with lesser acreage to minors and unmarried persons). After the president had authorized the survey of a reservation, individuals entitled to an allotment had four years to make a selection. If the person did not make a selection, the legislation empowered the secretary of the interior to order a special agent or agent of the tribe to make the choice. Once the selection was accomplished and approved by the secretary of the interior, the allottee received an inalienable title, or patent, for a twenty-five-year trust period that could be extended at the discretion of the president. Fee simple title would not be conveyed until the conclusion of this guardianship. Initially, the allottee was not only barred from selling the land, but also from executing leasing arrangements of any kind. The legislation intended to make good farmers of Indians, although much of the allotted land was inaccessible to the allottees and not suitable for farming.[66]

The Dawes Act also authorized the immediate sale of "surplus" reservation land to non-Indians. The capital generated from the sale of the surplus lands was to go into a trust account controlled by the United States government. It was not distributed to individual members of the tribe, nor was it given to the tribe's leadership as a central purpose of allotment was to break tribal organization and autonomy.[67] Finally, as promised, the Dawes Act extended citizenship to adult Indian allottees. The act also approved citizenship for non-allotment Indians who separated from the tribe and went on to "adopt civilized life."

The Law, As Written, Is Not Enough

The reformers had supported an allotment bill because they believed the legislation would be the vehicle to break tribal government, to make individual homesteaders of Native Americans, and to convey protective law and citizenship. All these policies were part of their program of acculturation and assimilation. But members of the Indian Rights Association quickly pointed out that the Dawes bill was primarily a measure to dispose Indian land in severalty. Assimilation – "becoming one of us" – would take time. Meanwhile, "it seems desirable to supplement [the bill's] provisions for the ultimate extension of law over the Indians . . . with some further legislation."[68] This was polite talk. The work of the reformers had fallen considerably short of its mark. Harvard Law School professor James Thayer, adviser to the Boston Citizenship Committee, picked up on this theme in his sharply critical *Atlantic Monthly* (1888) article: "So much for what the law [Dawes Act] accomplishes. Now consider what it does not accomplish, and does not aim at . . . [I]t does not cover the case of all the tribal Indians . . . [I]t provides them with no courts there (reservations, alloted or not), no means whatever of enforcing their rights there, and no system of law . . . [I]t leaves these land-owners with little power to use their land. . . . [S]ince their land is inalienable for a quarter of a century and untaxable, there is small inducement to any State . . . to do much for them . . . [T]he law makes no provision for the education of these new citizens."[69]

The reformers began drafting new legislation under Thayer's direction. Their purpose remained fixing "upon the Indian the same personal, legal, and political status which is common to all other inhabitants."[70] Thayer's bill, "An Act to establish courts for the Indian on the various reservations, and to extend the protection of the law of the States and Territories over all Indians, and for other purposes," was introduced into the Senate where it attracted little attention. In 1891, in an article pointedly entitled "A People without Law," Thayer attributed congressional disinterest to the absence of a single representative "deeply impressed with the importance of this particular step" and to the fact that the Indian question was "mired in detail" and "crowded aside by tariffs and silver."[71] Thayer failed to report that while the private Indian reform groups supported the bill, Dawes did not. Senator Dawes questioned the constitutionality of Thayer's legislation and contended that his own severalty bill was a sufficient mechanism for change and improvement.[72] The failure of the Thayer bill and similar legislation left these questions of law and citizenship to be addressed on an ad hoc basis.

Conclusion

Reformers had intended that the era opened by the Dawes Act would herald the birth of the citizen-Indian. In fact, it is necessary to concede the period after 1887 as one of the Indian as ward. The idea of the Native American as an inferior in need of improvement, of an immature "ward" needing the guidance of his American "father" was a staple of American social thought after 1887. The Dawes Act with its trust provisions, along with *Kagama's* statement of plenary power over "wards of the nation," trumpeted approval of the era of guardianship with its explicit rejection of the Indian as equal. Indian voices fought this status, but United States policy systematically opposed assertions of tribal autonomy. The insistent United States policy of acculturation left no room for any opposing Indian voice concerning the Indian's future. When, for example, large numbers of Cherokees, Choctaws, Chickasaws, and Creeks proposed selling their allotments and buying land communally in Mexico or South America as an alternative to land in severalty in the United States, Congress refused to remove the restriction against alienation of their land.[73] Yet, United States policy compromised its own commitment to acculturation when a 1906 amendment deferred the grant of citizenship to allottees until the expiration of the twenty-five-year trust period. In *U.S. v. Celestine* the Supreme Court upheld this withdrawal of citizenship rights stating that "Congress, in granting full rights of citizenship to Indians, believed that it had been hasty."[74] A general grant of citizenship to Native Americans did not occur until 1924.[75]

Where were the reformers who previously had been so committed to equality of status and immediate citizenship for Indians? A change in the purpose of the Lake Mohonk Conference in 1904 hints at what occurred: "[T]he reforms demanded in the Indian Service being practically realized, the Conference [has] decided to broaden its field to include the welfare of colonial peoples."[76] The name, henceforth, became "Lake Mohonk Conference of Friends of the Indian and Other Dependent Peoples." Perhaps they had become distracted by non-Indian reform issues; perhaps, they agreed with the increased use of trust powers and saw no need for further effort. Whatever the reason, the generation of "friends" responsible for allotment slipped away from the cause. With reform work "realized," the actual process of allotment proceeded without much fuss from their corner.

No simple statement can be made about about the work of the nineteenth-century friends of the American Indian. A number of reform groups existed. Their opinions differed and changed over time. Generally, however, the reformer can be portrayed as someone for whom law was a means and an end in the process of Americanizing the Indian. These men and women believed that law could guide an orderly and legal transformation of Native American culture and prevent the physical extinction of native people. They also anticipated that expanding U.S. power could be tamed by the higher principles of liberal constitutionalism and that, by the hand of U.S. law, the Indian could have procedural fairness and perhaps substantive justice as well.

In these beliefs, the nineteenth-century reformers were not different from that earlier reformer, Franciscus de Victoria. In the sixteenth century, the Spanish theologian recast oppressive, religiously based justifications for Europeans' treatment of Indians into a more protective, secular, modern law. Victoria reasoned that Indians were entitled to natural law rights, but in order to make their rights effective they had to join the Christian, European family of man. The Law of Nations, for which Victoria's writings lay the foundation, has been described as providing Victoria with "a mediating structure that enabled him to resolve questions concerning the legitimacy of Spanish interference with Indian autonomy."[77] Victoria concluded that the Indian was a child in need of a European father to educate him according to Western, Christian norms; in short, to civilize him. Three hundred and fifty years passed between the delivery of Victoria's radical lecture, "On the Indians Lately Discovered," and the major legislative work of the American reformers in the late nineteenth century. Yet their fellowship was clear. Both believed in the taming and legitimizing power of law. Both insisted that only by the adoption of European social, political, and legal norms could the Indian make his rights effective.

It is appealing that the reformers urged a process of order and law against the rhetoric of raw power and the willingness of many whites to use violence. Land, after all, was running out in the late nineteenth century but men's passion for it was not. Perhaps, then, the work of the reformers, as Victoria's, helped to prevent the total physical extinction of Native Americans. But the final policies endorsed by the reformers in the Dawes Act era were explicitly directed at the cultural destruction of Native American communities. Inept social engineers, in the second half of the nineteenth century the reformers vacillated in the policies they recommended, moving from approval of culturally isolated Indian reserves, to assimilation, to guardianship. Rather than creating social stability and a new Indian identity, their policies stripped away much of the existing social structure cementing native societies. At the 1900 Lake Mohonk Conference, reformer Merrill E. Gates characterized the Dawes Act as "a mighty pulverizing engine for breaking up the tribal mass."[78] In hindsight, that law did, indeed, do a mighty job of pulverizing the tribal mass and destroying tribal landbase, but the Dawes Act and its progeny did not assimilate the Indians, both because the legislation treated them as inferiors rather than citizen-equals and because most Native Americans did not want to be Americanized.

The reformers took satisfaction in the laws that they had helped to draft. Although they had once worried about binding treaty commitments honoring Indian land rights and Indian sovereignty, by the end of the nineteenth century what mattered was not the original principles of federal Indian law but the existence of what they deemed protective, and civilizing, American law. They hoped to create a citizen-Indian to be melted into the great American pot. In fact, however, the reform era ended not with a grant of unencumbered Indian citizenship but with the development of a trust doctrine that legally formalized a relationship of power imbalance between tribes and the United States. At the moment that the Lake Mohonk Conference pronounced reform "realized," the Indian found himself not an equal under the law but an exception in an extra-constitutional status that was defined not by civil rights, due process, and judicial review, but by wardship, plenary power, and the political question doctrine.

Notes

1. A. de Tocqueville, I *Democracy in America* 368–69 (New York, 1945).
2. Canfield, "The Legal Position of the Indian," 15 *Am. L. Rev.* 21 (1881).
3. See, in general, R. Berkhofer, *Salvation and the Savage: An Analysis of Protestant Missions and American Indian Response, 1787–1862* (Lexington, Ky., 1965); H. Fritz, *The Movement For Indian Assimilation, 1860–1890* (Philadelphia, 1963) (hereinafter cited as H. Fritz); W. Hagan, *The Indian Rights Association: The Herbert Welsh Years, 1882–1904* (Tucson, 1985); F. Hoxie, *A Final Promise: The Campaign to Assimilate the Indians, 1880–1920* (Lincoln, Nebr., 1984) (hereinafter cited as F. Hoxie); R. Mardock, *The Reformers and the American Indian* (Columbia, Mo., 1971); L. Priest, *Uncle Sam's Stepchildren: The Reformation of United States Indian Policy, 1865–1887* (Lincoln, Nebr., 1942) (hereinafter cited as L. Priest); F. Prucha, *American Indian Policy in Crisis: Christian Reformers and the Indian, 1865–1900* (Norman, Okla, 1976) (hereinafter cited as F. Prucha); *Americanizing the American Indians: Writings by the "Friends of the Indian," 1880–1900* (F. Prucha ed., Cambridge, Mass., 1973).
4. Abbott, "Indians and the Law," 2 *Harv. L. Rev.* 167 (1888).
5. The completion of the transcontinental railroad on May 10, 1869, immigration, and the exhaustion of land in the East rapidly altered the density of population west of the Mississippi. The population of the West, seven million in 1870, jumped to more than eleven million in 1880. Between 1870 and 1890 eight states – Utah, Wyoming, Idaho, North and South Dakota, Colorado, Montana, and Washington – joined the Union.
6. American Bar Association, 15 *Reports of the American Bar Association* (1892).
7. For the discussion of Protestantism below, see S. Ahlstrom, *A Religious History of the American People* I:182, 266 and II:252 (Garden City, N.Y., 1975).
8. *Dartmouth College v. Woodward*, 17 U.S. (4 Wheat.) 518, 527 (1819).
9. On August 13, 1946, President Harry Truman signed into law the Indian Claims Commission. In an accompanying statement, the president described the transfer of Indian land to white ownership as "the largest real estate transaction in history." *Public Papers of the Presidents of the United States, Harry S. Truman, 1946*, at 414 (1962).
10. K. Kickingbird and K. Ducheneaux, *One Hundred Million Acres* (New York, 1973).
11. F. Prucha, *supra* note 3, at 21.
12. Allotment of tribal land in severalty, or the conveyance of (individual) fee simple title, had a long history among the New World Europeans. A 1663 General Court of Massachusetts Colony Order, for example,

provided that any Indian coming to "live civilly and orderly" should have "allotments amongst the English according to the custom of the English." J. Kinney, *A Continent Lost – A Civilization Won* 82 (Baltimore, 1937). In the late eighteenth and early nineteenth centuries allotment was considered an alternative to policies of land trades with Indian nations or military action against them. Early nineteenth-century treaties set aside land from ceded tracts for individual Indians. F. Cohen, *Handbook of Federal Indian Law* 129 (Charlottesville, 1982). See generally M. Young, *Redskins, Ruffleshirts, and Rednecks: Indian Allotments in Alabama and Mississippi, 1830–1860* (Norman, Okla., 1961). In this period, however, allotment had not yet become a policy of broad application whose goals included the wholesale assimilation of Native Americans and the elimination of a tribal landbase. Extensive use of allotment by the United States occurred in a series of mid-1850 treaties with Indian nations. The policy proved a failure. Social chaos and near total loss of individual land title resulted among the affected Native Americans.

13. See generally J. Beeson, *A Plea for the Indians* (New York, 1857) and H. Whipple, *Lights and Shadows of a Long Episcopate* (New York, 1902).

14. H. Fritz, *supra* note 3, at 37.

15. Indians encountered problems obtaining wages from off-reservation employers because courts were not open to them and because they were treated as wards incapable of making contracts. In 1867 a joint congressional committee killed a proposal to admit Indian testimony in all trials involving Indians. *Id.* at 33.

    As late as 1879 in the famous Ponca trial, the United States district attorney attempted to block the testimony of Chief Standing Bear with the query "Does this court think an Indian is a competent witness?" T. Tibbles, *The Ponca Chiefs: An Account of the Trial of Standing Bear* 79 (Lincoln, Nebr., 1972) (hereinafter cited as T. Tibbles).

16. I. Morris, *Arguments Against Territorial Government Over the Indians* 17 (Washington, D.C., 1870). For a general discussion of the Indian citizenship debate, see generally L. Priest, *supra* note 3, ch. 16. Interesting dicta concerning Indian citizenship appeared in the infamous *Scott v. Sandford* 1857 opinion by Chief Justice Taney. Taney wrote that although Indians were not originally citizens in the constitutional sense, Congress had the power to naturalize Indians (in contrast to blacks), analogizing them for this purpose to aliens. *Scott v. Sandford* 60 U.S. (19 How.) 393, 403–4 (1857). Felix Cohen comments that "despite the dictum in *Dred Scott*, Indians lacking any tribal relationship were treated at times as citizens without naturalization, but some in turn were denied political rights because they were not white." F. Cohen, *supra* note 12, at 641.

17. Treaty with the Ponca Indians, 14 Stat. 685 (1867); Treaty with the Sioux Indians, 15 Stat. 635 (1869). See generally Lake, "Standing Bear!

Who?" 60 *Neb. L. Rev.* 451 (1981) (hereinafter cited as Lake).

18. Act of August 15, 1876, ch. 289, 19 Stat. 192.

19. On the question of whether U.S. agents had legal consent, Lake, *supra* note 17, at 467–68, note 37.

20. An excellent account of Tibbles's activities is found in T. Tibbles, *supra* note 15. See also Lake, *supra* note 17.

21. For an account of Webster and Poppleton's efforts in *Standing Bear* and other litigation organized by the Omaha Committee, see J. Norgren, "Personal Liberty and Political Rights: The Cases of Standing Bear and John Elk" (forthcoming).

22. T. Tibbles, *supra* note 15, at 34–35.

23. *Id.* at 35.

24. *Id.* at 38.

25. *Id.* at 79.

26. *United States ex. rel. Standing Bear v. Crook*, 5 Dill. 465; 25 F. Cas. 695 (C.C.D. Neb. 1879) (No. 14, 891).

27. 25 F. Cas. 695, 699 (C.C.D. Neb. 1879).

28. *Id.* at 700.

29. T. Tibbles, *supra* note 15 at 96; see also *id.* at 83–89, 93, 97, 101, and 105.

30. 25 F. Cas. 695, 697.

31. *Id.* at 699.

32. *Id.* at 698.

33. Indian Rights Association, *1st Annual Report* 6, 18 (1884). Reading the early annual reports and tracts of the IRA and the Women's National Indian Association best conveys the membership's concern for, on the one hand, keeping covenants and, on the other, protecting Indians through the extension of United States law, including a policy of land allotment. Despite a century of deceitful American diplomacy and the prophetic words of Bishop Whipple that U.S. treaties with Indians were at heart unilateral, many reformers believed in the legitimacy of bilateral agreements. They felt that the many Indian tribes would willingly consent to the termination of treaty-guaranteed lands in favor of land in fee simple and that tribal members would voluntarily take up United States citizenship. F. Prucha, *supra* note 3, at 64.

34. Harsha, "Law for the Indians," 134 *N. Am. Rev.* 272, 292 (1882).

35. *Id.* at 277–78.

36. *The Civil Rights Cases* 109 U.S. 3, 25 (1883).

37. F. Cohen, *supra* note 12, at 640.

38. L. Priest, *supra* note 3, at 209. An excellent account of the shift in racial attitudes toward the Native American is found in F. Hoxie, *supra* note 3. In particular, see chapters 3, 4, and 7.

39. Indian Rights Association, *Annual Report*, 16 (1885).

40. *Id.* at 16–17.

41. L. Priest, *supra* note 3, at 63.

42. *Id.* at 86, 178.
43. F. Prucha, *supra* note 3, at 166.
44. Canfield, *supra* note 2, at 21, 37.
45. Indian Rights Association, *1st Annual Report*, Appendix A and 24 (1884).
46. *Ex Parte Crow Dog* 109 U.S. 556 (1883); *Elk v. Wilkins* 112 U.S. 94 (1884). See generally S. Harring, *Crow Dog's Case: American Indian Sovereignty, Tribal Law, and American Law in the Nineteenth Century* (manuscript in preparation), especially ch. 3 (hereinafter cited as S. Harring). Harring argues convincingly that there was little popular pressure for the extension of United States law to Indian reservations. Rather he identifies the Bureau of Indian Affairs as the particularly strong agent of persuasion.
47. The Major Crimes Act, 18 U.S.C. Sec. 1153, 3242; The General Allotment Act, ch. 119, 24 Stat. 388 (1887) (codified as amended at 25 U.S.C. §§ 331–58 (1976).
48. V. Deloria, Jr. and C. Lytle, *American Indians, American Justice* 168–69 (Austin, 1983).
49. S. Harring, *supra* note 46, at 80; R. Barsh & J. Henderson, *The Road: Indian Tribes and Political Liberty* 86–88 (Berkeley, 1980). Harring reviews the sequence of events involved in finding Crow Dog, analyzes local newspaper accounts, and concludes that there was no "popular outcry." Rather, he argues that the BIA wanted a test case, an opportunity to clarify the meaning of treaty provisions with the Sioux in 1869 and 1877 concerning criminal jurisdiction. S. Harring, *supra* note 46, at 89. Harring's conclusion is further supported by news accounts reporting local white disapproval of the verdict and the sentence of death. *Id.* at 100. Harring also argues that if it had been up to the BIA, the case that would have defined the legal status of Native American criminal law would have been the case of the Creek Johnson Foster for the murder of a Pottowatomie. *Id.* at 195.
50. Sundry Civil Act, 22 U.S. Stat. (March 3, 1883).
51. 109 U.S. at 572.
52. 23 Stat. 385.
53. 118 U.S. 375 (1886).
54. *Id.* at 383–84. In the 1860s and 1870s U.S. Indian agents began to organize police forces and courts under their supervision, intended to extend the agents' – and the BIA's – control. Many tribal members resisted the imposition of such social and legal control. See generally W. Hagan, *Indian Police and Judges* (Lincoln, Nebr., 1966). S. Harring, *supra* note 46, ch. 5, 6.
55. Harsha, *supra* note 34 at 283 (quoting President Seelye of Amherst College).
56. 112 U.S. 94, 100.
57. *Id.* at 102.

58. *Id.* at 106–7.
59. L. Priest, *supra* note 3, at 210.
60. 112 U.S. 94, 122–23.
61. G. Hyde, *A Sioux Chronicle* 160 (Norman, Okla., 1956).
62. *Id.* at 160.
63. Lambertson, "Indian Citizenship," 20 *Am. L. Rev.* 183 (1886).
64. A. Debo, *And Still The Waters Run* 22 (Norman, Okla., 1984 ed.).
65. 24 Stat. 388. See generally D. Otis, *The Dawes Act and the Allotment of Indian Lands* (F. Prucha ed., Norman, Okla., 1973). Between 1887 and 1934 when Congress terminated allotment policy with the passage of the Indian Reorganization Act, Indian landholding was reduced from 138 acres to 48 million acres – nearly 20 million of which was useless for farming. V. Deloria, *supra* note 48, at 10. The allotment policy was formally abandoned "as a disaster" in 1934 when Congress enacted the Indian Reorganization Act (also known as the IRA or the Wheeler-Howard Act), 25 U.S.C. § 461 *et seq.*, which provided for the expansion of the tribal land base and the reestablishment of tribal governments abolished by Congress at will and over the resistance of tribes. See, e.g., the Curtis Act (1897), which allotted the lands of the Five Civilized Tribes who had been removed from their eastern homelands by force or threat of force on the promise that their new land would be theirs forever.
66. See, e.g., the allotments made to the Comanches where only 30 of the 320 allotted acres were suitable for agriculture, U.S. Congress, 56th Cong., 1st Sess., *Senate Doc. 76*; H.R. Doc. No. 333 (cited in *Lone Wolf v. Hitchcock*, 187 U.S. at 558). Similarly, the allotments made to the Quinault Indians were covered with forests so thick that the separate tracts were literally inaccessible to the allottees. For a detailed account, *Quinault Allottee Ass'n v. United States*, 485 F.2d 1391, 1394–95 (Ct. Cl. 1973). See also Hughes, "Can The Trustee Be Sued For Its Breach? The Sad Saga of United States v. Mitchell," 26 *S.D.L. Rev.* 447 (1981).
67. The trust fund was subject to appropriation by Congress for "Indian education and civilization." A year after passage of the Dawes Act, Professor James Thayer of the Harvard Law School wrote, "One would feel a good deal surer of the proper application of that money if it were to be put into some trust company, upon specific and defined trusts." Thayer, "The Dawes Bill and the Indians," 61 *Atlantic Monthly* 315, 318 (1888) (hereinafter cited as Thayer).
68. Indian Rights Association, *5th Annual Report*, 4, 6 (1888).
69. Thayer, *supra* note 67, at 320–21.
70. Abbott, "Indians and the Law," 2 *Harv. L. Rev.* 167, 174 (1889). A summary of the proposed Thayer bill appears in the Indian Rights Association, *6th Annual Report*, 26–27 (1889).
71. Thayer, "A People without Law," 68 *Atlantic Monthly* 676, 686 (1891).

72. F. Prucha, *supra* note 3, at 339–41.
73. A. Debo, *supra* note 64, at 58–60. Debo wrote that to save his own self-respect, the white man "could not permit them to flee from his benefactions." *Id.* at 60.
74. 215 U.S. 278, 291 (1909).
75. Act of June 2, 1924, ch. 233, 43 Stat. 253 (superseded 1940) (a general grant of United States citizenship naturalizing all native-born, noncitizen Indians). Felix Cohen estimated that prior to the Citizenship Act of 1924, approximately two-thirds of Native Americans in the United States had already acquired citizenship. F. Cohen, *Handbook of Federal Indian Law* 153 (Washington, D.C., 1942). The statutory approach differs from the constitutional amendments employed to guarantee full political rights to women and blacks and historically left Congress with considerable freedom to alter and amend prior citizenship legislation. See *supra* note 74 and accompanying text.
76. Frederick E. Partington, *The Story of Mohonk* 29 (Mohonk Salerooms, 1911).
77. Williams, "The Medieval and Renaissance Origins of the Status of the American Indian in Western Legal Thought," 57 *S. Cal. L. Rev.* 1, 91–92 (1983). The discussion of de Victoria's contributions in this paragraph draws upon Professor Williams' article.
78. F. Prucha, *supra* note 3, at 257.

3

The Transformation of Indian Law: Trusteeship, Plenary Power, and the Political Question Doctrine

. . . Congress possesse[s] a paramount power over the property of the Indians, by reason of its exercise of guardianship over their interests, and . . . such authority might be implied, even though opposed to the strict letter of a treaty with the Indians.

Justice Edward White, United States Supreme Court[1]
(1903)

Nothing is gained by dwelling upon the unhappy conflicts that have prevailed. . . . The generation of Indians who suffered the privations, indignities, and brutalities of the westward march of the whites have gone to the Happy Hunting Ground, and nothing that we can do can square the account with them. Whatever survives is a moral obligation resting on the descendants of the whites to do for the descendants of the Indians what in the conditions of the twentieth century is the decent thing. It is most unfortunate to try to measure this moral duty in terms of legal obligations. . . . The Indian problem is essentially a sociological problem, not a legal one.

Justice Robert Jackson, United States Supreme Court[2]
(1944)

Historical Prelude

At the turn of the eighteenth century the vast preponderance of white power that was to determine American-Indian relations from the latter part of the nineteenth century did not yet exist. "[T]oo powerful and brave not to be dreaded as formidable enemies,"

109

Indian tribes were recognized as separate and distinct political entities in American law.[3] By the end of the nineteenth century, however, federal Indian law had changed fundamentally. At that time once firmly fixed legal principles of tribal land ownership and occupancy rights had been converted to allow the large scale taking of Indian land wherever and whenever it was expedient or convenient to do so. Tribes, respected as nations "retaining their original natural rights, as undisputed possessors of the soil"[4] at the beginning of the century, were treated as "unfortunate," "ignorant," and "dependent" wards of the United States by the end of the nineteenth century.[5] Half a century after the Supreme Court had held Indian occupancy rights to be "as sacred as the fee simple of whites,"[6] ninety million acres – two-thirds of all tribal lands – had been declared surplus land open for non-Indian settlement by simple congressional fiat in the Dawes Act and ensuing executive action.

United States policy in the early nineteenth century had reflected both a respect for the power of Indian tribes and an appreciation that legal principles, the doctrine of discovery in particular, were well suited to accomplish the primary goals of American domestic and foreign policy. Early judicial decisions reflected this understanding. *Fletcher v. Peck, Johnson v. M'Intosh*, and the 1830s Cherokee cases established two fundamental propositions.[7] The first was that Indian title "[was] certainly to be respected by all courts"[8] and that Indians as "occupants [of the soil]" had "a legal as well as just claim to retain possession of it, and to use it according to their discretion."[9] Tribes, therefore, had a "right to the lands they occupy, until that right shall be extinguished by a voluntary cession to our government."[10] Indian title of occupancy was a fully recognized and fully protected property right.

The second principle was the recognition of tribal autonomy. In *Cherokee Nation* and *Worcester*, the Court accepted as well established that from the settlement of our country [the Cherokee Nation has] been uniformly treated "as a state, as a distinct political society, separated from others, capable of managing its own affairs and governing itself."[11] There was no disagreement that Indian people were "capable of maintaining the relations of peace and war, of being responsible in their political character for any violation of their engagements."[12]

The Court's respect for Indian autonomy and property rights was explicitly based on the doctrine of discovery. As interpreted by Marshall, the doctrine of discovery provided a legal framework for regulating both the competing claims of European discoverers and the relation of the discoverer and the Indian tribes within the boundaries of the claimed territory. Among the Europeans, the principle of discovery "gave to the nation making the discovery the sole right of acquiring the soil from the natives and establishing settlements upon it."[13] The first discoverer could, therefore, preempt competing claims of other nations: latecomers were barred from dealing with Indian tribes on their own; tribes were not to be available as allies in inter-European conflicts.

In relations between the discoverer and Indian tribes within the discovered territory, tribal property rights and autonomy were initially respected. It was a respect warranted by Indian power. Since Indians "were ready to repel by arms every attempt on their independence,"[14] "[t]hat law which regulates and ought to regulate in general, the relations between the conqueror and the conquered, was incapable of application to a[n Indian] people under such circumstances."[15] While conquest of Indians "too powerful and brave not to be dreaded as formal enemies" was an impossibility, peace and friendship with tribes occupying the discovered and claimed territory were possible, but only by adapting legal principles so as to assure Indian property rights and by protecting Indian land from white encroachment.

Legal recognition of the extraterritoriality of Indian tribes – both in terms of autonomous governmental structure and tribal property – was reconciled with the first discoverer's preemptive sovereignty claims against that of competing latecomers by modifying the scope of tribal sovereignty and property rights in two crucial aspects. Discovery imposed on sovereign tribes the political dependence of "domestic, dependent nations" and the acknowledgment that the ultimate sovereign controlled the external relations of the tribes.[16] It was a necessary corollary of such control that Indian tribes were "deemed incapable of transferring . . . absolute title to others."[17] They were, consequently, barred from alienating their land to anyone but the ultimate sovereign, who had acquired the exclusive right of purchase by discovery. As a result of these restrictions the Indians' rights to complete sovereignty, as independent nations, were necessarily diminished.

Although the "peculiar" mix of Indian sovereignty and dependence was to become the foundation for the systematic dispossession of the Indian later in the nineteenth century, the fact that tribes were "necessarily considered, in some respects, as dependent, and in some respects, as a distinct people"[18] did not derogate from the sanctity of their title or the strength of their autonomy in relation to American society. Under the legal principles accepted

by the American government during the first third of the nineteenth century, "[Indian] rights to complete sovereignty were only
diminished by the distributional preference of the discovery
principle."[19] Dependency for foreign relations purposes, Marshall
made clear, did not detract from the Indians' autonomy, for "[a]
weak state . . . may place itself under the protection of one more
powerful, without stripping itself of the right of government, and
ceasing to be a state."[20] Although the chief justice had opened the
possibility of misinterpretation by referring to the federal government's right of "regulating the trade with the Indians, and managing all their affairs," he was careful to foreclose any assertion of
federal management power over matters other than trade with the
Indians. "To construe the expression . . . into a surrender of self-
government, would be, we think, a perversion of their necessary
meaning, and a departure from the construction which has been
uniformly put on them."[21] To the extent that Marshall's own
equivocal formulations in *Fletcher* and *M'Intosh* had left open how
Indian title could be legitimately abolished, the *Worcester* decision
established unequivocally that it could be done only with Indian
consent.

Discovery gave European nations no more than the "right of
purchasing such lands as the natives were willing to sell."[22] The
requirement of Indian consent had been an integral element of
white-Indian land dealings from the earliest laws of the new European colonies in North America to the enactment of the Northwest
Ordinance in 1787 and Marshall's decision in 1832.[23] The Supreme
Court's affirmation of the "unquestioned" and "therefore unquestionable rights of the Indians in their land" confirmed the governmental policy of land acquisition through formal treaties of cession.
The treaty system, the policy of purchasing Indian lands, and the
enactment and reenactment of statutes and treaties respecting the
intratribal jurisdiction of Indian governments attested to the recognition of Indian power during the first third of the nineteenth
century and to the fact that legal principles of autonomy and
property rights were at that time not a legal fiction but a practical
reality.

Adherence to the law of discovery provided an efficient route in
foreign policy. Successor to the defeated England, the United
States could assert the rights of the discoverer over Indians while
the principle of preemption served to dampen the competing claims
of European states. The law of discovery was equally advantageous
for accomplishing domestic policy objectives. As acknowledgment
of the Indian right to own, use, and dispose of their lands[24] did not

bar the acquisition of Indian land by treaty or purchase, it imposed no intolerable restraints on the new nation bent on economic expansion and growth. Where tribes were willing to sell or cede their land for money or other consideration, the process of trading with the Indians offered an efficient and inexpensive way for the acquisition of vast new lands for expansion and growth.

The advantages of this policy were not initially negated by the one clear restraint that the law imposed on the acquisition of Indian land – the requirement of Indian consent. Since the lands white society wanted for settlement and exploitation could be bought without much difficulty from the tribes who owned and occupied them during the first several decades after independence, the American government proceeded to acquire vast expanses of Indian land by treaty and by purchase and opened them to white settlement.[25] Purchase freed Indian land from the cultural encumbrances that set it apart from the rest of society and opened millions of acres for white settlement or speculation. Neither the size of Indian land holdings nor the nature of its use were, therefore, regarded as immediate or insurmountable obstacles to progress. As long as Indians were ready to cede their land, compliance with the requirement of Indian consent did not conflict with either the economic needs or the legal requirements of American land policy.

It was only when Indians began to resist trading their land that the original legal protections for tribal land became incompatible with white America's notions of economic and political progress. Adherence to principles of Indian occupancy and consent when and where tribes were opposed to trading their land at any price and where they insisted on using it in ways contrary to the demands of a market economy meant that the exceptional economic and cultural status of Indian land could become a permanent barrier to economic growth. How much Indian consent was the centerpiece of the booming land trade as well as the foundation of its legality became clear once Indian willingness to give up their land came to an end. When tribes began to realize that no cession – no matter how large or how "final" – would ever end white demands for more land, they resisted further cessions, and the happy marriage of political convenience and legal principle broke asunder. Without Indian consent the transfer of title to vast tracts of land from Indian to non-Indian ownership presented intractable legal problems. If tribes refused to treat land as a market commodity and could not be enticed to sell or cede it, the trade in Indian land would either have to come to an end or proceed in open violation of the law.

No case made this point more clearly than that of the Cherokee when they resisted Georgia and President Jackson. When the Cherokee refused to sign treaties relinquishing their land, they were removed from it by force. The import of the Cherokee's resistance to further land cessions during the second half of the nineteenth century was unmistakable. Indian refusal to sell land entailed a lasting withdrawal of large areas from the real estate market at the very time when non-Indian demands for the acquisition of these lands was growing – the result of the rapid pace of westward migration, the discovery of gold, and the building of railroads. As more tribes followed the logic of the Cherokee's determination and attempted to halt further trade in their land, legal guarantees for Indian occupancy threatened to become an insurmountable and permanent obstacle – unless they were changed. The course of, and solution to, the Cherokee's legal confrontation with Georgia over their property rights presaged the direction of that change.

Despite the fundamental shift in the direction and spirit of American-Indian relations revealed in the Cherokee crises, the typical pattern of federal land policy during the second half of the nineteenth century was not characterized by the same open defiance of the law that marked Jackson's response to the Cherokee's legal victory. To the contrary, the single most important aspect of the new federal policies affecting Indian land rights was that they were justified through a dramatic – though gradual – revision of the central concepts of Indian law. Instead of flaunting the law openly – as state and national government had done without hesitation in the Cherokee cases – American policy proceeded to take Indian land under cover of legal principle, albeit legal principles transformed to accommodate economic and political pressure.

The loss of legal protection for Indian land and sovereignty after 1830, as described earlier, was neither a unilinear nor a uniform development; nor did it occur all at once. Indian resistance to land trades materialized at different times in different regions – a function of their repeated exposure to additional demands for more land and of white pressure.[26] It was possible, therefore, that the government could deal with tribes who had not yet experienced or understood the full dimensions of the demand for land on the basis of consent in one area, while it ignored the absence of consent at the same time in another place. The original legal principles of Indian consent were abandoned where they proved to be obstacles to trades or treaties, but they remained intact where they could be accommodated.

The fact that the outcome of the Cherokee conflict did not at once become the signal for the immediate seizure of all desirable

114

Indian land also demonstrated the remaining strength of the earlier commitment to established international and domestic legal principles in dealing with the Indian.[27] Insistence on a decent respect for Indian rights remained a significant concern as countervailing sentiment for the dispossession of the Indian grew louder and stronger. Protest over the lawless treatment of the Cherokee reflected the sharp divisions that the new Indian removal policy had already provoked. As a result of the Indians' uneven pattern of resistance to further land trades and the considerable disapproval of the government's lawlessness by the newly forming reformist organizations, the unilateral and nonconsensual taking of Indian land and encroachment on tribal sovereignty proceeded slowly after the Cherokee crisis. At the core of the revision of Indian property rights during the second half of the nineteenth century was the weakening and, eventually, the elimination of the once firmly held requirement that Indian land could only be taken with Indian consent, by mutual agreement. This was accomplished not by the explicit abandonment of precedent or the sharp reversal of the basic principles of Indian property rights, but through the introduction of new legal concepts into federal Indian law that undermined the consent requirement, and Indian autonomy, by outflanking them.

Trusteeship: "An Illusion Unsupported by Legal Authority"[28]

The legal transformation of the federal government's limited *guardianship* over Indian tribes into an unlimited *trusteeship* accomplished a fundamental reallocation of Indian property rights and undermined tribal autonomy.[29] The transformation reflected the continued, unflinching demand for tribal land coupled, at the end of the nineteenth century, with an intensified ethnocentrism within the United States with respect to Indian peoples and the increased willingness of the United States to assert power over Indian governments. It is critical that while the United States consistently chose to express this new relationship in law, the relationship had no legitimate legal basis. Lacking legal doctrine, the legal expressions relied upon the assertion of moral obligations anchored in the cultural imperialism of white Americans. As the Indians' trustee, the federal government not only assumed the authority to interfere with internal tribal affairs but also asserted the right to dispose of tribal property as it chose.[30] Under the guise of morality and the newly claimed trust authority, the American government could substitute unilateral action for the earlier bilateralism.[31]

By the end of the nineteenth century this United States' Indian trust doctrine had become the legal foundation for the intervention of the federal government in every detail of tribal life – and in particular the control of tribal property.[32] Reflecting the advent of social theories that defined Indians as infants and incompetents, members of the lower races of the world, paternalistic power to take unilateral action for the sake of the "unfortunate" members of this "ignorant and dependent race" replaced the limited legal authority based on treaties and the international law of discovery. However, in passing on the extravagant new guardianship claims of the federal government, United States courts examined neither the lack of historical and legal foundation for such sweeping powers nor defined an exact source for them.[33]

Instead of doctrine and precedent, inchoate notions provided that "the recognized relation between the Government and the Indians [was] that of a superior and an inferior,"[34] and the exercise of governmental power over Indian tribes was justified on the premise that "[t]he Indian tribes *are* the wards of the nation [and] communities dependent on the United States."[35] It followed that "from their very weakness and helplessness . . . there arises the duty of protection, and with it the power."[36] Justified only by reference to the Indians' inferiority, the trust relationship asserted by Congress in the 1887 Dawes Allotment Act became the source of largely unrestrained federal power to regulate all aspects of tribal existence – from the management and disposal of Indian land and resources,[37] to the imposition of federal criminal jurisdiction over tribal members,[38] and even the dissolution of tribal government.[39]

The lack of a firm legal foundation for the assertion of federal trusteeship was paralleled by the absence of legal standards defining the fiduciary duties of the trustee. Although the guardian-trust powers asserted by the federal government by the end of the nineteenth century were far larger in scope and far more pervasive in kind than the clearly delineated dominion of the ultimate sovereign claimed earlier in the same century, the courts imposed on it few restraints other than the pious judicial "presumption" that "the United States would be governed by such considerations of justice as would control a Christian people in their treatment of an ignorant and dependent race."[40] Positing that the United States as trustee would act "in perfect good faith in dealing with the Indians,"[41] the courts set neither constitutional limitations nor traditional common law standards – no conflict of interest, no self-dealing – of fiduciary conduct.

Judicial decisions fashioned no other external restraints to replace the inherent limitations previously imposed by legal respect for tribal sovereignty. To the contrary, Congress's power over tribal relations and property was deemed "political" and, therefore, not subject to control by the judicial department.[42] Questions of the "proper" or "just" uses of the trustee's uncurbed authority, the Supreme Court held, were a matter of "governmental policy" not open to discussion.[43] Courts were, and often continue to be, oblivious to the inherent and unavoidable conflicts of interest of the Indians' trustee. In particular, there has been little legal clarity about the role of the Department of Interior, which acts as trustee for tribes at the same time that it acts as representative of the United States government. Necessarily responsive to the political interests of the American people, the commitment of the executive branch to this peculiar trust institution has incorporated into the trust relationship precisely the conflict of interests that originally threatened Indian land and resources. It would be difficult to imagine courts tolerating that kind of conflict in a trustee in any other area – be it corporate ownership, personal, or charitable trusts.

Conflict in the U.S.-Indian trust relationship is not theoretical or historical. It is expressed routinely – almost daily – in decisions made by the trustee caught between the department's trust obligation to the tribes and the pressures of non-Indian constituents who want access, on good terms, to tribal resources including water, land, gas, oil, and uranium.[44] The ongoing, everyday, and contemporary nature of this conflict is exemplified by litigation brought by the Pyramid Lake Paiute. The Paiute argued that the secretary of the interior created a breach of trust by diverting water from the lake, which was rich in fishlife, for a United States Bureau of Reclamation irrigation project, although it was in the tribe's interest to keep Pyramid Lake full.

In 1973 a federal court acknowledged this conflict in *Pyramid Lake Paiute Tribe v. Morton*, an opinion that suggested considerable government deference was owed to Indian trust responsibilities. Judge Gesell determined, first, that a burden rested with the secretary of the interior to justify with "precision" any diversion of water from the tribe rather than to continue to use an arbitrary "judgment call" and reaffirmed more broadly that trust dealings with Indians should be judged by the "most exacting fiduciary standards."[45] In Paiute water rights litigation a decade later, however, Justice Rehnquist established a new rule to govern trust situations where, according to the Court's poetic imagery, the interior secretary "was requir[ed] . . . to carry water on at least both shoulders."[46] Faced with conflicting trust obligations to Indians and non-Indians, the secretary-trustee need not, the Supreme Court held, follow

> the fastidious standards of a private fiduciary, who would breach his duties to his single beneficiary solely by representing potentially conflicting interests without the beneficiary's consent. The government does not "compromise" its obligation to one interest that Congress obliges it to represent by the mere fact that it simultaneously performs another task for another interest that Congress has obligated it by statute to do.[47]

Assessing Rehnquist's opinion, a leading Native American public-interest law organization concluded, "[T]he Court's decision says that the federal government is not bound by traditional rules of ethics and justice and fairness when it represents Indian interests which conflict with other federal interests which Congress has required it to represent."[48] The Court's opinion in this case, *Nevada v. U.S.*, highlights how fragile tribal reliance on trust protection is in the face of the powerful interests and the dramatic fears that dominate, in this instance, the question of water rights.

Without the imposition of fiduciary obligations concomitant to the qualitatively and quantitatively changed dimensions of federal trusteeship, the trust doctrine has proved to be a pliable instrument of nearly unlimited federal control – and neglect. Where Indian land has been the issue, reliance on federal trust authority also effectively circumvented the requirement of Indian consent and resulted in the massive transfer of Indian land to non-Indian ownership. The sweeping powers of the trustee and its underlying premise of Indian inferiority made it possible for the government to take Indian land without Indian consent in the name of fulfilling its trust responsibilities. In its 1903 *Lone Wolf* decision, the Supreme Court rejected the principle that Indian interest in the common lands fell within the protection of the Fifth Amendment to the Constitution on the grounds that Congress could dispose of tribal property in the exercise of its "full administrative power."[49] On this premise, a congressional taking of treaty-guaranteed tribal land for minimal monetary compensation without tribal consent was "mere[ly] [a] change in the form of the investment" of the property of the government's ward.[50] To support the government's claim of such extraordinary powers over Indians, the courts examined neither the lack of historical and legal foundation for the extravagant claims nor defined an exact source for it but were content to found the government's assertion of sweeping trust powers on amorphous notions of racial and social superiority. Guardianship decisions made at this time relied nearly exclusively on contemporary precedent whose broad confirmation of powers for the federal government was unsupported by prior judicial opinions or the Constitution. Where the Marshall Court's affirmation of Indian occupancy rights in *M'Intosh* and *Worcester* – which remained binding precedent – were acknowledged, they were interpreted to hold merely that the permanent or perpetual occupancy rights of the Indians were valid only as against the states and individuals but not the United States, which was, therefore, free to abrogate them at will.[51]

That the United States may take Indian land by paternalistic prerogative continues to be maintained. In language reminiscent of the temper of nineteenth-century superiority, the federal government argued in 1979 that "Indian tribes have been incapable of prudent management of their communal property" and that the United States has, therefore, the corresponding duty to manage it for them as their trustee. From this it followed that the "disposal of tribal property in the discharge of this responsibility to manage property for the tribe's benefit is an act on behalf of the tribe and, in effect, a disposal by the tribe."[52] Rephrased, the government asserted – nearly a century after *Lone Wolf* – "a proper exercise of this [trust authority] is no more a taking than would be a sale by the tribe itself."[53] Discussing the *Fort Berthold* "good faith effort" test, the *Sioux Nation* Court stated that Congress may seize Indian property and "transmute [it] from land to money" and that, if carried out in what Congress believes to be "the benefit of the Indian," there is no "taking" in violation of the Fifth Amendment.[54] Under this interpretation of the trust theory governmental alienation of Indian land cannot constitute a taking and requires no Indian consent.

The introduction of the trust doctrine into federal Indian law and its expansive judicial interpretation obviated the need to reject formally the original principles of Indian property rights or to abrogate explicitly the pivotal requirement of Indian consent. As decisions legalized the "purchase" of Indian land even when the Indians themselves opposed and resisted such trades, the massive seizure of Indian land without Indian consent did not suffer the public stigma among non-Indians of the Cherokee cases – that of the government placing itself above the law. Once the Supreme Court began to sanction in the name of trusteeship what it had refused to sanction in the name of discovery or conquest in the Cherokee cases – the taking of tribal land without Indian consent – the United States could pride itself on acquiring Indian land in lawful real estate transactions long after the Indians had become involuntary and disenfranchised participants in it. However much federal trust powers were "an illusion unsupported by legal authority," they served well to provide a legal cover for the breach of the legal standards the government had originally set for itself.

The nature and abuses of the trust relationship have not gone without challenge from Native Americans. In particular, beginning in the 1960s, tribal efforts to establish that federal trust power carried fiduciary duties led to legal judgments of equitable relief and, occasionally, money damages, in a handful of breach of trust cases.[55] By the 1970s it appeared that a change had occurred and that the trust relation, long a source of unsatisfactory United States intrusion into Indian life, included an anodyne doctrine of obligation. Court decisions supported tribal claims that the United States government had ignored its fiduciary duties failing, for example, to invest tribal funds held in trust, to pay interest on money held in the United States Treasury, to supervise mineral rights leases in the interest of the tribe, to prevent trespass on tribal land, and to pursue water rights policy in the interest of the tribe.[56] Extensive publicity surrounding the land claims of the Passamaquoddy and Penobscot Indians, which proceeded only after a federal court agreed that the United States had a fiduciary obligation to file protective suits on behalf of the tribes, encouraged the American public to embrace this view of trust responsibility.[57]

Quite suddenly in 1980, however, the Supreme Court anesthesized the new direction of trust doctrine. In *U.S. v. Mitchell* (*Mitchell I*), the Court cut back on the tendency of the Court of Claims to permit trust suits or creation of a cause of action for money damages and placed a narrow construction on a broad statute (the General Allotment Act) creating a trust relationship.[58] Three years later, without expressly overruling *Mitchell I*, the Supreme Court's *Mitchell II* decision supported the principle that the United States, as manager of Indian property, acts as trustee and is liable for violations of breach of express statutory duties as well as common-law fiduciary duties.[59] Where *Mitchell I* appeared to "spell the end of the trust relationship as a doctrine enforceable against the federal government,"[60] *Mitchell II* not only established that the United States was liable for money damages for mismanagement – in this case, of Quinault timber resources – but also held open the possibility of long-term protection of tribal interests where United States trust powers have been asserted.

The changing membership of the Supreme Court and the short duration of time since *Mitchell II* make it impossible to tell whether Native Americans will be frustrated in their attempts to impose common-law fiduciary standards on the federal trustee. According to a prominent student of federal Indian law, the trust relationship has been "a source of enforceable rights against the executive branch and has become a major weapon in the arsenal of Indian rights."[61] But this same observer reminds us that the trust relationship is not constitutionally based and thus not enforceable against Congress.[62]

Without constitutional anchor, and often still without a foundation in ordinary trust principles, even the strongest judicial insistence on "moral obligations of the highest responsibility"[63] for the federal trustee cannot alter the abuses of the use of trust powers or transform trust authority into a limitation of the plenary power of the United States over Indians. As long as trusteeship is not conditioned on adherence to explicit fiduciary standards, the only legally enforcible duties that the United States government has toward Indians are those that it chooses to impose on itself, by itself.[64] Whatever humanitarian impulses the United States follows in the exercise of its trust relations with Indians, the Indians enjoy not by right but by their guardian's good grace. If there continues to be a trust relationship, the history of its use since the late nineteenth century argues eloquently for the development of fiduciary standards that are neither vague, nor self-servingly ethnocentric, nor unduly protective of the federal treasury.

Plenary Power and the Political Question Doctrine

The weakening of Indian sovereignty and property rights through the invocation of federal trusteeship was supported by a far-reaching expansion of plenary federal power over Indian tribes. While the "plenary" character of federal power with respect to Indian tribes had originally been understood to demarcate the exclusive nature of the federal authority over Indian affairs against competing state laws and private deals, the reach of the government's plenary power came to be understood as "nearly absolute" with respect to the tribes themselves by the end of the nineteenth century.

The concept of plenary power, which frames the legal authority of the federal government in Indian affairs and supports its trust power, derives from two constitutional sources, the Indian commerce clause and the treaty clause.[65] Indians are specifically mentioned only in the commerce clause, which authorizes Congress "[t]o regulate Commerce with foreign Nations, and among the several States, and with the Indian Tribes."[66] The treaty clause grants the national government exclusive authority to enter into treaties,[67] and together with the Indian commerce clause it has served as the principal foundation for the exercise of federal power over Indian affairs.

The original delineation of the scope and limits of the federal power that derived from these two constitutional sources was shaped by the historical conditions framing Indian-American relations during the formative decades of federal Indian policy-making.[68] Before, and for several decades after, the founding of the new Republic, the most salient element of that relationship was the recognition of the distinct and separate sovereignty of Indian tribes, who were largely considered independent nations, capable of governing themselves. It was consistent with the prevailing political conditions to equate Indian with foreign relations and to define the relationship with them by treaty. Both foreign and domestic policy reflected that understanding.

Relations with the Indians were administered by the War Department from the first administration in 1789[69] until half a century later in 1849 when Indian affairs were transferred to the Interior Department.[70] Treaties with Indian tribes were accorded the same dignity as that given to treaties with foreign nations.[71] They were largely treaties of peace and friendship;[72] some included mutual assistance pacts,[73] others provided for the restoration and exchange of prisoners,[74] for extradition,[75] and for relations with third powers.[76] During the early period, it was generally undisputed that Indian affairs were an aspect of military and foreign policy rather than of domestic law.

The allocation of civil and criminal jurisdiction reflected the initial recognition of, and respect for, tribal autonomy. Until the second half of the nineteenth century, treaties left internal tribal matters to the tribes, in particular the jurisdiction over intratribal crimes. Although tribal criminal jurisdiction over non-Indians soon became subject to a maze of treaty-based exceptions,[77] jurisdiction over offenses committed by Indians against non-Indians and by non-Indians against Indians originally followed commonly accepted principles of international law.[78] Hostilities against the United States were not considered treason. Criminal and civil laws generally treated persons in Indian country – whether Indian or white – as no different from persons in Canada or Mexico,[79] acknowledging, and at the same time buttressing, the foreign nation status of Indian tribes. Judicial decisions did not question the parallels between Indian treaties and treaties with foreign nations.[80] The power to make treaties with Indians was regarded as "coextensive with that to make treaties with foreign nations,"[81] and it was a power specifically allocated to the federal government.[82]

The foreign affairs focus entailed by the location of federal power to deal with Indians in the treaty clause had two principal corollaries. The first was that Indian affairs were the exclusive prerogative of the federal government: federal treaties and other federal actions preempted state laws in Indian country. The second was that the power of judicial review over the substantive content of federal Indian policy was limited to the same extent as judicial power to review foreign affairs decisions was limited. In analogy to legal concepts governing foreign relations, the federal government's power to make treaties with the Indians was considered a political question, beyond judicial examination.[83]

Monopolization of the power over Indian affairs by the federal government was a course persistently and consistently pursued before, during, and after the adoption of the Constitution.[84] Almost immediately after enactment of the Constitution, Congress seized its constitutional prerogative to monopolize Indian land and other trade in the hands of the federal government – at the expense of the states and private speculators. The Indian Trade and Intercourse Act of 1790 barred states from engaging in land treaties with Indian tribes within or outside their boundaries and adopted a federal licensing scheme to control and supervise the activities of traders, which had often been the cause of friction with Indian tribes. Early decisions of the nineteenth century, therefore, not surprisingly focused on the allocation of the power over Indian affairs to the national government and delineated the exclusive nature of that power as against the states.[85]

The commerce clause basis for the exercise of federal authority over Indian tribes similarly provided a foundation for exclusive federal power over all matters affecting Indian trade. In addition to locating the power of dealing with the Indians in the hands of the federal government as opposed to those of the states, allocation of the power to conduct trade with the Indians in the commerce clause of Article I, Section 8 of the Constitution created the legal underpinning of Congress's authority over Indian tribes. Since Congress's power over "Indian Tribes" was placed in the same category as its power over "foreign Nations" and the "several

States," it served as the underpinning for the understanding that federal legislative authority over Indian affairs was plenary. Parallel to Congress's power over interstate commerce, congressional authority over Indian tribes was considered plenary in the sense that all of the power to regulate intercourse with the Indian tribes rested in the hands of Congress. The combination of exclusive plenary power and its legal conceptualization as an essentially political power assured that federal Indian policy would remain virtually free from judicial scrutiny and exempt from external standards until well into the twentieth century.

In the historical context of separate sovereign Indian status and within the legal framework of the commerce and the treaty clauses, the grant to Congress of plenary – meaning exclusive – power over Indian affairs and the corollary exemption of federal Indian treaty policy from judicial review were not marked deviations from the ground rules of the constitutional and political system. Within this framework the grant to the federal government of exclusive and nearly unreviewable power was linked inseparably, however, to the foreign nation status of tribes and was justifiable only as long as Indian tribes maintained their independence and remained outside the control of American political institutions.

By the end of the nineteenth century that context had changed dramatically. Using physical confrontation and economic pressure in conjunction with legal and bureaucratic manipulation, the United States and its citizens pressed in on Indian communities, weakening and destabilizing them.[86] Soon the United States claimed that these new political realities undermined the premise of separate Indian sovereignty. The power of Indian tribes, which had once impressed on the first generation of American leaders the necessity and wisdom of seeking peaceful agreement with them, had been weakened irrevocably. Regardless of how Native Americans saw themselves, in the United States the status and position of the tribes had changed from that of independent nations to dependent wards of federal government.

Fundamental changes in federal Indian policy had both reflected and promoted the decline of the autonomy of Indian tribes and caused the United States to abandon the foreign relations approach to Indian affairs. Congress abolished the treaty system in 1871[87] and shortly embarked on its most sustained and systematic policy of land allotment and forced acculturation through the Dawes Act, one of whose aims was to destroy the tribal unit altogether. A year prior to passage of the Dawes Act, in a sharp break with the original legal principles respecting the separate autonomy of the tribes, they were subjected to federal criminal jurisdiction.[88] Although these policies ignored and undermined the original foreign relations and treaty basis of the federal government's plenary power, the exercise of that power remained exempt from external standards and continued to be used unchecked.

Late nineteenth-century judicial decisions increasingly sanctioned uses of power premised on legal assumptions invalidated by political realities that the United States had brought about. In a setting of explicit disregard for the sovereign nation status of Indian tribes by the federal government, the Supreme Court not only reconfirmed but expanded the scope of federal power (so as to be "nearly absolute" rather than merely exclusive). And as the foreign relations justification for exempting the exercise of federal power over Indians from judicial review was undermined, judicial decisions nevertheless relied on the political question doctrine to insulate federal Indian policy from meeting constitutional standards.

No case better illustrates this fusion of the plenary power and political question doctrines that augmented the near absolute and unreviewable power of Congress, while it deprived Indian tribes of legal possibilities to resist its arbitrary exercise, than the 1903 Supreme Court decision in *Lone Wolf v. Hitchcock*.[89] No case more clearly raises the question whether the law, indeed, was the "better way." No case better solicits sympathy or demands outrage than the betrayal of the confederated tribes of Kiowa, Comanche, and Kiowa-Apache by Indian agents and by the United States Congress.

The 1867 Treaty of Medicine Lodge established a reservation for the Kiowa and Comanche.[90] Article six provided for the allotment of land. Article twelve established that no subsequent cession of reservation land would be valid unless consented to by three-quarters of male tribal members. In 1892 the United States negotiated an agreement of land cession with the confederated tribes. This agreement, however, violated the terms of the treaty: it did not have the consent of the required number of tribal members and, it was charged, fraud and deceit had been used to acquire what Indian signatures had been obtained. Tribal members, supported by the Indian Rights Association as well as cattlemen interested in protecting their grazing privileges on the reservation, lobbied against the necessary congressional ratification. But even after the secretary of the interior certified that three-fourths of eligible members had not signed the agreement, Congress sanctioned legislation that broke the treaty and approved the taking of the Indians' land.[91]

Faced with exhaustion of political remedies these tribes – not unlike the Cherokee seventy years before – turned to the courts. Yet while the Supreme Court in the Cherokee cases had eventually been unwilling to sanction the use of political power, in *Lone Wolf* the justices found the unilateral and arbitrary abrogation of Indian treaties within Congress's "[p]lenary power over the tribal relations of the Indians."[92] Congress, according to this American Court, had the power to appropriate the treaty-held Indian lands. The appropriation did not irritate the Fifth Amendment because "Congress purported to give an adequate consideration" for the land.[93] Yet, as the tribal petitioners argued in *Lone Wolf* and in litigation half a century later, they had received only 50 percent of the fair value of their lands as compensation for this taking by the federal government.[94]

The *Lone Wolf* Court did not content itself with approval of this congressional power to abrogate treaties and control (lease, sell, or allot) tribal property without tribal consent. It also deemed this "plenary authority . . . [to be] a political one, not subject to be controlled by the judicial department of the government."[95] Certainly there was supreme irony in an opinion that, invoking a doctrine based on the foreign nation status of Indian tribes, simultaneously described Indians as "wards of the nation . . . dependent . . . for their daily food . . . [and] political rights.[96] Without reluctance or comment, Justice White and his colleagues applied a rule of law to circumstances, and a relationship, that in no way resembled those that had given rise to the original development of the rule. *Lone Wolf*, in 1903, exempted the exercise of this nearly absolute congressional power from judicial review at the very time when the original constitutional justification for judicial abstention – the foreign policy character of federal Indian policy – had been explicitly abandoned.

The Court's application of treaty law concepts to the relations between the federal government and Indian tribes left the plaintiff tribes with neither external nor domestic remedies against congressional abuses of the treaty power. Implied foreign nation status in this context did not set Indians free to act on their own and to leave the compact as other foreign nations could under international law. Indian weakness, and federal Indian policy built on it, assured that diplomatic alternatives open to foreign states in retaliation for unilateral and unprovoked treaty violations – war, boycott, attachment of assets or other international legal or diplomatic remedies – were not available to Indian tribes. At the same time, judicial attribution of foreign nation status to Lone Wolf's tribe barred them from domestic legal remedies for breach of contract or promises. Domestic political redress could be won only from Congress, the very institution that had chosen in the first place – unilaterally – to ignore or abrogate its "solemn" treaty obligations, be it for reasons of public policy, popular pressure, white greed, or no reason at all.

In order to justify the exercise of plenary power and its exemption from judicial review, judicial decisions following *Lone Wolf* had to maintain as real what was by then legal fiction – the foreign nation status of Indians. The imposition of that legal fiction on Indian-American relations at the turn of the century did not serve the interests of Indian tribes. Their independence and self-government had by then been systematically undermined by congressional policies beginning with, and extending, the Major Crimes and Allotment Acts, which treated Indians as inferior and incapable wards of the federal government and which, cavalierly, disregarded the tribes' residual autonomy.[97] The legal fiction served well, however, the interests of the government by sustaining uses of power over Indians that would scarcely have been tolerated if used against non-Indians.

The legal consequences of the metamorphosis of the plenary power concept in the course of the nineteenth century was to legitimize the exercise of unilateral and *standardless* power by the United States over Indian tribes whose lack of recourse was confirmed by this one-sided allocation of power. The unreviewable power to abrogate treaties, which *Lone Wolf* left to Congress, made tribes captive to the will and whim of the legislature. It is in this sense fitting that *Lone Wolf*, which perfected the combination of near absolute congressional power with its exemption – until recently[98] – from judicial review, was recognized as the "Indian's *Dred Scott* decision."[99]

Conclusion

Despite some taming of federal plenary power over Indian tribes through breach of trust litigation and the recent repudiation of political question doctrine, plenary power is alive and well. Judicial attitudes of nonintervention remain and federal courts continue to support – indeed increasingly, to lead – the federal government in the assertion of inherent powers of almost unlimited scope in the areas of tribal property rights and, in particular, tribal sovereignty.[100] With troubling regularity, for instance, the Supreme

Court has described tribal sovereignty recently as existing "only at the sufferance of Congress," which has plenary power over them.[101] While individual Indians now hold the same constitutional rights as other Americans, and it is claimed that Congress does not have the power under plenary power "to deny due process or equal protection or the freedom of religion and speech,"[102] many Native Americans reject an individual rights focus. For them, group – that is, tribal – rights constitute the critical issue. The protection and perpetuation of the tribe matters. Failure to acknowledge this concedes the superiority of a Western-oriented, individual rights perspective and denies the cultural pluralism and political rights of Indian societies.[103]

Scholars and lawyers concerned with plenary power present an array of conclusions about its reach in the modern era and its future. For some, the contours of the power have been judicially refigured in ways that impose protective legal standards: *"Morton v. Marcari, Delaware Tribe* and *Sioux Nation . . .* modernized judicial review of congressional action in Indian law . . . and are polite but firm warnings to Congress that care must be taken in-house."[104] This observer concedes, however, that "regardless of whatever protections and advances the tribes may have achieved in the courts in modern times, Congress remains the fount of most Indian law." Congressional power "may no longer be absolute but by any mark it remains uncommonly broad."[105] That the plenary power-political question doctrine has been narrowed is acknowledged but how meaningfully remains a contentious point. One expert in the field of federal Indian law writes, "[T]he scuttling of *Lone Wolf* in the name of review for rationality amounts to recognition that the familiar constitutional framework for ordering congressional action through limited judicial oversight applies to the making of Indian laws;"[106] but a noted constitutional scholar hazards: "[T]here is abundant other evidence of the present vitality of *Lone Wolf*'s theory of plenary power and superiority. In *United States v. Sioux Nation*, for example, Justice Blackmun maintained 'the Lone Wolf holding [has been] often reaffirmed'."[107] This analyst asserts that while "Congress's power over Indians has met with some judicial narrowing [this] does not mean that federal plenary or implied power over Indians is contracting. Far from it. The power continues to expand. Now it is taking place in the Supreme Court rather than in Congress."[108]

The array of prescription is equally dazzling. A recent law journal article admonishes Native Americans and the federal Indian law community to "learn to live with plenary power." It concedes that Indian law recognizes the "co-existence of two absolutely contradictory tenets: the sovereign status of Indian tribes and the plenary power of Congress over them . . . plenary power is acceptable, but only in direct proportion to the extent that it is counterbalanced by a conflicting, and inconsistent, recognition of inherent tribal sovereignty."[109] This commentator's nemesis, however, counsels that we not learn "to live with Eurocentric myopia," argues that the plenary power is an unprincipled embodiment of the doctrine of discovery, and urges the unqualified recognition of tribal sovereignty.[110] Where the one writer has "some faith in the ability of the United States Congress and federal court system to exercise the plenary power with a delicate touch,"[111] the other – a scholar whose work is deeply rooted in European and North American history – rejects any optimistic belief in the "ability of Congress and the courts to handle the plenary power with care."[112] Delicate touch or not, some experts urge tribal litigation strategies that "challenge this practically unlimited power of Congress to run Indian affairs,"[113] while a long-time practitioner in the field of Indian law flatly asserts that plenary power is "a relic of the nineteenth century."[114] This attorney makes the following straightforward argument: "[I]t is time for lawyers to stop repeating by rote that Congress has plenary power over Indian affairs. The Plenary Power Doctrine has no sound basis in American Constitutional Law. It was a doctrine of raw political power and it remains today a doctrine of colonialism."[115]

Notes

1. *Lone Wolf v. Hitchcock*, 187 U.S. 553, 565 (1903).
2. *Shoshone v. U.S.*, 324 U.S. 335, 355 (1944) (concurring).
3. *Johnson v. M'Intosh*, 21 U.S. (8 Wheat.) 543, 596–97 (1823); *Worcester v. Georgia*, 31 U.S. (6 Pet.) 515, 559 (1832).
4. *Worcester*, 31 U.S. at 559.
5. *Beecher v. Wetherby*, 95 U.S. (5 Otto) 517, 525–26 (1877).
6. *Mitchel v. United States*, 34 (9 Pet.) 711 (1835).
7. Our outline of these two fundamental propositions here and in chapter 1 does not mean to suggest perfect agreement of their legitimacy, either then or now. The early cases gave rise to sharply differing interpretations. Marshall's conclusion that Indian land title was, by historical necessity, diminished by restrictions on the In-

dians' right of alienating their land – leaving tribes with less than a fee simple absolute – was by no means universally accepted. Justice Johnson's dissent in *Fletcher v. Peck*, 10 U.S. (6 Cranch) at 146, argued in favor of the Indians' "absolute proprietorship of their soil" and denied that another sovereign could share the Indians' fee simple. Dissenting in *Cherokee v. Georgia*, 30 U.S. (5 Pet.) at 75–80, both Justice Thompson and Justice Story argued that the Cherokee Nation retained foreign nation status in the full sense of international law.

Students of federal Indian law have, in particular, criticized Marshall's derogation from absolute Indian title as unsupported by historical fact or prior legal doctrine. See, e.g., Berman, "The Concept of Aboriginal Rights in the Early Legal History of the United States," 27 *Buffalo L. Rev.* 637 (1978); R. Barsh & J. Henderson, *The Road: Indian Tribes and Political Liberty* (Berkeley, 1980); and Ball, "Constitution, Court, Indian Tribes," 1987 *Am. B. Found. Res. J.* 1 (1987).

It is a philosophical and moral critique of the pretensions of discovery that echoes Marshall's own admission that neither "natural law [nor] the usages of civilized nations" supported such a restriction on the Indian right of transfer but condemns as unjustified and unjustifiable Marshall's pragmatic acceptance of it as an indispensable adaptation to the actual condition of European and Indian people. *Johnson v. M'Intosh*, 21 U.S. at 591–92. Yet while there is disagreement over the moral and historical justification for Marshall's definition of less than fee simple absolute Indian title, there is no disagreement that the "lesser" protected occupancy rights that Marshall's decisions established were indefensible. Thus, even Marshall's least protective definition of Indian property rights as "mere" occupancy rights is explicit in establishing that these occupancy rights were permanent and secure – "as sacred as fee simple of whites," *Mitchel*, 34 U.S. (9 Pet.) at 711 – and could not be extinguished unless the tribes agreed to it. See above Berman, at 649, whose careful reading of the judicial texts rejects a hierarchical ordering of the terms "absolute title" and "occupancy rights."

8. *Fletcher*, 10 U.S. at 142–43.
9. *Johnson*, 21 U.S. at 574.
10. *Cherokee Nation*, 30 U.S. at 17.
11. 30 U.S. at 16.
12. *Cherokee Nation*, 30 U.S. at 16.
13. *Johnson*, 21 U.S. at 573.
14. *Id.* at 590.
15. *Id.* at 588.
16. *Cherokee Nation*, 30 U.S. at 17. Much has been written about the arrogance of European power on which the restrictions on Indian sovereignty and property rights were premised and on their lack of foundation in natural and international law. Williams, "The Algebra

of Federal Indian Law: The Hard Trail of Decolonizing and Americanizing the White Man's Jurisprudence," 1986 *Wis. L. Rev.* 219
(hereinafter cited as Williams, "Algebra") and *supra*, note 7. Since our
analysis examines the adherence of American law to its own founding
principles, this study accepts restrictions on Indian title and sovereignty – however ill-founded – as given in the sense that they form
the baseline against which departures from original principles of
federal Indian law are measured. The focus of this analysis is how and
why federal Indian law departed from those very standards that were
adopted and accepted as binding by the new American state itself.

17. *Johnson*, 21 U.S. at 591–92.
18. *Id.* at 596–97. See also Frederick E. Hoxie, *A Final Promise: The Campaign to Assimilate the Indians, 1880–1920* (Lincoln, Nebr., 1984).
19. Berman, *supra* note 7, at 649.
20. *Worcester*, 31 U.S. at 561.
21. *Id.* at 553–54.
22. *Id.* at 544–45.
23. Three years after the sale of Manhattan Island, the colony of the New Netherlands wrote into law the principle that Indian lands should be acquired only with Indian consent, and with the exception of Massachusetts and North Carolina, all of the colonies adopted similar laws. The Northwest Ordinance established as national policy that "Indian land and property shall never be taken from them without their consent." Cohen, "Original Indian Title," 32 *Minn. L. Rev.* 28, 39–40 (1947).
24. *Johnson*, 21 U.S. (8 Wheat) 543; *U.S. v. Alcea Band of Tillamooks*, 329 U.S. 40, 46 (1946).
25. For example, the United States entered into several treaties with the Cherokee under which the Cherokee would cede tracts of land east of the Mississippi River in exchange for lands west of the Mississippi. *Cherokee Nation* 30 U.S. (5 Pet.) at 5 (indicating treaties between the United States and the Cherokee). The Cherokee also ceded large portions of land to the United States in exchange for carrying out earlier promises that the Cherokee who remained east of the Mississippi might rely on the aid of the United States. *Id.* at 5–6 (citing Treaty between the United States of America and the Cherokee Tribe of Indians, July 8th, 1817, 7 Stat. 156, reprinted in 2 *Indian Affairs, Laws, and Treaties* (C. Kappler, ed. 1904). The Cherokee were not alone in their relinquishment of large tracks of land to the United States. In his dissent in *Cherokee Nation*, Justice Thompson observed that "the whites have been gradually pressing upon [the Oneida], as they kept receding from the approaches of civilization. We have purchased the greater part of their lands, destroyed their hunting grounds, subdued the wilderness around them, overwhelmed them with our population, and gradually abridged their native indepen-

dence." *Id.* at 67. See also *Massachusetts v. New York*, 271 U.S. 65, 83 (1925) (describing a large portion of upstate New York that had been ceded to Massachusetts by the Treaty of Hartford, July 8, 1788 by the Mohawks, Oneidas, Onandagas, Cayuga, and Senecas).

26. The Sioux, for example, were still willing to make treaties ceding millions of acres in the 1850s, twenty years after the Cherokee had already understood that the demand for land was neverending and that treaties would not be honored. By the late 1860s, when the Sioux understood what the Cherokee had had to learn before them, the Sioux, too, refused to make further cessions. And so it went as the westward drive of the white population moved toward the Pacific.

27. Strickland, "The Absurd Ballet of American Indian Policy," 31 *Me. L. Rev.* 219 (1979).

28. Cohen, "Indian Wardship: The Twilight of a Myth," 6 *Amer. Indian* at 11 (1953).

29. *In re Heff*, 197 U.S. 488, 496 (1905). ("The continuance of the relation as wards relates both to property and personal protection.") The etiology of the "trust" concept is treated variously in the federal Indian law literature. It is often presented as synonymous with a guardian-ward relationship or, alternatively, as having been parented by the guardian-ward relationship between the United States and Indian governments invented by Marshall in *Cherokee Nation*, 30 U.S. at 17 ([the tribes'] "relation to the United States resembles that of a ward to a guardian.") See Ball, *supra* note 7, at 62–66. Marshall's text indicates that he was employing "suggestive analogy" and did not say that tribes are wards of the United States. Indeed, no aspect of the economic, political, or military condition of Cherokee society at the time of *Cherokee Nation* qualified as existing within such a relationship.

30. The imposition of federal criminal jurisdiction over tribes in 1885, the alienation of ninety million acres of tribal "surplus" land, and much more rested on the power of the guardian, soon-to-be trustee, "to manage the Indians' affairs" for them.

31. Haas, "The Legal Aspect of Indian Affairs from 1887 to 1957," 311 *Annals* (AAPSS) 12–13 (May 1957). The use of morality as a cover for the exercise of self-interest may be explored in F. duc de Larouchefoucauld, *The Maxims* (New York, 1959) (L. Krononberger trans.); N. Keohane, *Philosophy and the State in France* (Princeton, 1980).

32. The BIA and other federal agencies interfere with tribal governments with respect to questions of jurisdiction, domestic relations, relations with state and local governments, commercial activity of all kinds, education of Indian children, and religious ceremonies and practices. The United States as trustee regulates virtually every form of activity related to the land: the BIA leases Indian lands (*Davis v. Morton*, 469 F.2d 593 (10th Cir. 1972)); regulates grazing (25 C.F.R. § 166 (1988))

(General Grazing Regulations); regulates mineral development (*Jicarilla Apache Tribe v. Supron Energy Company*, 728 F.2d 1555 (10th Cir. 1984), *on rehearing*, 782 F.2d 855, *modified*, 793 F.2d 1171 (10th Cir. 1986) (*en banc*), *cert. denied*, 107 S. Ct. 471 (1986)) and has the power to approve (for form) the wills of allottees that devise interests in allotments. See also, F. Hoxie, *supra* note 18, in particular ch. 5, "The Emergence of a Colonial Land Policy."

33. Although the courts rested the proposition that the United States – as the Indians' trustee – had unlimited powers over them and their property on Marshall's characterization of Indian tribes as "domestic dependent nations" in a "state of pupilage," *Cherokee Nation*, 30 U.S. at 17, they did not acknowledge the Marshall Court's explicit limitation of the concept of American guardianship over Indian nations by conceding the internal autonomy and property rights of Indian nations, which "had always been considered as distinct, independent, political communities, retaining their original natural rights, as the undisputed possessors of the soil." *Worcester*, 21 U.S. at 559. The Supreme Court itself had earlier rejected the suggestion that federal management of Indian trade could be construed "as a surrender of [Indian] self-government," *Worcester*, 31 U.S. at 553–54. Instead, judicial decisions made during the last quarter of the nineteenth century took for granted the federal guardian's power "to manage all tribal affairs." And despite Marshall's explicit admonition that tribes had not stripped themselves of the right of government or ceased to be states by placing themselves under the protection of the United States, *Worcester*, 31 U.S. at 561, the Indians' disinterest in Western values and comparative weakness, along with American ethnocentrism, became the justification for the government's assertion of total control. For a review of the origins of the trust relationship, see American Indian Policy Review Commission, *Report on Trust Responsibilities and the Federal-Indian Relationship, Including Treaty Review* (Task Force One) 47–53 (Washington, D.C., 1976).

34. *In re Heff*, 197 U.S. at 498.

35. *United States v. Kagama*, 118 U.S. 375 (1886).

36. *Id.*

37. See, e.g., *Lone Wolf v. Hitchcock*, 187 U.S. 553 (1903) (power to dispose of Indian lands as guardian of the tribe); *Cherokee Nation v. Hitchcock*, 187 U.S. 294 (1902) (power to lease Indian land as guardian).

38. *United States v. Kagama*, 118 U.S. 375 (1886) (upholding constitutionality of the Major Crimes Act as an exercise of congressional guardianship power).

39. See Act of March 1, 1901, ch. 676, § 46; 31 Stat. 861, 872. (Creek Nation tribal government to cease as of March 4, 1906 – unless extended by Congress). In correspondence, Richard W. Hughes,

Esq. points out that this proposition was "popularly believed, and was the proposition acted upon by the BIA," but that in *Harjo v. Kleppe*, 420 F. Supp. 1110 (D.D.C. 1976), *affirmed sub nom. Harjo v. Andrus*, 581 F.2d 949 (D.C. Cir.) (1978) the Court held that the government of the Creek Nation was never lawfully terminated by Congress and that the tribe continued to possess full powers of self-government. (Letter of September 14, 1989). See also Act of June 28, 1898, 30 Stat. 495 (providing for the end of the tribal governments of the Choctaws and Chickasaws).

40. *Beecher*, 95 U.S. at 525–26.
41. *Lone Wolf*, 187 U.S. at 568.
42. *Id*. at 565.
43. *Beecher*, 95 U.S. 517 at 525.
44. Both at the beginning of contact with Europeans and in the modern era, tribes have had resources wanted by non-Indians. BIA official David Harrison recently described the situation this way: "It is beginning to look like the Indians have most of what is running short in the rest of the country – water, oil, gas, uranium, and tremendous amounts of western coal . . . Indian resources are extensive: 52 million acres . . . 30 per cent of the country's strippable coal; 15 per cent to 40 per cent of the nation's uranium; an annual timber harvest of 1 billion board feet; 6 million to 8 million acres of grazing land . . ." P. Wiley & R. Gottlieb, *Empires in the Sun: The Rise of the New American West* 220 (New York, 1982).
45. *Pyramid Lake Paiute Tribe v. Morton*, 354 F. Supp. 252, 256 (D.D.C. 1973). See generally Chambers & Price, "Regulating Sovereignty: Secretarial Discretion and the Leasing of Indian Lands," 26 *Stan. L. Rev.* 1061 (1974); Chambers, "Judicial Enforcement of the Federal Trust Responsibility to Indians," 27 *Stan. L. Rev.* 1213 (1975); and Newton, "Enforcing The Federal-Trust Relationship After Mitchell," 31 *Cath. U. L. Rev.* 635 (1982) (hereinafter cited as Newton, "Enforcing Trust").
46. *Nevada v. U.S.*, 463 U.S. 110, 128 (1983). See generally W. Veeder, *Indian Water Rights in the Concluding Years of the Twentieth Century* (Chicago: Newberry Library, Center for the History of the American Indian, Occasional Papers No 5, 1982); Native American Rights Fund, *The NARF Legal Review* (Boulder, Summer 1983; Spring 1986; Fall 1986) (review of tribal water rights).
47. 463 U.S. 110, 128.
48. Native American Rights Fund (Summer 1983), *supra* note 46 at 2.
49. 187 U.S. at 564, 568.
50. 187 U.S. at 568.
51. *Lone Wolf*, 187 U.S. at 564–65.
52. Brief for Petitioner at 48, *United States v. Sioux*, 448 U.S. 371 (1980) (No. 79–639).

53. *Id.*
54. *United States v. Sioux Nation of Indians*, 448 U.S. 371, 408–9. Five years later, in the Dann sisters' land litigation, the Supreme Court concluded that a "payment" had been effected, although the Shoshone received no money and opposed the conversion of their land. As described by one legal scholar, the Court said that "[t]he United States was not only the judgment debtor to Indians, but was also trustee to Indians. Therefore the United States as debtor can pay itself as trustee, say this change in bookkeeping constitutes payment to Indians, and [courts] will certify the fiction as reality." Ball, *supra* note 7, at 65 (referring to *United States v. Dann*, 470 U.S. 39, 42) (1985).
55. Newton, "Enforcing Trust," *supra* note 45, 635, 636–37, n. 10.
56. *Id.* at 645–51.
57. *Joint Tribal Council of Passamaquoddy v. Morton*, 522 F.2d 370 (1st Cir. 1975).
58. 445 U.S. 535 (1980). See generally Newton, "Enforcing Trust," *supra* note 45; Hughes, "Can the Trustee Be Sued For Its Breach? The Sad Saga of United States v. Mitchell," 26 *S. D. L. Rev.* 447 (1981) and Note, "Indians May Sue for Breach of Federal Trust Relationship: United States v. Mitchell," 26 *Boston C. L. Rev.* 809 (1985). Charles Wilkinson concludes that *Mitchell I* "is unlikely to have broad impact . . . the holding in *Mitchell I* is . . . made effectively irrelevant by *Mitchell II*." C. Wilkinson, *American Indians, Time, and the Law* 84 (New Haven, 1987).
59. *United States v. Mitchell*, 463 U.S. 206 (1983) (*Mitchell II*) (at issue were specific timber management statutes). *Mitchell II* acknowledges that the Tucker Act does now waive sovereign immunity.
60. Newton, "Enforcing Trust," *supra* note 45, at 680.
61. Newton, "Federal Power over Indians: Its Sources, Scope, and Limitations," 132 *U. Pa. L. Rev.* 195, 233 (1984) (hereinafter cited as Newton, "Federal Power").
62. Newton, "Federal Power," *supra* note 61, at 233. Wilkinson is somewhat more sanguine, arguing that "since *Delaware Tribe*, tribal representatives have made repeated use of the rational basis test in advocating against bills deemed to be detrimental to Indian interests. The new cases have been argued in the legislative forum with particular vigor in defining Congress's trust duties." *Supra* note 58, at 83. Ball questions whether this new protection will extend beyond the five purposes of trust doctrine outlined in the *Mitchell II* dissent. Ball, *supra* note 7, at 64. Casting a bright light on past, and possible future, failure of breach of trust litigation, other scholars have argued that tribes would also do well to pursue strategies based upon the assertion of tribal sovereignty rather than trust relationship. Newton argues that tribes might cease to concede federal plenary power,

invoke tribal sovereignty, and rely less on "the trust relationship with its patronizing, colonial overtones." Newton, "Enforcing Trust," *supra* note 45, at 680–81.

63. *Seminole Nation v. United States*, 316 U.S. 286, 297 (1942).

64. *Report on the Progress of the Special Committee on Investigations of the Select Committee on Indian Affairs and to Provide Additional Funding*, Senate, 100th Cong., 2d Sess. (1988). S. Res. 381 21(c) (100th Cong., 2d Sess., Feb. 26, 1988) provided that the Special Committee on Investigations is authorized to "study or investigate any and all matters pertaining to problems and opportunities of Indians and the Federal administration of mineral resources, including but not limited to resource management and trust responsibilities of the United States Government, Indian education, health, special services, and other Federal programs, and related matters." Late in 1989, the special investigative committee issued a final report and legislative recommendations calling for "a new federalism for American Indians." The proposal awaits congressional action. *Final Report and Legislative Recommendations. A Report of the Special Committee on Investigations of the Select Committee on Indian Affairs*, Senate, 101st Cong., 1st Sess. (1989).

65. In *McClanahan v. Arizona State Tax Commission*, 411 U.S. 164 (1973), the Court observed: "The source of federal authority over Indian matters has been the subject of some confusion, but it is now generally recognized that the power derives from federal responsibility for regulating commerce with Indian tribes and for treaty making." *Id.* at 172 n. (citations omitted). Ball observes, however, that this analysis by Justice Thurgood Marshall was subsequently modified when Marshall dropped the reference to treaty power and added the "superior position" of the United States as a source of its authority. Ball, *supra* note 7, at 50 citing to *Merrion v. Jicarilla Apache Tribe* 435 U.S. 130, 155 (1980). Newton situates plenary power in commerce power as well as "the treaty, war and other foreign affairs powers [and] the property power." "Federal Power," *supra* note 61, at 199.

66. U.S. Const. art. I, sec. 8, cl. 3. The only other express reference to Indians is the exclusion of "Indians not taxed" from the apportionment of taxes and representatives to Congress. U.S. Const. art. I, sec. 2, cl. 3, amend. XIV, sec. 2.

67. U.S. Const. art. II, sec. 2, cl. 2. See, e.g., *Morton v. Mancari*, 417 U.S. 535, 551–52 (1974); *Board of County Comm'rs v. Seber*, 318 U.S. 705, 715 (1943).

68. *Cherokee Nation*, 30 U.S. (5 Pet.) at 43; *The Kansas Indians*, 72 U.S. (5 Wall.) 737, 757 (1867); *United States v. Forty Three Gallons of Whiskey*, 93 U.S. 188, 195 (1867); *Morton v. Mancari*, 417 U.S. 535, 553 n. 24 (1974).

69. Act of August 7, 1789, ch. 7, § 1, 1 Stat. 49.

70. Act of March 3, 1849, ch. 108, § 5, 9 Stat. 395.
71. *Forty Three Gallons of Whiskey*, 93 U.S. 188.
72. See, e.g., Treaty with the Sacs, May 13, 1816, 7 Stat. 141; Treaty with the Choctaws, January 3, 1786, 7 Stat. 21 (Treaty at Hopewell); Treaty with the Delawares, September 17, 1778, 7 Stat 13.
73. See, e.g., Treaty with the Kansas, August 16, 1825, art. 3, 7 Stat. 270, 271; Treaty with the Wyandots, Delawares, Shawanoese, Senecas, and Miamies, July 22, 1814, art. 2, 7 Stat. 118; Treaty with the Great and Little Osages, November 10, 1808, art. 12, 7 Stat. 107, 110.
74. See, e.g., Treaty with the Cherokee, July 2, 1791, art. 3, 7 Stat. 39.
75. See, e.g., Treaty with the Choctaws, September 27, 1830, art. 8, 7 Stat. 333, 334 (Treaty of Dancing Rabbit Creek).
76. See, e.g., Treaty with the Kioway, Ka-ta-ka, and Ta-wa-ka-ro Nations, May 26, 1837, art. 9, 7 Stat. 533, 535 (recognizing relations between the tribes and the Republic of Mexico); Treaty with Comanche and Witchetaw, August 24, 1835, art. 9, 7 Stat. 474, 475 (recognizing friendly relations between those tribes and the Republic of Mexico).
77. See, e.g., Treaty with the Choctaws, September 27, 1830, arts 6–8, 7 Stat. 333, 334. See also Clinton, "Criminal Jurisdiction over Indian Lands: A Journey through a Jurisdictional Maze," 18 *Ariz. L. Rev.* 503 (1976).
78. Non-Indians who settled and committed crimes within Indian country were subject to punishment by the Indian tribes just as Indians committing offenses against state and Indian law were subject to punishment by non-Indian courts. See, e.g., Treaty with Wyandots, Delawares, Shawanoes, Ottawas, Chipewas, Putawatimes, Miamis, Eel-river, Weeas, Kickapoos, Piankashaws, and Kaskaskias, August 3, 1795, art. 6, 7 Stat. 49, 52). See also, Treaty with the Delawares, September 17, 1778, 7 Stat. 13 (for punishment of offenders by both treaty parties, according to their laws and customs and natural justice).
79. F. Cohen, *Handbook of Federal Indian Law* 5 (Washington, D.C., 1982).
80. *Holden v. Joy*, 84 U.S. (17 Wall.) 211, 242–43 (1872); *Worcester*, 31 U.S. at 559.
81. *Forty Three Gallons of Whiskey*, 93 U.S. at 197.
82. See, e.g., *McClanahan*, 411 U.S. 164; *Kansas Indians*, 72 U.S. 737.
83. *Mancari*, 417 U.S. 535, 553 n. 24 (1974).
84. The Albany Plan of Union (1754), reprinted in 1 W. Swindler, *Sources and Documents of United States Constitutions*, Second Series, 155 (W. Swindler ed. New York, 1982); Articles of Confederation, art. 9.; U.S. Constitution art. I, sec. 8. See, however, a federal appeals court decision holding that, under the Articles of Confederation, a

state need not have received central government permission for the purchase of Indian land. *Oneida Indian Nation of New York v. New York*, 860 F.2d 1145 (2d Cir. 1988).

85. The *Fletcher, Johnson, Cherokee Nation*, and *Worcester* decisions discussed in chapter 1 indisputably stand for this principle. Similarly, later nineteenth-century Supreme Court decisions held that tribes were free from state jurisdiction. *The Kansas Indians*, 72 U.S. (5 Wall.) 737 and *The New York Indians*, 72 U.S. (5 Wall.) 761 (1866).

86. An "Indian department" responsible for the execution of United States Indian policy – political, military, and "education and civilization" – had been established in the War Department by Congress because many Indians had fought with the British in the revolutionary war. The creation of the Interior Department in 1849 provided an opportunity to move the Office of Indian Affairs out of the War Department. This bureaucracy became an ever-more ubiquitous presence in the lives of Natives Americans both as a buffer to, and as an agent of, "manifest destiny." Act of March 3, 1849, ch. 108, § 5, 9 Stat. 49. F. Prucha, 111–15 *The Great Father* (abr. ed. Lincoln, Nebr. 1984).

87. 16 Stat. 544; 25 U.S.C. § 71.

88. Major Crimes Act, 18 U.S.C. § 1153 *et seq.*

89. 187 U.S. 553 (1903).

90. Treaty between the United States of America and the Kiowa and Comanche Tribes of Indians, October 21, 1867, 15 Stat. 581. By a separate treaty the Apache tribe was incorporated with the Kiowa and Comanche and became entitled to share in the benefits of the reservation created by Medicine Lodge. Treaty between the United States of America and the Kiowa, Comanche, and Apache Tribes of Indians, October 21, 1867, 15 Stat. 589.

91. 187 U.S. at 557. For a discussion of the various lobby groups which appeared before Congress in this conflict, see W. Hagan, *The Indian Rights Association: The Herbert Welsh Years, 1882–1904* (Tucson, 1985).

92. 187 U.S. at 565.

93. *Id.* at 568.

94. 187 U.S. at 561; *United v. Kiowa, Comanche and Apache Tribes*, 163 F. Supp. 603, 608 (Ct. Cl. 1958), *cert. denied*, 359 U.S. 934 (1959).

95. 187 U.S. at 565.

96. *Id.* at 567.

97. American Indian Policy Review Commission, *Final Report* at 130 (Washington, D.C., 1977); see generally Chambers, *supra* note 45.

98. Only in 1977, commenting on *Lone Wolf's* non-justicibility doctrine, the Supreme Court said, "[T]he statement . . . has not deterred this Court, particularly in this day, from scrutinizing Indian legislation to determine whether it violates the equal protection component of the

Fifth Amendment." *Delaware Tribal Business Committee v. Weeks*, 430 U.S. 73, 84 (1977). Three years later the Court further repudiated this use of the political question doctrine: "[I]t has long since been discredited in takings cases, and was expressly laid to rest in *Delaware Tribal Business Comm. v. Weeks.*" *Sioux Nation*, 448 U.S. 371, 413 (1980). While repudiated, it is essential to remember that the doctrine has been of central importance in modern litigation, including a case denying the native peoples of Alaska their claim to most of Alaska's 272 million acres. *Tee-Hit-Ton Indians v. United States*, 348 U.S. 272 (1955). Ball comments that "the announced new policy of review, however, has not resulted in any action of Congress being struck down by the Court. The Court has never limited Congress's will with the tribes." *Supra* note 7, at 56–57. But, see Laurence, "Learning to Live with the Plenary Power of Congress over the Indian Nations: An Essay in Reaction to Professor Williams' Algebra," 30 *Ariz. L. Rev.* 413, 418 n. 34 (1988) (arguing that plenary power is acceptable and that congressional plenary power and tribal sovereignty must coexist as contradictory tenets in a legal system that must be flexible enough to accommodate such contradictions).

99. *Sioux Nations of Indians v. United States*, 601 F.2d 1157, 1173 (Ct. Cl. 1979) (Nichols, J. concurring).

100. Newton, "Federal Power," *supra* note 61, at 233, 261; Ball, *supra* note 7, at 57.

101. *Encondido Mutual Water Co. v. LaJolla Band of Mission Indians*, 466 U.S. 765, 787–89 n. 30 (1984) (quoting *U.S. v. Wheeler*, 435 U.S. 313, 323 (1978): "all aspects of Indian sovereignty are subject to defeasance by Congress"); *National Farmers Union Insurance Co. v. Crow Tribe of Indians*, 471 U.S. 845, 851 n. 10 (same); *Rice v. Rehner*, 463 U.S. 713, 719 (1983) (same).

102. Laurence, *supra* note 98, at 419. Roberts Williams, Jr. reminds us that the Supreme Court's form of Indian equal protection, articulated in its 1974 *Morton v. Mancari* decision, 417 U.S. 535, creates *sui generis* treatment of Indians. Williams, "Learning Not to Live with Euro-centric Myopia" 30 *Ariz. L. Rev.* 439, 445–46, n. 29 (1988) (hereinafter cited as Williams, "Learning Not to Live").

103. See, e.g., Williams, "Learning Not to Live," *supra* note 102, at 447.

104. Wilkinson, *supra* note 58, at 81–82. Newton agrees that *Mancari* "broke important ground [by attempting] to fit Indian legislative classifications within the equal protection framework" but concludes that "cases subsequent to *Mancari* have unfortunately ignored many of the signals of judicial activism in the *Mancari* decision and have cut back on the promise of that decision." Newton, "Federal Power," *supra* note 61, at 272, 274. She underscores that *Mancari* and *Weeks* involved equal protection challenges raised by individuals and describes the general failure of the equal protection argument to date

when raised by tribes. *Id.* at 281–86. Newton argues, however, for persistence in the use of both equal protection and due process litigation by tribes. *Id.* at 286–88.

105. Wilkinson, *supra* note 58, at 81.

106. *Id.* at 82.

107. Ball, *supra* note 7, at 55. Professor Ball also argues that Justice Thurgood Marshall finds *Lone Wolf* "viable and acceptable as indicated by one of his footnotes." *Id.* at 54, citing to *Solem v. Bartlett*, 465 U.S. 463, 470 n. 11 (1984) and that Justice Stevens makes "favorable use of *Kagama* and *Lone Wolf*" in his *Merrion* dissent. *Id.* at 55.

108. Ball, *supra* note 7, at 56. Professor Ball sees the demise of the *Lone Wolf* political question doctrine in federal Indian law as having presented the Court with the opportunity to enhance and embed plenary power in the federal system, to conduct what he calls "independent operations." "Little notice is then taken when the Court begins to wield this power on its own, moving by itself against the tribes where Congress has held back." *Id.* at 57. This is an important caveat at a time when other experts conclude that Congress is where the action is: "Congress remains the fount of most Indian law. It is on Capitol Hill that it all can be lost and that most of it can be preserved." Wilkinson, *supra* note 58, at 82.

109. Laurence, *supra* note 98, at 422.

110. See generally Williams, "Learning Not to Live," *supra* note 102 and Williams, "Algebra," *supra* note 16.

111. Laurence, *supra* note 98, at 424.

112. Williams, "Learning Not to Live," *supra* note 102, at 452.

113. Newton, "Enforcing Trust," *supra* note 45, at 682.

114. "Plenary Power Over Indians: A Doctrine Of Colonialism" at 3 (n.d.).

115. *Id.* at 8. See also Ziontz, "Indian Litigation," in S. Cadwalader and V. Deloria, Jr. eds., *The Aggressions of Civilization* (Philadelphia, 1984).

4

The Indian Claims Commission: Politics as Law

It would be a miracle if in the course of these [Indian land]
dealings . . . we had not made some mistakes and
occasionally failed to live up to the precise terms of our
treaties and agreements with some 200 tribes . . . [the
Claims Commission is proof that we] stand ready . . . to
correct any mistakes we have made.

> Statement of President Truman upon Signing
> Bill Creating the Indian Claims Commission,
> August 13, 1946[1]

Introduction

When the Indian Claims Commission (ICC) was established after
World War II, it was greeted as one of the most imaginative and
generous initiatives by the American government for dealing with
the legacy of claims arising from the government's past relations
with Indian tribes. Hailed as a measure giving Indians their long
delayed "day in court," the ICC was to serve as the "legal conscience" of the nation.[2] Twenty-five years later, when the ICC
ceased to operate, its performance and decisions were again hailed
as major accomplishments in providing justice for the American
Indian.

Underlying the pervasive praise of the land claims process is the
assumption – not always stated explicitly – that the United States
voluntarily went beyond established legal principle to allow Indians
to assert claims against it that would not ordinarily be cognizable in
a court of law. By guaranteeing Indians access to a forum in which
even hundred-year-old land claims could be asserted, the United
States waived its sovereign immunity, which had until then been a
barrier to Indian land claims. Most extravagantly, the claim is made
that the establishment and performance of the ICC demonstrate the

141

perfectability of liberal law in allowing *ex post facto* rectification of what are now generally admitted to be grievous lapses from the norms and principles of the rule of law.

Although the acclaim for the commission's achievements is strong, it is not unanimous. Among those who are less sanguine about the role of the ICC are Indian tribes who contend that the commission – far from righting old wrongs – actually created additional obstacles for full legal vindication of tribal land rights. Continuing litigation challenging various aspects of ICC proceedings in the United States Court of Claims – charged by Congress with the completion of cases before the ICC at the time of its dissolution – attests to the existence of unresolved legal claims. In addition, new lawsuits filed in federal courts over claims already adjudicated by the ICC and the Court of Claims present a fundamental challenge to the legality and legitimacy of the ICC land claims process established by Congress.[3]

The essence of the Indian challenges is that the land claims process forced Indian tribes to exchange valid land claims for money damages, therefore precluding Indians from regaining land rights vital to their continued tribal existence. In addition, ICC procedures are attacked as lacking full due process guarantees. At the heart of these claims is the contention that the ICC process was so flawed in substance and procedure that it cannot be accepted as a binding legal solution to Indian land claims.

Whether or not the ICC remedied – in the full legal sense of that word – the illegal takings of Indian land or whether it merely served as a convenient mechanism to absolve the United States, with finality, from full legal responsibility is central to any assessment of what role the law played in Native American-United States relations. Against the background of Indian powerlessness, an evaluation of the ICC raises fundamental questions about the ability of the American legal system to realize its principal claims to autonomy, neutrality, and fairness. The political and legal use made of the ICC as a purported example of the invocation of liberal legal principle on behalf of a politically and economically weak minority deserves special attention.

Answers to the question of what role federal Indian law played range from the contention that liberal law protected the American Indian against all political odds to the opposite claim that liberal law is the root cause of Indian powerlessness to resist oppression.[4] The first argument is based on the proposition that law was the only barrier to tribal extinction at a time when the imbalance of power between Indian and white society was vast and when pressures for the wholesale expropriation of Indian land were overwhelming. The contrary view holds that in the unequal relation of Indian tribes and white society, liberal law was no more than the handmaiden of power, providing a convenient instrument and a cosmetic facade for the dispossession of the American Indian. This debate joins the history and impact of the Indian Claims Commission to the larger question of whether federal Indian law ought to be praised or cursed for what it has done to the Indian.

History

When the ICC was established in 1946,[5] Indian litigation over illegal takings of tribal land was not new to the American legal system. For more than half a century Indian tribes had sued the United States with varying degrees of success for the seizure of Indian land in violation of treaties, without proper legal authority, or as a result of fraud.

Resort to the court in these cases was possible only with explicit authorization from Congress in order to overcome the barrier of sovereign immunity. Indians had to rely on special jurisdictional acts because their treaty-based claims had been specifically excepted in 1863[6] from the jurisdiction of the Court of Claims, established in 1855 to hear all claims against the United States.[7] Congressional consent to Indian lawsuits was thus a prerequisite to all Indian land claims litigation against the U.S. before the establishment of the ICC at the end of World War II.

The built-in difficulties of securing separate congressional permission for the bringing of each tribal claim are readily apparent. Access to court depended on sufficient Indian influence in Congress to lobby for the requisite special jurisdictional acts. Since the initial taking of Indian land in violation of law often reflected nothing so much as the political powerlessness of Indian tribes, premising subsequent Indian legal redress on Indian political power to move Congress was inherently contradictory. The implementation for those legal gains that tribes succeeded in making presented the same dilemma. Since the final resolution of such cases depended on congressional willingness to appropriate – on a case by case basis – such funds as the Court of Claims awarded, even victorious tribes were thrown back on the political good will of Congress.

For Congress, in 1946, a more compelling reason for changing the ad hoc nature of the Indian claims process was that it had proved to be unwieldy and time consuming as well as unproductive. Resolution of claims in this manner involved long delays before the desired legislation was enacted. The jurisdictional acts thus obtained did not always permit the presentation of all the claims the Indians felt entitled to have settled judicially.[8] In such cases, as well as those in which Congress had considered but not enacted special jurisdictional bills, requests for such legislation were almost invariably introduced in succeeding Congresses.[9]

For both Congress and the federal executive branch, a systematic final claims process was also congruent with the recommendations of the earlier Meriam report and the longstanding United States goal of assimilating Native Americans. The Meriam report,[10] the most authoritative assessment of the government's Indian policy before World War II, had stressed that final claims settlements were a prerequisite for removing the last and most insurmountable obstacle to a final assimilation of the Indian.[11] From the perspective of the United States, the settlements would clear the slate with respect to past dealings. But, more important, the settlements would encourage Indians to become part of American society once title to Indian land had been irrevocably terminated by payment. The more extensive formalization of this new phase of a United States assimilation program – called termination and relocation policy[12] – was put in place a few years after the passage of the Indian Claims Commission Act (ICCA). The ICCA and termination policy fit together naturally. In a 1957 article on termination policy, Senator Arthur V. Watkins linked the purpose of the ICC and termination: "[A] basic purpose of Congress in setting up the Indian Claims Commission was to clear the way toward complete freedom of the Indians."[13] Like supporters of the Dawes Allotment Act seventy years before, the freedom that Watkins envisioned anticipated the Native American as an assimilated citizen with all the rights, and obligations, of other Americans whose land could now be transferred from Indian ownership to non-Indian ownership.[14]

Not unlike the sorcerer's apprentice, Congress found it impossible to control the forces it had unleashed by denying Indians routine access to the Court of Claims and assuming legislative responsibility for policing Indian access to judicial remedies. Claims litigation up to World War II thus proved to be both cumbersome for Congress and less than satisfactory to Indian tribes. It was to eliminate the inherent political liability of this process for Indians, to increase the efficiency of the adjudication of Indian land claims, and to support the incorporation of Indian people and land into the dominant culture that the ICC was established.

The 1946 act gave the commission jurisdiction over five categories of claims: (1) claims in law or equity arising under the Constitution, laws or treaties of the United States, as well as executive orders of the president; (2) all other claims in law or equity, including those sounding in tort, with respect to which the claimant would have been entitled to sue in a court of the United States if the United States were subject to suit; (3) claims that would result if the treaties, contracts, and agreements between the claimant and the United States were revised on grounds of fraud, duress, unconscionable consideration, mutual or unilateral mistake, whether of law or fact or any other ground cognizable by a court of equity; (4) claims arising from the taking by the United States, whether the result of a treaty of cession or otherwise, of lands owned or occupied by claimant without the payment for such lands of compensation agreed to by the claimant; and (5) claims based upon fair and honorable dealings that are not recognized by any existing rule of law or equity.[15]

Provision for Indian suits on claims where the government's dealings with tribes did not satisfy standards of fair and honorable dealings was regarded as proof of the extraordinary readiness of the United States to correct its mistakes and to compensate for past injustices. The same generosity of approach was evident in other provisions of the act. Neither statutes of limitations nor the defense of laches was to bar the resolution of Indian claims.[16] In determining the amount of damages suffered by a claimant tribe the commission was not, as a general rule, to offset "gratuitous" payments by the United States to a tribe.[17]

Provisions for the establishment of an investigative division as an adjunct of the ICC were to assure that claims could be prepared with speed and without imposing large financial burdens on Indian claimants. For similar reasons the operating procedures of the commission were to be informed by principles resembling arbitration more than adjudication. Although not precise in its formulation, the operating mode of the commission appeared to be defined in deliberately nonadversarial terms.

Other provisions of the act were less generous toward Indian claimants. Monetary compensation for wrongful takings of Indian land was to be determined on the basis of market price at the time of taking. The negative fiscal results of that rule were magnified by express prohibitions on adding interest to awards from the time of taking until the award would be paid.

The notice provisions of the act were restrictive. Tribes had only five years from the time of enactment in 1946 until the time for filing claims expired in 1951. All claims not filed by that date were forever barred. Given the complexity and magnitude of many of the claims, the lack of legal experience by many tribes, and the dearth of information, the pressure for filing claims was immense. The filing deadline was only one example of an order of priorities in which the government's desire for finality prevailed over genuine concern for justice. Pressure to resolve specific cases and the urgency of completing the work of the commission were the reasons given again and again by the commission in routinely denying unrepresented tribal groups the right to intervene in litigation already in progress. The need for finality was also the reason for refusing to allow tribes to disavow legal strategies pursued by their attorneys without their knowledge or consent.

The original plan for the claims process thus had the potential both for genuine generosity in "righting old wrongs" and for the imposition of narrow and grudging restrictions on Indian redress. Once the commission was established and operating, however, its potential for generosity and justice was almost immediately undermined by excessively narrow interpretations of the provisions favoring Indian tribes and by the commission's readiness to use implied restrictions to limit severely Indian rights and remedies under the act. In part this development can be attributed to external political pressures to minimize Indian gains. When an unexpectedly large number of claims was filed during the last months of the filing period,[18] attempts to extend the filing period by one year faltered on the opposition of the Senate and the Justice Department.[19]

The commission had barely begun to operate when inveterate congressional opponents of Indian claims tried to abolish it.[20] Even though these attempts failed, they showed the extent of congressional hostility to the new direction of Indian affairs for which the ICC stood.[21]

The more important reason, however, that the restrictive elements of the act would prevail over its more generous features lay in internal procedural decisions of the commission; these assured that the fact-finding commission model envisioned by the Claims Act was replaced by a judicial framework emphasizing adversarial over cooperative procedures.[22]

Although all of the proposed Indian claims legislation since 1935 and the ICC Act itself had deliberately opted to make the claims forum a commission rather than a court, the procedures and rules adopted by the commission in June 1947 eliminated the formal distinction between commission and court.[23] In effect, under the new rules and procedures the commission worked like a court, a reality formally acknowledged by Chief Commissioner Witt soon after the ICC began processing claims.[24]

The reasons the commission leaned toward the judicial model were mixed. In large part they were historical. Since Indian claims had been handled since 1881 by the Court of Claims, it was only natural for the commission to look for reference to that institution, its rules, and the body of decisions and legal theories it had developed. The Justice Department, mindful of the restrictive approach the Court of Claims had pursued in Indian claims cases and fearful of the fiscal threat of prospective Indian claims, backed the commission's choice to limit its own discretion. Not surprisingly, the claims attorneys favored procedures that maximized the need for their services. The Indians themselves, long accustomed to unilateral Bureau of Indian Affairs (BIA) decision making, also appeared to welcome a process that promised to guarantee them active participation.

One of the immediate results of the commission's adoption of the judicial model was that its work was slow. Extensions of time were granted liberally. Between 1947, when the first seventeen claims were filed, and 1956, the Justice Department alone received over five thousand extensions of time to file pleadings. Of the 852 claims filed by the 1951 deadline, almost 200 remained unanswered five years later.[25] The claims attorneys made equally liberal use of procedures permitting delay. Aside from the immediate effect of the perpetual delays on the expectations of the Indian plaintiffs, their cumulative impact on Indian claims litigation made clear that the commission could not complete its work in the time Congress had allotted. As a result the commission had to ask for extensions of time every five years until 1976, creating an image of unending and unmanageable Indian claims.[26]

The negative consequences of the commission's adoption of the judicial model went beyond the costs of inefficient litigation. For the Indians the commission's turn away from the less adversarial alternative had several important implications. In rejecting the role of an "impartial fact-finding commission,"[27] the ICC never established the independent governmental investigative division called for by the Claims Act.[28] The resultant unavailability of governmental fact-finding made claims litigation much more expensive for the tribes by putting the burden of getting and paying for experts on them.

Eventually the costs of expert testimony and investigation were financed through government loans to claimant tribes, which were then offset against whatever award a tribe won.[29] While this procedure made it possible for tribes to hire the necessary experts, its effect was to decrease the value of claims awards – in many cases by considerable amounts. As expert witnesses became part of the arsenal of the adversarial process put in place by the ICC's choice, expert expenses became an increasingly substantial part of claims litigation costs. This revolving loan fund, established by Congress in 1963 for the payment of a tribe's expert witnesses, had to be increased by 300 per cent during the first decade of its existence.[30]

Failure to establish the investigative division also made it much more difficult for Indian claimants to get access to information in Interior Department files that they needed to present their cases properly. Without the help of an investigative division whose primary task was to have been the "complete and thorough search for all evidence affecting each claim, utilizing all documents and records in the possession of the Court of Claims and the several Government departments,"[31] tribes soon found it difficult, if not impossible, to gain access to crucial Interior Department files. The BIA, in particular, refused Indian requests for information on the ground that government employees could not "aid or assist in the prosecution or support of claims against the United States."[32]

The Role of the Lawyers

Possibly the most important consequence of the commission's embrace of full-scale adversary forms and procedures for claims adjudication, however, was to give lawyers the most salient role in the claims process. From the beginning, the role of lawyers proved to be one of the most problematic aspects of the claims process. Both sets of lawyers – the claims lawyers representing the tribes and the Justice Department lawyers representing the U.S. government – pursued interests not necessarily congruent with the Claims Act's goal of "righting old wrongs."

Definition of their posture as purely adversarial made it easy for the government's lawyers to emphasize their role as aggressive defenders of the government's fiscal interests and that of non-Indian property owners. Conversely, it allowed them to ignore that the claims process was "primarily designed to right a continuing wrong – for which no possible justification [could] be asserted."[33] With the inexorable logic of the adversarial party, Justice Department lawyers thus spent years "to build arguments which would confine the Commission's jurisdiction, to object to various theories, to attempt to maximize offsets, to discourage tribal expenditures for expert witnesses, to confine notice and to drive harsh settlement bargains" as part of their protection of non-Indian interests.[34]

It was a mode of representation that fit well into past patterns of Indian claims litigation. In fighting tribal claims before the Court of Claims in the last several decades before the establishment of the ICC, United States attorneys had prided themselves on their record of either defeating Indian claims completely or, alternatively, of successfully off-setting tribal awards through governmental counter claims. The government's lawyers, one critic pointed out, did not like to lose "even in a just cause."[35] With the adoption of an adversarial framework, United States attorneys could safely regard themselves not as participants in a benevolent process of claims settlement but rather play an aggressive role as opponents of any possible Indian gain.

The prominent role in ICC proceedings of attorneys who had traditionally specialized in representing Native American claims before the Court of Claims was to become as problematic as that of the United State's lawyers. The source of the problem was the fact that the lawyers who specialized in representing tribal claims before the Court of Claims had accepted – if not promoted – the fundamental premise that Indian land claims litigation could only result in a trade of Indian title and land claims for monetary compensation. While this trade was of questionable interest to Indian tribes whose survival as distinct cultures depends on a land base,[36] it served well the material interests of their non-Indian lawyers. The statutory rules governing ICC procedures perpetuated this conflict of interest by establishing a contingency fee system for paying attorneys out of the monetary proceeds of tribal awards.[37] In the process of claims litigation, Indian tribes eventually had to give up claims of millions of acres of land while claims lawyers collected between eighty and one hundred million dollars in fees.[38]

While profitability per se is hardly an unusual feature of legal business, the tying of attorney's fees to monetary compensation raised particularly troublesome issues in the context of land claims litigation. The most important of these are Indian charges that the claims lawyers pursued strategies that maximized their own interests rather than that of their Indian clients. Such strategies, Indian critics contend, were responsible for the commission's development of substantive legal doctrines that served to confirm – and even strengthen – Indian legal disabilities in the claims process. At its sharpest point the conflict of interests between tribes and their attorneys can be considerable. In the Santo Domingo Pueblo's suit seeking permission to withdraw from a stipulation entered into by its former lawyers, Judge Nichols of the Court of Claims stated, in dissent, it is "the attorney's interest, but not the tribe's . . . to effect a judicial sale, as it were, of tribal land at values of some historic past date, not of the present, to be set by the Commission, whether or not the Indians may in reality ever have had their title extinguished except by the ICC proceeding itself."[39]

Another consequence of this conflict of interest could always be that "the counsel's interest on the usual contingent fee basis turns only on the amount of the award to be extracted from defendant [government]; yet the tribe's interest is not only in the amount of the award, but also in minimizing what land title or claim thereto it has to give up, which may be substantial";[40] that is, the attorney fee structure provided incentives for litigation that maximized rather than minimized the area of Indian title extinguishment, thus increasing the monetary award for the tribe and the proportionate share of the attorney, but only at the price of taking more Indian land.

Although Congress never confronted the conflict of interest problems raised by the attorney contingent fee provisions of the ICC Act, it enacted legislation to deal with that issue in the context of expert testimony. Employment of expert witnesses on a contingency fee basis, it was feared, might lead to testimony weighed in light of the financial interest of the witness in the outcome of the case.[41] Even payment for experts by claims attorneys was thought to be questionable in light of the lawyers' own contingent contract.[42] Establishment of a revolving fund for expert assistance loans[43] to impecunious tribes was to prevent the feared conflict of interest. There is some irony in the fact that Congress acted to prevent conflicts of interest with respect to experts but failed to focus on the much larger issue of attorneys' conflicts of interest.

The Claims Process and Indian Interests

Regardless of the extent to which the legal strategies of claims lawyers were determined by self-interest, it is clear that their strategies influenced the substantive approach of the ICC to questions of crucial importance to Indians. Early on its decisions on these questions established that the potential for generosity and substantial redress inherent in some of the provisions of the Claims Act was not likely to be realized. The commission adopted the monetary-compensation-only approach of past claims litigation in the Court of Claims; it generally worked on the presumption that all land outside established reservation boundaries had somehow been taken by the United States; and it accepted stipulated dates of taking or extinguishment having scant – if any – relation to the date when Indians had last made use of the land. Judged in light of its legal outcomes the adversarial model of claims litigation adopted by the commission served to confirm, rather than to ameliorate, the development of legal doctrines fundamentally adverse to Indian interests.

One of the earliest decisions of the commission eliminated Indian hopes for return of any Indian land.[44] Although the commission acknowledged that the Indian Claims Commission Act did not specifically state the character of the relief the commission could grant, if found nevertheless that the act's provisions "plainly limit the relief to that which is compensable in money."[45] This reading of the statute relied on language that spelled out specific requirements in monetary terms, e.g., that the "final determination" shall state the "amount" of relief or that "payment of any claim . . . shall be a full discharge" of all claims.[46] Although it is not clear why such language could not also be read restrictively as being limited to those relief provisions that deal with the disposition of monetary claims, the *Osage Nation* decision established the subsequently unchallenged rule that Indian tribes cannot recover land even where that would be plausible.[47] In order to reach the conclusion that land itself could not be regained by the Indians, the commission departed from the well-established rule of federal Indian law that doubtful terms of treaties or statutes are to be construed in favor of the Indians.[48] For Indian claimants the decision provided an early indication that the "legal conscience" of the nation had material limits.

Given the ICC's premise that valid Indian claims to land had to be traded for cash settlements, the process of determining how much of a tribe's land was taken, and when and how became of vital significance. With respect to these issues the ICC developed a body of legal doctrines fundamentally prejudicial to Indian interests. The substantive rules developed by the commission for defining what constituted a taking deviated in major respects from constitutional standards. Instead the commission substituted factual and legal tests that effectively barred Indians from establishing that they had never lost title to their land.

Most devastating in this regard was the willingness of the commission to presume that all land outside established reservation boundaries had *somehow* been taken by the United States and to accept stipulated taking dates or presume extinguishment, even when there was no evidence that tribes had ever relinquished title to their land or had stopped using it. Claims lawyers' interest in establishing that title had been lost may explain why "[t]he alternative that Indians might still own the land was likely not to be seriously urged by any party."[49] Instead of presenting evidence of actual takings, claims attorneys relied on such general and non-specific concepts as "white encroachment" on Indian land to show that it had been taken.[50] Similarly, passage of the Taylor Grazing Act in 1934 or the U.S. Forest Act in 1911 were accepted as establishing implicit U.S. takings.[51]

Against the background of the legal limitations imposed by the ICC on the presentation of Indian land claims and the fact that reliance on the claims process would automatically extinguish all tribal claims to Indian title land, the question of who would litigate tribal claims took on vital significance. On this issue the ICC followed procedures that allowed any individual member or any group of tribal members to file claims on behalf of the entire tribe without any formal authorization by the tribe as a whole.

The traditional Hopi and Seminole peoples, the Western Shoshones, and most recently the Oglala and Rosebud Sioux repeatedly tried to convince the ICC that the attorneys purporting to represent all members of their tribe only spoke for one faction.[52] Although the traditional Hopi formally protested the filing of any claims on their behalf,[53] claims attorney John Boyden of Salt Lake City nevertheless filed a claims petition in which he represented himself as attorney for all Hopis. Nearly twenty years later, after the ICC had extinguished Hopi title to more than four million acres in return for a $5 million settlement, Boyden urged the commission to award him the full 10 per cent, or $500,000 in attorney's fees, because the lack of cooperation and the persistent opposition of "a major, traditional faction of the Hopi population had made his lawsuit that much more difficult."[54]

The Miccosukee Seminoles protested to no avail the filing of claims not authorized "by them or for them" according to provisions they would not accept "now" or "in the future."[55] In 1980 the Pueblo of Santo Domingo petitioned the Court of Claims to protect them from their ex-lawyers' unauthorized legal concessions.[56] In 1981 a group of Western Shoshone people accused their former attorneys of an "unconscionable history of attorney malpractice and misconduct" in pursuing claims disavowed by most of the tribe.[57] Even after the award of $110 million, the Oglala Sioux contended that their claims attorney had "prosecuted the claim for money without proper authorization and without the understanding and consent of the Dakota people" to whom the nature and the consequences of the money claim had been "totally misrepresented" ever since it was first filed in 1923.[58]

The readiness of the commission to hear claims presented by individual Indians on behalf of a tribe without that tribe's authorization proved to be devastating to a number of tribes. In some cases tribes may not even have known of ongoing litigation pursued by some of their individual members.[59] Where additional tribal groups tried persistently to intervene in such cases they generally met firm resistance from the commission.

The combination of legal rules encouraging tribes to trade land claims for money, the expansive legal approach to Indian land takings and final adjudication of tribal claims litigated without explicit tribal consent assured that the claims process did not impinge on any vital property interests of white society. For Indians that approach confirmed the historical relegation of their property interests to an extraconstitutional status. This served effectively to establish takings where none had occurred or to advance a taking date to a point earlier than when it had occurred.[60]

The use of the act's "gratuitous offset" provisions by the commission betrayed an equally firm determination to protect the fiscal interests of the government. The act specifically provided that "gratuitous" payments by the United States to the tribes should not, as a general rule, be offset against awards made to the tribes unless the commission found that the nature of the tribe's claims and the entire course of dealings between the United States and the tribe warranted the offset.[61] Despite this provision the ICC initially allowed offsets for a large variety of U.S. government expenses on behalf of Indian tribes, regardless of whether the tribes had asked for such expenditures or whether they would have needed any U.S. assistance at all if their land had not been taken or if they had been paid in full for its value.[62]

Only after tortuous efforts in the late 1960s did the commission begin to scrutinize the government's offset requests more closely, reasoning that "[t]here is a causal relation between the original Government failure of full payment, and the subsequent need for various types of gifts now commonly claimed as general gratuities by the Government."[63] Although the commission's decision was reversed,[64] it continued to reduce materially the effects of the gratuitous offsets demanded by the United States, disallowing, finally, as gratuitous offsets in the award of claims, burial expenses for individual Indians paid for by the federal government.[65]

Conclusion

Both substantive rules and procedures of the claims process demonstrate the extent of the influence of political priorities on the ICC. The operation and results of the claims process were marked and marred by the ready accommodation of legal procedures to the exigencies of political power.

The role of the ICC demonstrates how successfully political goals and priorities can be masked by legal procedure. In original plan and structure the new claims forum was political and administrative rather than judicial. In and of itself the commission structure followed the administrative agency mold; the commission was to operate for only ten years, and its three members were appointed by the president with advice and consent from the Senate for fixed terms. Provision for a governmental investigative division was to assure the fact-finding role of the commission and to assist Indian tribes in the presentation of their claims. There is little evidence that Congress intended to create an adversary process of the kind the commission itself opted to pursue.

The settlement of outstanding political claims was essential and necessary for political reasons and went beyond the need to rationalize past claims procedures. The Meriam report urged final claims settlements to foster the final assimilation of Native Americans – the goal of the soon to be enacted termination legislation. From a foreign policy perspective it was seen as important that the establishment of the Indian claims process would serve to "strengthen our moral position in the eyes of many minority peoples."[66]

Against the background of these political goals the change in the commission soon after its establishment from a primarily administrative to a largely judicial institution is important. It reflects a pattern typical of U.S.-Indian relations: the resort to judicial forms serves to disguise the tension between law and power, but it cannot resolve it – as the Indian claims process demonstrates. The ICC is a striking example of the consequences that the reliance on legal form had for resolving tribal claims. When the ICC began to wrap itself in a judicial mantle, it followed the time-honored course of U.S.-Indian relations in which the exercise of power is disguised by a cloak of legal principle. Since the obfuscation of its political role could not, however, relieve the ICC from the need to tailor its legal process to respond to political pressures, the legal charade ultimately worked to discredit the work of the commission.

Any suggestion that acknowledgment of the political role and function of the ICC would have avoided the taint of illegitimacy and provided a more honest setting for its work, however, cannot imply that such a political framework would have been more in the interest of the Indians. Given Congress's historic record of disregard for Indian rights, reliance on political remedies seems unwarranted.

Whether their land is taken in the name of law or in the name of power may matter little to Indians left without land. The only benefit for Indians of establishing the political nature and core of the claims process is that it would make explicit the long-standing premise of U.S. policy: that in Indian affairs, land rights must yield to power and that legal forms will not change that outcome. It would prevent the United States from absolving itself of responsibility for the fate of the Native American in his own land. It is necessary in the sense that history, too, has its claims.

Notes

1. *Public Papers of the Presidents of the United States, Harry S. Truman* 414 (Washington, D.C., 1962).
2. Barker, "The ICC: The Conscience of the Nation," 20 *Fed. B.J.* 240 (1960).
3. *Osceola v. Kuykendall*, 4 *Ind. L. Rep.* F80.
4. Compare, e.g., Cohen, "Original Indian Title," 32 *Minn. L. Rev.* 28 (1947) and Coulter, "Lack of Redress," *Civil Rights Digest* 30 (Spring 1978).
5. Act of August 8, 1946, ch. 907, 60 Stat. 939 (codified at 25 U.S.C. § la). See also Lurie, "The Indian Claims Commission," 436 *Annals of the American Academy of Political and Social Science* 97 (1978); H. Rosenthal, "Their Day in Court: A History of the Indian Claims Commission" (Ph.D. diss., Kent State University, 1976) (hereinafter cited as Rosenthal, "Their Day"); Rosenthal, "Indian Claims and the American Conscience: A Brief History of the Indian Claims Commission," in *Irredeemable America: The Indians' Estate and Land Claims* (I. Sutton ed. Albuquerque, 1985) (hereinafter cited as Rosenthal, "Indian Claims").
6. Act of March 3, 1863, ch. 92, § 9, 12 Stat. 765, 767 (codified as carried forward and amended at 28 U.S.C. § 1502). (Section 1502 was amended in the 1949 revision of Title 28, at 63 Stat. 89, to delete the reference to treaties with Indian tribes, thus bringing this section into conformance with Section 24 of the Indian Claims Commission Act

(28 U.S.C. §1505).) Indian tribes were denied access on the theory that, like foreign nations, their treaty-based claims against the United States that "often partake of a political character," were best settled by Congress through bilateral negotiations. 62 *Cong. Globe* 124 (April 12, 1862).

7. Act of February 24, 1855, ch. 122, § 1, 10 Stat. 612 (codified as carried forward and amended at 28 U.S.C. § 171).

8. Flickinger, "The American Indian," 20 *Fed. B.J.* 212, 214–15 (1960). During hearings on the various legislation for a claims commission, Congressman Henry Jackson, chairman of the House Committee on Indian Affairs, outlined the problem and his solution: "We are being harassed constantly by various pieces of legislation and we plan to dispose of all those routine claims and let the Commission decide what the obligation is of this Government to the Indians . . . and appropriate the money." *Hearings on H.R. 1198 and H.R. 1341 before the House Comm. on Indian Affairs*, 79th Cong., 1st Sess. 68 (1945).

9. Editorial Note, "Section 2 of the Indian Claims Commission Act," 15 *Geo. Wash. L. Rev.* 388 (1946–47).

10. Institute for Government Research, *The Problem of Indian Administration* 805–811 (L. Meriam ed. Baltimore, 1928).

11. W. Washburn, *Red Man's Land/White Man's Law* 266 (New York, 1971).

12. Termination policy followed, with some changes in direction, from the assimilationist legislation of the late nineteenth century. The 1928 Meriam report enumerated the disastrous conditions afflicting Indians and pronounced the policy of forced assimilation a failure, but "it did not challenge ultimate assimilationist goals." United States Commission on Civil Rights, *Indian Tribes: A Continuing Quest for Survival* 21 (Washington, D.C., 1981) (hereinafter cited as *Indian Tribes*). As a result of the Meriam report and other contemporary investigations United States Indian policy shifted in the early 1930s. Through the Indian Reorganization Act (25 U.S.C. Sect. 461) the restoration of tribal resources and self-government would be supported *but still* as "transitional devices for the complete assimilation of Indian life into the dominant white society." *Id.* at 22.

Following World War II members of the now conservative Republican Congress began calling for the immediate diminution of federal supervision of tribes as a cost-saving program, as emphasis on Indian incorporation, and as an action intended to "dismantle New Deal programs." V. DeLoria & C. Lytle, *American Indians, American Justice* 16 (Austin; 1983). The 1953 House Concurrent Resolution 108 (67 Stat. B132) encapsuled the new policy urging it desirable "as rapidly as possible, to . . . subject [Indians] to the same privileges and responsibilities as are applicable to other citizens of the United States, [and] to end their status as wards of the United States" F. Prucha, *Documents of*

United States Indian Policy 233 (Lincoln, Nebr., 1975). Supported by a number of subsequent bills terminating federal responsibility for designated tribes, as well as by Public Law 280 (67 Stat. 588), which permitted state governments to assume civil and criminal jurisdiction over Indian reservations in five states and the territory of Alaska, termination legislation set out to end *rapidly* the trustee relationship between the federal government and Indian people, remove the tax-exempt status of Indian land, end federal responsibility for the economic and social well-being of Indian people, undercut tribal government, and promote assimilation by dividing tribal property among individual members. *Id.* at 257–58. Termination legislation was then enhanced by a program of physical relocation of Indian people from reservations to urban areas. For an overview of termination and relocation policy and its repudiation beginning in 1958 and finalized in President Nixon's July 8, 1970 "Special Message on Indian Affairs," see primary documents in Prucha, *Documents* at 233–41, 256–58, and 263–64. For a brief discussion of the impact of termination policy on one tribe, see League of Women Voters, "The Menominee: A Case against Termination," in *The American Indian Past and Present*, (2d ed. R. Nichols ed. New York, 1981). Tribal consent to state jurisdiction imposed by Public Law 280 has only been required since passage of the Indian Civil Rights Act of 1968. 25 U.S.C. §§ 1321–22, 1326 (1982).

13. Prucha, *supra* note 12, at 239.

14. The U.S. Commission on Civil Rights reports that some 133 separate bills were introduced in the period of termination legislation to permit the transfer of trust land from Indian ownership to non-Indian ownership. *Supra* note 12, at 22–23, citing to Task Force Ten, *Report of Terminated and Nonfederally Recognized Indians: Final Report to the American Indian Policy Review Commission* 1632–33 (Washington, D.C., 1976).

15. Ch. 959, § 1, 60 Stat. 1049, 1050 (codified at 25 U.S.C. § 70a).

16. § 2, 60 Stat. at 1050 (codified at 25 U.S.C. § 70a).

17. *Id.* Once a jurisdictional act had been won in the pre-ICC period, one of the greatest dangers that faced Indian claims was that of court-imposed deductions of millions of dollars against awards made to Indians. This practice was called the "off-set of gratuities," i.e., the deduction of those monies that the United States claimed it had given to the Indians under no obligation, but simply through altruistic sentiments. It became a means to limit the recovery due the tribe. Until 1935 the Court of Claims had no guidelines as to what might be considered a proper deduction from an award. In *Duwamish Tribe et al. v. United States*, 79 Ct. Cl. 530, for example, the deduction of administrative expenses completely off-set a considerable award from the court. In other cases, administrative costs were disallowed. Between 1929 and 1935 "in every case but two where a recovery has been won

in the court the petition has been dismissed because the recovery was exceeded by the off-sets." *Hearings before the Senate Comm. on Indian Affairs on S. 2731,* 74th Cong., 1st Sess. 9 (1935) (testimony of Assistant Solicitor Poole).

In 1940 Commissioner of Indian Affairs John Collier testified that

> [T]he set-off against a claimant of gifts made to him by the defend-
> ant is found nowhere else in the law outside of Indian claims. It has
> been adopted there not because of any legal justification but as a
> practical device to reduce the obligations of the United States . . .
> Gratuities are funds expended by the United States to carry out its
> governmental function of administering Indian affairs and civilizing
> the Indians. The expenditures may or may not have been actually
> beneficial to the Indians; sometimes they were hurtful; in most cases
> they were made without the Indians' consent. It is a fiction to call
> them payments upon a claim as they were not made as such and
> were often made before any claim was formulated.

Limiting the Jurisdiction of the Court of Claims in Indian Cases: Hearings before a Subcomm. of the Senate Comm. on the Judiciary, 76th Cong., 3d Sess. (February 13, 1940).

18. The reasons for the last minute rush were that some tribes had difficulty securing legal representation, that for many of the claims the case workup was a difficult and lengthy process, and that some claims attorneys apparently held off on filing to await the outcome of the early claims.

19. Rosenthal, "Their Day," *supra* note 5, at 147.

20. Even before the new commissioners were appointed, Senator Harlan J. Bushfield of South Dakota and E.H. Moore of Oklahoma intro-duced a bill to repeal the Indian Claims Commission. S. 405, 80th Cong., 1st Sess., 93 *Cong. Rec.* 596 (1947). Senators unfamiliar with the act, though they had voted for it, were outraged to discover that it barred defenses based on statutes of limitation or laches. *Hearings on Independent Offices Appropriations Bill, 1949 Before the Subcomm. of the Senate Comm. on Appropriations,* 80th Cong., 2d Sess. 101–2 (1948) (statement of Senator McKellar: "I do not see how it is possible for a bill like that to have gotten through Congress. I cannot conceive of a bill to give claims of that kind to people so far back as 1801 and 1865, with interest thereon during all that time. It looks like a scheme, really, to defraud the Government.") But see *Loyal Creek Indians v. U.S.,* 97 F. Supp. 426 (Ct. Cl.), *cert. denied,* 342 U.S. 813 (1951) (prohibiting the awarding of interest to ICC awards from the time of taking to the time of payment). See also *Extension of the Indian Claims Commission: Hearings on S. 2408 Before the Subcomm. on Indian Affairs of the Senate Comm. on Interior and Insular Affairs,* 92nd Cong., 1st Sess. 47 (1971)

(testimony of Robert C. Bell asserting that not allowing interest to be paid on the claims deterred the government from quickly resolving the claims). After describing a visit to the ICC's office, which revealed that none of the employees were engaged in any work, one Senate report concluded that the ICC was an unnecessary agency and recommended its dissolution. S. Rep. No. 778, 80th Cong., 1st Sess. (1947).

21. Rosenthal, "Their Day," *supra* note 5, at 140–45.
22. H.R. Rep. No. 1466, 79th Cong., 2d Sess., reprinted in 1946 *U.S. Code. Cong. & Admin. News* 1347.
23. Barney, "Indian Claims or the Historical Appraisal," 31 *Appraisal Journal* 170 (1963).
24. *Hearings on Interior Department and Related Agencies Appropriations Bill for 1956 Before the Subcomm. of the House Comm. on Appropriations*, 84th Cong., 1st Sess. 573–80 (1955).
25. *Hearings on H.R. 9390 for Appropriations for Interior and Related Agencies for 1957 Before the Subcomm. of the Senate Comm. on Appropriations*, 84th Cong., 2nd Sess. 552–58 (1956).
26. Rosenthal, "Their Day," *supra* note 19, at 281. As the end of the ICC's term approached, it became obvious that the commission would be unable to complete its work. Of the 852 claims filed with the ICC only 102 had been disposed of. S. Rep. No. 1727, 84th Cong., 2d Sess. (1956). Initially, the Senate proposed a two-and-a-half-year extension of the commission; however, after negotiations with the House, a five-year extension was granted. See H.R. Rep. No. 2719, 84th Cong., 2d. Sess. (1956). In 1961, Congress authorized another five-year extension to the ICC. Fourteen years of operation had apparently granted the ICC legitimacy and the extension was passed with little dissent. Rosenthal, "Indian Claims," *supra* note 5, at 58.

By March 1, 1967, the ICC had adjudicated 236 dockets of the original 583 dockets, which represented the 852 claims filed. Of the adjudicated dockets, 103 resulted in awards for the Indians for a total sum in excess of $200 million. Congress manifested its frustration with the ICC's inability to dispose of claims with more expediency when it amended the act and issued another extension in 1967. Although the Subcommittee on Indian Affairs expressed sympathy for the difficulties inherent in the ICC's work, the subcommittee warned all participants "that their full cooperation [was] expected" for the ICC to complete its work by 1972. H.R. Rep. No. 132, 90th Cong., 1st Sess. reprinted in 1967 *U.S. Code Cong. & Admin. News* 1106, 1107. To facilitate the disposal of claims, Congress increased the number of commissioners from three to five. *Id.* Congress also limited the number of continuances that would be permitted in a given case. If the claimant failed to proceed on the trial date without a showing of good cause, the case would be dismissed with prejudice. Congressional scrutiny proved to be successful – all other things being equal – for the years immediately following the 1967 extension. In the two years preceding this extension twenty-three dockets were completed, whereas in the two years following the extension seventy-three dockets were completed. Indian Claims Commission, *Final Report* 125 (Washington, D.C., 1978) (hereinafter cited as ICC, *Final Report*).

Indian frustration with both the slow pace of adjudication and the minimal impact of the awards was also apparent by 1967. In his testimony before the Senate Subcommittee on Indian Affairs, Hank Adams, a member of the board of directors of the National Indian Youth Council declared:

> Few people in the United States would permit themselves to be bought out with their own resources, but for the Indian it has come to be expected as a matter of course. And should the awards of the Indian Claims Commission continue to be used as the government's money, merely as supplemental appropriations to the BIA's budget or even displacement, to sustain the proven failures, or failure-ridden programs, then perhaps the Commission should be terminated.

Indian Claims Commission Act Amendments: Hearings on S. 307 Before the Subcomm. on Indian Affairs of the Senate Comm. on Interior and Insular Affairs, 90th Cong., 1st Sess. 91 (1967).

In 1971 Congress once again began consideration of another five-year extension for the ICC. At this time there was a sense that the remaining claims should be transferred to the Court of Claims for more expedient disposal. *Extension of the Indian Claims Commission: Hearings on S. 2408 Before the Subcomm. on Indian Affairs of the Senate Comm. on Interior and Insular Affairs*, 92nd Cong., 1st Sess. 43–44 (1971). Ultimately, Congress reluctantly granted another extension and imposed stricter controls on the commission including an automatic transfer provision for remaining dockets to go to the Court of Claims, close oversight of the appropriations to the commission, and the requirement that the ICC report on its progress at the beginning of each session of Congress. H.R. Rep. No. 894, 92nd Cong., 2d Sess. 2 (1972).

Congress granted a final eighteen-month extension to the commission in 1976. This final extension was justified on the grounds that it would be more efficient to have the ICC complete as many dockets as possible before turning them over to the Court of Claims. This final extension was not granted without dissent. The extension was opposed on the grounds that the ICC was only interested in self-perpetuation, rather than the interests of the Indian claimants. S. Rep. No 705, 94th Cong., 2d Sess. 27–28 (minority views of Senators Fannin, Hansen, and McClure). Additionally, there was dissent in the

House of Representatives because, in the view of one member, "[t]o continue this 30-year-old Commission further is a waste of taxpayer's money. The Congress has been more than generous to the American Indian tribes and their attorneys in allowing them adequate time to prepare and present their claims." H.R. Rep. No. 1150, 94th Cong., 2d Sess. 11 (1976) (minority view of Chairman Haley).

27. H.R. Rep. No. 1466, *supra* note 22, at 1349.

28. Ch. 959, § 13 (b), 60 Stat. at 1053.

29. In 1963 a revolving fund was established for loans to Indian groups for use in obtaining expert assistance, other than counsel, to prepare and try cases before the commission. Act of November 4, 1963, Pub. L. No. 88–168, 77 Stat. 301 (codified as amended at 25 U.S.C. §§ 70n–1 to 70n–7). Numerous excellent accounts are available describing the role of the ethnologist-expert witness in the claims process. See, e.g., Beals, "The Anthropologist as Expert Witness," in *Irredeemable America: The Indians' Estate and Land Claims* (I. Sutton ed. 1985); Jennings, "A Growing Partnership: Historians, Anthropologists, and American Indian History," 29 *Ethnohistory* 21 (1982); Lurie, "Epilogue," also in *Irredeemable America*; Stewart, "Kroeber and the Indian Claims Commission Cases," 25 *Kroeber, Anthropological Society Papers* 181 (1961). See also *Index to the Expert Testimony Before the Indian Claims Commission* (N. Ross, ed. New York, 1973).

30. Funding in 1964 was $900,000. It was doubled in 1966 and reached $2.7 million by 1973. 77 Stat. 301, November 4, 1963; 80 Stat. 814, September 19, 1966, and P.L. 93–97, May 24, 1973.

31. *Id.*

32. Cohen, "The Erosion of Indian Rights, 1950–1953: A Case Study in Bureaucracy," 62 *Yale L. J.* 348, 372 (1953).

33. H.R. Rep. No. 1466, *supra* note 22, at 1.

34. M. Price, *Law and the American Indian* 503 (Indianapolis, 1973).

35. *Hearings on S. 2408: A Bill to Extend the Indian Claims Commission Before the Subcomm. on Indian Affairs of the Senate Comm. on Interior and Insular Affairs*, 92d Cong., 1st Sess. 46 (October 21, 1971).

36. *Report to the Hopi Kikmongwis and Other Traditional Hopi Leaders on Docket 196 and the Continuing Threat to Hopi Land and Sovereignty* (Indian Law Resource Center, Washington, D.C., 1979) (hereinafter cited as *Hopi Report on Docket 196*). See also P. Matthiessen, *Indian Country* (New York, 1984).

37. Sec. 15 of the Indian Claims Act, ch. 959, 60 Stat. 1049, provided for a maximum 10 percent contingency fee of the amount recovered in any case in addition to payment of all reasonable expenses. See also Gamino, "ICC: Discretion and Limitation in the Allowance of Attorney's Fees," 3–4 *Am. Ind. L. Rev.* (1975).

38. ICC, *Final Report, supra* note 26, at 24.

39. *Pueblo of Santo Domingo v. United States*, 647 F.2d 1087, 1090 (Ct. Cl.

1981) (Nichols, J. dissenting) *cert. denied* 456 U.S. 1006 (1982).

40. *Id.* at 1091.

41. ICC, *Final Report, supra* note 26, at 14.

42. *Id.*

43. 77 Stat. 301, November 4, 1963.

44. *The Osage Nation of Indians v. United States*, 1 Ind. Cl. Comm. 54 (December 30, 1948), reversed on other grounds, 119 Ct. Cl. 592, *cert. denied* 342 U.S. 896 (1951).

45. *Id.* at 65.

46. *Id.*

47. The Western Shoshone, for example, claim title to unoccupied land leased by the U.S. as grazing land to ranchers. Recognition of Indian title would neither have dislocated anyone nor disrupted current economic uses of the land, since the same ranchers could have continued to lease from Indian landlords. See generally Mander, "This Land is Whose Land," *The Village Voice* (December 10, 1979) and Thorpe, "The Destruction of a People," 13 (No. 1) *Akwesasne Notes* (Early Spring 1981).

48. *Carpenter v. Shaw*, 280 U.S. 363 (1930); *United States v. Dann*, 706 F.2d 919, 932 (1983).

49. *Western Shoshone Identifiable Group v. U.S.*, No. 80–326–K (D. Nev. May 23, 1980).

50. See, e.g., *Dann*, 706 F.2d 919. An exception is suggested in the case of *Yakima Tribe v. United States*, 158 Ct. Cl. 672 (1962), *on remand*, 16 Ind. Cl. Comm. 536 (1966). See Hughes, "Indian Law," 18 N. *Mex. L. Rev.* 403 (1988), at 421–22.

51. *Id.* at 928–33. See also *Dann*, 873 F.2d 1189, 1198.

52. See generally *Hearings on S. 2000 and S. 2188: Distribution of Seminole Judgment Funds Before the Senate Select Comm. on Indian Affairs*, 95th Cong., 2d Sess. 27 (March 2, 1978) and Exhibit 31: Letter of Morton Silver to Attorney General of the United States (October 1, 1953) (hereinafter cited as *Seminole Hearing*). See also *Hopi Report on Docket 196, supra* note 36; Motion for Leave to File Papers in Opposition to Motion for Attorney's Fees, *Sioux Nation v. U.S.*, App. No. 148–78, filed December 22, 1980 (hereinafter cited as Sioux Motion).

53. *Hopi Report on Docket 196, supra* note 36, at 81, quoting a petition of protest from Hopi religious leaders to President Truman, March 28, 1949 (Exhibit 38). The issue of wrongfully binding unrepresented claimants to a judgment in what amounts to a class action is explored thoughtfully in Orlando, "Aboriginal Title Claims in the Indian Claims Commission: *United States v. Dann* and Its Due Process Implications," 13 *B.C. Env. Affairs L. Rev.* 241 (1986).

54. *Hopi Report on Docket 196, supra* note 36, at 188; see also *id.* at 93–94.

55. *Hearings on S. 2000 and S. 2188: Distribution of Seminole Judgment Funds Before the Senate Select Comm. on Indian Affairs*, 95th Cong., 2d Sess. 27

(March 2, 1978).

56. *Memorandum in Support of Petitioner's Motion to Vacate, Pueblo of Santo Domingo v. United States*, No. 80–355 (November 23, 1980).

57. *Reply to Answering Brief of Claims Attorney to Request for Review of Decision, Western Shoshone Indentifiable Group v. United States*, No. 80–326K, filed February 13, 1981, at 3.

58. Sioux Motion, *supra* note 52.

59. See, e.g., *Temoak Band of Western Shoshone Indians, Nevada v. the U.S.*, 228 Ct. Cl. 26 (1981). Thus, despite objections from a *very early* moment, the efforts of these groups to take steps to correct the course of the litigation were thwarted by the combination of the BIA, the ICC, the Claims Court, and the claims attorneys.

60. In the complex Dann Sisters' and Western Shoshone litigation, the 9th Circuit firmly rejected the legal theory that Indian property interests held an extraconstitutional status. *Dann*, 706 F.2d 919. Their decision, however, was reversed by the U.S. Supreme Court. *U.S. v. Dann*, 470 U.S. 39 (1985). In 1989 the 9th Circuit followed the higher Court, stating, "[W]e reject . . . the Danns' attempt to continue to rely on the defense of tribal aboriginal title." *Dann*, 873 F.2d 1189, 1194–95. This decision forecloses any further claims by the Dann sisters through their tribe.

It has been alternatively suggested that it was the claims attorneys who made the decisions to trade land claims for money and that the jurisdictional grant to the ICCA would have allowed that body to hear claims founded upon theories of extant title on the part of the tribes. Richard W. Hughes, Esq. to author, September 14, 1989.

61. § 2, 60 Stat. at 1050 (codified at 25 U.S.C. § 70a).

62. See, e.g., *United States v. Kiowa, Comanche & Apache Tribes*, 166 F. Supp. 939 (Ct. Cl. 1958), *cert. denied*, 359 U.S. 934 (1959).

63. *Delaware Tribe of Indians v. United States*, 21 Ind. Cl. Comm'n 18 (1969).

64. *United States v. Delaware Tribe*, 427 F.2d 1218 (Ct. Cl. 1970).

65. *Lummi Tribe of Indians v. United States*, 24 Ind. Cl. Comm'n 21 (1970).

66. ICC, *Final Report, supra* note 26, at 5 (statement by Secretary of the Interior Julius Krug).

5

Federal Courts, Tribal Sovereignty, and Indian Civil Rights

We think, "what fools were these nineteenth-century men who did not see that cultural values differ from group to group." How quaintly dated, how Victorian, we muse. And yet, when we look at the present era we find, for example, much of this same attitude emerging in the Indian Civil Rights Act of 1968.

Rennard Strickland[1]

Introduction

When the Supreme Court decided *Santa Clara Pueblo v. Martinez*[2] in 1978, it faced an issue of paramount importance for federal Indian law – the applicability of United States constitutional standards to intratribal relations. In *Santa Clara* the Court held that the Indian Civil Rights Act (ICRA),[3] enacted by a Congress using its plenary power and trust powers only a decade earlier, did not extend federal civil jurisdiction to disputes between members and governments of Indian tribes. The Court's narrow construction of the ICRA gave new life to federal Indian law principles that had long held that Indian tribes are not bound by the U.S. Constitution.[4] The Supreme Court reached its conclusion in the face of a widely held assumption – shared by legislators, lower federal courts, and Indian people themselves – that the ICRA had been passed precisely to end or overcome the insulation of intratribal affairs from constitutional standards.

Although *Santa Clara* has been both praised and criticized,[5] the decision constituted neither a victory for those who had opposed passage of the act as an unwarranted interference with tribal sovereignty nor a defeat for those who had welcomed it as a long overdue reform of federal Indian law. *Santa Clara* was in essence a

164

compromise: the Court accepted without qualification the mandate of Congress that a tribe must respect the constitutional rights and liberties of persons coming under its authority. But it held that tribal governments themselves, not the federal courts, were the exclusive forums for deciding issues of tribal adherence to the constitutional standards imposed by the Indian civil rights legislation.

More than a decade later there is much evidence that the compromise the Court sought to strike between the competing demands of tribal sovereignty and constitutional rights has not proved entirely workable. Indians and non-Indians continue to seek relief from arbitrary tribal action in federal court.

What went wrong? The essence of the problem, as several lower federal courts have pointed out in criticizing *Santa Clara*, is that the decision created "rights while withholding any meaningful remedies." Increasing tribal interaction with non-Indians – be it as a result of economic development or assertions by Indian governments of dormant powers long unexercised – is likely to raise the question of remedies more frequently and with greater urgency. In response to considerable publicity about incidents of alleged miscarriages of tribal justice, pressure has mounted to provide for external review of tribal action. As a result it is likely that renewed efforts will be made to extend federal court jurisdiction over intratribal affairs.[6]

This chapter argues against legislative revocation of the Supreme Court's decision to entrust ICRA enforcement to the tribes themselves. As long as federal Indian policy continues to foster Indian self-determination, tribal courts must have the flexibility to depart from constitutional norms on condition that they can articulate why such deviation is essential to protect traditional and still extant autonomous cultural values. If necessary, the *Santa Clara* compromise can be modified by the Supreme Court itself to provide for primary tribal definition of individual rights standards under the ultimate supervision – if needed – of federal courts. Such an interactive process should not require ICRA standards to mirror constitutional guarantees operative outside the tribal context in every aspect and every detail in every tribe.

The Supreme Court's *Santa Clara* approach to reconciling constitutional values and tribal sovereignty has not been wholly successful. First, the Court's decision assumed that the enforcement of constitutional rights and liberties by the tribes could be severed from the institutional underpinning of an independent judiciary on which civil rights enforcement rests outside the tribal context. That assumption was flawed. Second, the failure of the Court to state explicitly why and on what condition ICRA standards may differ from constitutional rules applicable in federal courts has prevented the evolution of a flexible accommodation of constitutional rights and Indian autonomy. Nevertheless, we conclude that the principles underlying the Court's *Santa Clara* approach to Indian civil rights are viable despite the particular shortcomings revealed by Indian rights litigation following that decision. Modified by provision for federal court review only if tribal courts fail to articulate why cultural values demand deference, the *Santa Clara* approach can lead to the evolution of a legal doctrine that accommodates both Indian self-determination and constitutional rights.

Whether tribal courts will be able to formulate individual rights standards compatible in essence with core values of the ICRA as well as Indian cultural autonomy will depend on two factors. One is the development of tribal judicial systems with some independence from, and review power over, the actions of tribal councils. The other factor will be the readiness of Congress and federal courts to accept tribal implementation of constitutional standards not in all aspects identical to the substantive and procedural norms of American society. Both will take time and tolerance.

Enactment of the ICRA

Enactment of the Indian Civil Rights Act (ICRA) in 1968 was generally thought to create a watershed in federal Indian law. Section 1302 of the ICRA makes many of the constitutional guarantees of the United States Bill of Rights binding on Indian tribes.[7] The legislation enumerates specific rights that are not to be abridged by Indian tribal governments. While exempting the prohibition against the establishment of religion, the Congress "incorporated" the remainder of the First, Fourth, Fifth, Sixth, Seventh and Eighth Amendments for Indian reservations in language taken almost verbatim from the Bill of Rights. In addition, a tribe is required not to "deny to any persons within its jurisdiction the equal protection of the laws" and is prohibited from passing bills of attainder or ex post facto laws. With the exception of a narrow provision for federal habeas corpus review of detention, the act contains no reference to enforcement procedures.

The ICRA broke with long-standing principles and traditions of federal Indian law. Before the passage of the act, it was well established that Indian tribes were not bound by the United States

Constitution. The principle of Indian sovereignty, on which the insulation of tribal governments from U.S. constitutional standards is premised, had been accepted early in the relationship between the federal government and Indian nations. In the Cherokee cases,[8] Chief Justice John Marshall affirmed the status of Indian tribes as distinct and independent political entities, capable of governing their own affairs. Half a century later, in *Talton v. Mayes*,[9] the Supreme Court reconfirmed that the powers of tribal self-government existed prior to the adoption of the United States Constitution and that tribal laws were neither created by nor flowed from the Constitution. Native Americans living under tribal jurisdiction were, logically, not accorded constitutional protections but had to rely upon tribal customs and traditions in their dealings with tribal authorities.

Lower federal courts, too, have consistently acknowledged the special legal-political status of tribes. Recognizing and deferring to concepts of tribal sovereignty, *Native American Church v. Navajo Tribal Council* held in 1959 that "[n]o provision in the Constitution makes the First Amendment applicable to Indian nations."[10] So clear had been the consensus on Indian autonomy over internal tribal affairs that federal Indian law authority Felix Cohen could state unequivocally that "[t]he provisions of the Federal Constitution protecting personal liberty or property rights, do not apply to tribal action."[11]

Despite the strength of the legal principles insulating the intra-tribal relationship of Indian governments and tribal members from the imposition of external standards, the premise of tribal sovereignty and the corollary concept of the exceptionalism of federal Indian law had come under increasing pressure during the two decades preceding the enactment of the ICRA.[12] It was reflected most clearly in Congress's adoption in 1953 of the policy of "termination," aimed at assimilating Indian tribes by discontinuing their special legal status.[13] Later, during the Nixon administration, the tide of federal policy turned back again to favoring a policy of self-determination.[14] But even then concern over the inapplicability of the Bill of Rights and the Fourteenth Amendment to Indian tribes remained. During the course of congressional hearings on the Indian Civil Rights Act, Senator Sam Ervin of North Carolina, the chief sponsor of the act, was "astounded to learn that . . . reservation Indians do not possess the same constitutional rights which are conferred upon all other Americans" and Senator Roman Hruska of Nebraska was "jarred and shocked by the conditions as far as constitutional rights for members of the Indian tribes are concerned."[15] The exemption of tribal power from constitutional limitations imposed on all other governmental authority was regarded in Congress, and elsewhere, as being in conflict with fundamental principles of limited power inherent in liberal constitutional government.[16] Tribal governments – whether legislative councils, chiefs, or courts – were no less given to abuses of authority than their non-Indian counterparts.[17]

Since Indian tribes provide vital governmental services to their members,[18] arbitrary and discriminatory tribal action could have a significant negative effect on the three-quarters of a million Indians living under tribal jurisdiction. The argument was made that if federal courts were powerless to intervene in cases where members of tribes claimed to have been imprisoned or expelled for arbitrary or capricious reasons, where freedom of expression was curtailed by fiat, or where equal protection was denied on account of race or sex, individual Indians were left without redress.[19]

Judicial decisions – in part reflecting, in part spurring the concern over the extraconstitutional nature of intratribal relations – added to the pressure for change. In 1965 the Ninth Circuit decided to grant the habeas corpus petition of an Indian woman alleging unlawful detention by her tribe.[20] The court expressed doubt about "the present validity" of the broad proposition that "the Constitution applies to the Indians, in the conduct of their tribal affairs, *only* when it expressly binds them, or is made binding by treaty or act of Congress."[21] Although the decision did not depart in principle from the well-established judicial "hands-off" approach to internal tribal affairs,[22] it did not hide a broader judicial discomfort with the "pure fiction" of independent tribal sovereignty.[23] Judge Duniway's opinion relied on two factors: (1) the incongruity of the Indians' historic claim to sovereignty and their position as "wards of the nation" and "communities dependent on the United States," and (2) the evidence of pervasive federal support for and regulation of the Indian courts on the Fort Belknap Reservation. The court concluded that the current status of Indian tribes generally, and that of the Fort Belknap Indian court in particular, did not provide a sufficient factual basis for exclusive tribal jurisdiction: "We know that in the one hundred and thirty years that have since passed, the 'independence' of the Indian tribes has decreased, and their dependency has increased."[24] From these facts it followed that "the status of the Indians today" undermined what might have been valid reasons for jurisdictional abstention "one hundred years ago."[25] Similar questions were increasingly raised by other courts as well as by Congress. The congressional response to the complaints about civil rights violations and arbitrary tribal action was to try to set constitutional limits to the exercise of tribal governmental power.[26] The enactment of the ICRA in 1968 must be seen against this background.

From a tribal perspective, the imposition of constitutional rights and liberties standards on tribes was in direct conflict with principles of Indian sovereignty and tribal self-determination. Meaningful self-determination must preclude appeal to external authorities by reference to rules not congruent with traditional tribal concepts of authority and justice. Critics of the pending ICRA legislation objected that efforts to restrict tribes in the same way as the Bill of Rights restricts the United States government presupposed structures that were unlikely to exist in tribal governments. "Applying every limitation of the Bill of Rights to the acts of Indian tribes," one prominent Indian claims attorney argued, "could destroy tribal self-government, while the economic and social advancement of reservation Indians clearly is tied to the maintenance of strong tribal institutions."[27] Application of equal protection principles to voting rights was bound to conflict with tribal selection of leaders by elders or priests of a tribe. Similarly, tribal discretion with respect to the determination of membership on the basis of racial criteria would be unlikely to withstand scrutiny.[28] Fifth Amendment property protections would be likely to be inapposite to communal property.

In response to what were considered legitimate concerns raised over the imposition of external constitutional standards on tribal autonomy, Congress modified some of the provisions of the proposed Indian civil rights legislation.[29] Responding to pressure from the theocratic Pueblos, the ICRA explicitly exempted tribal governments from the constitutional prohibition against the establishment of religion.[30] The Fifteenth Amendment prohibition on racial classification voting was omitted because the tribes, as ethnic or racial units, were required to restrict voting to an ethnically determined, rather than to a geographically defined, community.[31] Assistance of counsel was not mandated in deference both to the traditionally nonadversarial nature of tribal court proceedings and to the unmanageable administrative and fiscal burdens it would place on tribal court systems.[32] Yet while congressional sensitivity to cultural and political differences of tribal organization satisfied some of the concerns over Indian cultural autonomy, the limited legislative concessions to tribal self-determination could not and did not veil the fact that the ICRA was a significant intrusion into the independence of tribal governments.

As a result, passage of the ICRA was both praised and condemned. Proponents hailed the bill as a long overdue extension of
constitutional protections to individual tribal members often subjected to arbitrary and capricious actions by tribal governments.
From this perspective enactment of the ICRA finally ended the
anomalous and inchoate legal position of Native Americans who
were guaranteed basic civil rights as American citizens in a national
setting but who could be denied the protections of these same basic
rights by their own tribal authorities. By contrast, critics of the
ICRA viewed the creation of new rights against tribal governments
as an unwarranted invasion of Indian sovereignty. From their
perspective the extension of constitutional standards to Indian
tribes threatened to undermine the autonomy of Indian people to
maintain and foster cultural institutions of their own.[33]

Interpretation and Application of the ICRA in the Lower Courts

With the passage of the Indian Civil Rights Act Congress relieved
the federal courts of some of the pressure for a complete judicial
solution for reordering the relation between the Constitution and
Indian tribes with respect to individual rights. Yet while the act
addressed itself broadly to the problems that had plagued courts
when individual tribal claimants sought to invoke constitutional
protections against tribal governments, it did not resolve the
underlying tension between respect for tribal autonomy and culture
on the one hand and compliance with constitutional requirements
of due process, equal protection, and individual rights guarantees
on the other hand. In addition the absence of enforcement mechan-
isms – with the exception of habeas corpus review – confronted
courts with the task of resolving some of the most contentious
questions left open by the the legislation. The necessity of deciding
when and what constitutional restrictions were applicable to tribal
governments and how they were to be enforced, therefore, posed
complex challenges to the lower federal courts.

Only the provision for habeas corpus review of detention under
tribal orders was resolved clearly and early. Section 1303 was tested
in federal court soon after the enactment of the ICRA and found
constitutional.[34] It was a result virtually unavoidable based on both
the explicit language of the law and the long-standing history of
federal court responsibility for the adjudication of "major" criminal
offenses committed within areas under tribal jurisdiction.[35] The

availability of federal court habeas corpus review of tribal detention is, therefore, considered well settled.[36]

Less clarity prevailed over the less specific congressional directives on the civil jurisdiction of federal courts, and the first years of litigation against tribal governments under the ICRA produced initial uncertainty over the reach of the act. Several courts found that the Civil Rights Act of 1968 vested civil jurisdiction in federal courts,[37] but other courts denied that the ICRA gave them jurisdiction over "intra-tribal" disputes.[38] By the time *Santa Clara* reached the Supreme Court, however, a good deal of consensus existed in the lower federal courts that the ICRA created a federal cause of action and waived tribal immunity from suit.[39] Four circuits agreed that the ICRA provided a jurisdictional basis to protect substantive rights guaranteed by the ICRA.[40]

Yet just as court decisions began to establish a judicial consensus on the jurisdictional reach of the ICRA, the litigation that built on these decisions deepened the disagreement over the permissible reach of external intervention into tribal affairs. As lawsuits against Indian tribes and their officers multiplied,[41] Indian tribes asserted with increasing urgency that civil remedies imposed under the ICRA undermined their cultural and political autonomy. Such an outcome, tribes argued, posed the same concerns that were raised when the ICRA was enacted a decade earlier.

The ICRA in the Supreme Court

When Julia Martinez filed her civil lawsuit in 1975, she sought to invoke the help of the federal district court in New Mexico on behalf of her eight children who were barred from full membership in her own tribe, the Santa Clara Pueblo.[42] The sole reason for the tribal council's denial of membership to the Martinez children was that Julia Martinez, a full member of the tribe, had married a Native American man from another tribe. Had it been the children's father – and not their mother – who married outside the tribe, the Pueblo's patrilineal rules of descent, expressed in a tribal ordinance, would have allowed the children full membership and eligibility to inherit property.

To civil rights and civil liberties organizations in the United States – and an American public newly attentive to problems of sex discrimination – the membership rules of the Santa Clara Indians were an egregious example of an unjustifiably discriminatory practice.[43] Even if the Pueblo's rules were based on long-standing tradition – and there were arguments that this was not so[44] – it did not follow that such discrimination should still be permitted in the last quarter of the twentieth century.[45] From this perspective Julia Martinez's case was a classic example of the practices the ICRA was enacted to prevent.

To Indian governments and advocates of tribal self-determination Julia Martinez's invocation of federal judicial power under the ICRA presented a grave threat to a principle crucial to the survival of Indian culture.[46] A federal court decision to intervene in the internal affairs of the Santa Clara Pueblo would diminish the autonomy and sovereignty of *all* Indian tribes. If Mrs. Martinez succeeded and federal courts were to dictate to the Santa Clara Pueblo constitutional standards alien to its own customs and culture, the very autonomy that had allowed the Pueblo in the past to maintain and foster a culture, language, and religion of its own would be destroyed. To force the admission of her children into the Pueblo on the authority not of her own people but of outsiders would be a Pyrrhic victory for Julia Martinez – undermining that Indian way of life of which she wanted her children to be part.

The progress of the Martinez case through the federal courts reflected the complexity of the process of resolving the competing Indian rights and tribal sovereignty claims. This district court held that it had civil jurisdiction under the ICRA to intervene in tribal membership decisions but found in favor of the Pueblo on the merits.[47] The Tenth Circuit affirmed federal court jurisdiction but reversed on the merits and ordered the Pueblo to admit the Martinez children as members of their tribe.[48] In granting *certiorari* the Supreme Court implicitly recognized the necessity of resolving the conflicting legal claims raised by the ICRA.[49]

In a seven to one decision written by Justice Thurgood Marshall the Court reversed the holding of the Tenth Circuit and offered its own compromise interpretation of the ICRA. The Court ruled that the act did not give federal courts jurisdiction over Indian tribes or their officers except for the narrow remedy of habeas corpus to test the legality of detention.[50] The decision turned on the Court's reading of congressional intent underlying the ICRA. Justice Marshall's analysis of the legislative history of the act focused on the "dual statutory objectives"[51] through which Congress tried to accomplish both the protection of individual tribal members and the furthering of tribal self-government. "In addition to its objective of strengthening the position of individual members vis-à-vis the tribe, Congress also intended to promote the well-established federal policy of furthering Indian self-government."[52]

On the jurisdictional issue the absence of any provisions explicitly waiving tribal immunity from suit or directly providing for a cause of action against tribal officials was considered fatal to claims brought under the act. "In the absence here of any unequivocal expression of contrary legislative intent, we conclude that suits against the tribe under the ICRA are barred by its sovereign immunity from suits."[53] The Court also declined to overcome the obstacle of legislative silence by implying a private cause of action because such an implication would result in significant interference with tribal autonomy.[54]

In contrast to the congressional silence on the crucial questions of tribal immunity and the creation of a cause of action, the Court found much strong and explicit congressional intent to preserve Indian self-determination and to respect tribal sovereignty. To transfer jurisdiction for dispute resolution among Indians from tribal institutions to federal courts, the Court feared, would undermine the authority of tribal courts and infringe on the Indians' right to govern themselves.[55] External enforcement of constitutional standards, Justice Marshall concluded, would constitute such a pervasive interference with tribal self-government that its detrimental consequences would go beyond any changes in substantive law that the ICRA could have intended.

The Court's rejection of the expansive federal jurisdiction concepts that had evolved in the lower federal courts in the course of the decade following enactment of the ICRA was based on the Supreme Court's understanding of the destructive institutional and political impact of external ICRA enforcement on Indian self-determination. The Court saw no such danger to tribal sovereignty, however, in a reading of the act which left enforcement of the ICRA's substantive constitutional standards to the tribes themselves. The decision left no doubt, therefore, that tribal governments were obligated to adhere to the mandate of the ICRA in settling disputes between themselves and tribal members under their jurisdiction: "Tribal forums are available to vindicate rights created by the ICRA, and Section 1302 has the substantial and intended effect of changing the law which these forums are obliged to apply."[56]

In trying to reconcile principles of Indian self-determination and respect for constitutional norms protecting individual rights, the Supreme Court in *Santa Clara* attempted to strike a compromise between two sets of legitimate yet competing concerns. The Court's repeated expression of respect for Indian autonomy and self-government was a "major restatement of the vitality of tribal sovereignty."[57] The Court's allocation of ICRA enforcement responsibility to the tribes themselves was an explicit expression of confidence in the willingness and ability of the latter to do so. Reference to the acceptability of nonjudicial enforcement schemes[58] indicated the Court's sensitivity to the fact that cultural differences were likely to influence the character of tribal enforcement and signaled its readiness to allow variations as long as the substance of the act's constitutional norms was respected.

At the same time as the Court declared its respect for tribal sovereignty, it left no doubt that Congress's passage of the ICRA was indeed an important new development in federal Indian law that made the United States Constitution binding on Indian tribes for the first time. The Court made clear that Congress was ultimately free to impose an external constitutional rights enforcement scheme, but only in the absence of tribal compliance with ICRA standards.[59] The decision thus left the Pueblo free to implement constitutional protections on its own and without federal court intervention, but it did so only conditionally.

Santa Clara thus offered a method for political accommodation of the goals of the ICRA and Indian self-determination in which Indian tribes were to play a leading role. The decision left no doubt that the viability of the compromise rested on the willingness and ability of tribes to enforce constitutional norms.

Problems of Tribal ICRA Enforcement

Once the Supreme Court had taken the federal courts out of the enforcement of the ICRA, tribal governments were unavoidably put to the test of "applying and enforcing its substantive provisions."[60] The Civil Rights Division of the Department of Justice, which had been active in ICRA litigation before *Santa Clara*,[61] dismissed all its cases pending before federal courts.[62] With few exceptions federal courts dismissed ICRA complaints – although frequently not without misgivings. Tribal institutions were left quite free, therefore, to implement ICRA provisions on their own.

More than a decade after *Santa Clara* there is a good deal of evidence that the potential for a tribal solution offered by the Court's compromise has not – yet – been realized. A 1984 Presidential Commission found that "[b]oth Indians and non-Indians complain of political discrimination against them by tribal courts which are arms of tribal governments" and expressed "doubts about the fairness and the rule of law on reservations."[63] After eight years of telling Indians that it was not taking any action on Indian civil rights, the Justice Department still received forty-five ICRA complaints alleging tribal court disregard of due process, voting fraud and malapportionment, discriminatory hiring or failure to provide tribal benefits equally to all members.[64]

Federal courts have expressed substantial criticism of the inadequacy of tribal enforcement of the ICRA.[65] Although they have, with few exceptions,[66] followed *Santa Clara* and dismissed the ICRA complaints of individual Indians against their tribes, they have often done so reluctantly. Thus the Eighth Circuit expressed frustration at not being able to provide a remedy for a non-enrolled member of the Oglala Sioux Tribe seeking election to the tribal council.[67] The candidate's right to run in the election had been initially confirmed by the chief judge of the tribal court. But that ruling was subsequently reversed by a second tribal judge chosen to replace the chief judge by a tribal council displeased with the initial ruling.[68] "Such actions," the unanimous court stated, "raise serious questions under the Indian Civil Rights Act, but because the Supreme Court determined in *Martinez* that there is no private right of action under the ICRA [the plaintiff] has no remedy."[69] After expressing "serious concern that [the plaintiff's] rights under Section 1302 of the Indian Civil Rights Act may never be vindicated," the Eighth Circuit questioned "whether such a result is justified on the grounds of maintaining tribal autonomy and self-government: it frustrates the ICRA's purpose of 'protect[ing] individual Indians from arbitrary and unjust actions of tribal governments,' and in this case it renders the rights provided by the ICRA meaningless."[70] In *Garreaux v. Andrus* the court held that the "[Supreme] Court's language in *Santa Clara* precludes a writ of mandamus or any other action" to require the recalcitrant tribal council to hold an election to allow changes in the tribal constitution.[71] Although the court recognized "that the plaintiffs are being treated unfairly by the tribal council," it found that the plaintiff was left only with tribal remedies of uncertain efficacy.[72]

A more recent Eighth Circuit decision echoed what has become a familiar theme for federal courts dismissing ICRA complaints despite their misgivings over an enforcement scheme in which violation of ICRA-protected rights by tribal governments may only be pursued in tribal forums. Recalling Justice White's dissent in *Santa Clara* the court felt that it was "improbable that Congress desired enforcement of [ICRA] rights to be left to the very tribal authorities alleged to have violated them."[73] In *Committee to Save*

Our Constitution a South Dakota district court concluded that complaints alleging tribal council violation of election rules and improper interference with tribal court decisions could not be reviewed by the Department of the Interior because "under the language of *Santa Clara* [the Department of the Interior and the Bureau of Indian Affairs] were not permitted to act as a reviewing court as to the jurisdiction or correctness of the [tribal judge's] ruling."[74] The court recited at length the facts of the case. These showed that the tribal council immediately removed the tribal judge who had made the election ruling adverse to the council's interest and replaced him with a new judge directly related to the chairman of the council. He promptly reversed the first judge. Despite these events the district court concluded that the correctness of this reversal "was to be accepted at face value as the law of the Tribal Court of the Cheyenne River Sioux Tribe."[75] Another court dismissing a complaint arising out of an election dispute found that exclusive allocation of ICRA enforcement responsibility to tribes created "a vacuum with the potential for chaos" instead of fostering self-government.[76] In a case alleging bad faith on the part of the tribal council in a child custody matter, a federal court found that "plaintiff's available tribal forums seem limited indeed . . . [and] it certainly may be argued that the effect, after *Santa Clara*, of the ICRA is to create rights while withholding any meaningful remedies."[77]

Although federal courts have, as a general rule, dismissed ICRA complaints in accordance with *Santa Clara*, frustration with their inability to provide remedies for what were considered egregious violations of ICRA-protected rights has led to some avoidance of the "restrictive rule in *Santa Clara*"[78] by finding jurisdiction despite *Santa Clara*.[79] Thus, the United States Court of Appeals for the Tenth Circuit fashioned an exception to the Supreme Court's federal jurisdiction bar for civil cases in the so-called *Dry Creek Lodge* litigation. It found federal jurisdiction to consider an ICRA complaint for damages against the tribe because the matter was "outside of internal tribal affairs" and concerned a non-Indian who lacked access to tribal court.[80] Since plaintiffs were non-Indians, who alleged violation of their personal and property rights under the Constitution and denial of access to tribal court, the Tenth Circuit found that the "limitations and restrictions present in *Santa Clara* should not be applied." "To hold that [plaintiffs] have access to no court is to hold that they have constitutional rights but no remedy. The self-help [suggested in Council minutes] does not appear to be a suitable device to determine constitutional rights."[81]

Judge Holloway, in dissent, reluctantly disagreed with the majority but found that the district court had been correct in dismissing "this most disturbing case" because the dismissal was compelled by *Santa Clara*.[82]

So far application of the *Dry Creek Lodge* exception has been very limited. Other courts have implicitly,[83] or explicitly,[84] rejected it. The Tenth Circuit itself has been careful to limit the scope of the exception it created.[85] Despite its limited application, *Dry Creek Lodge* is a striking example of the frustration federal courts express over the fact that "constitutional guarantees are not applicable to the exercise of governmental powers by an Indian tribe."[86]

Several developments are likely to increase judicial frustration with the *Santa Clara* rule and, by the same token, increase the pressure for change. During the last decade Congress has allocated to Indian governments themselves the responsibility for providing federally funded services until then directly provided by the Bureau of Indian Affairs (BIA) or other federal agencies. Reflecting its commitment to self-determination and sustained criticism of BIA paternalism and mismanagement, Congress in the 1970s enacted legislation giving tribal governments vastly enhanced authority over child welfare, education, and health services. Although these measures reflect Congress's commitment to, and support for, self-determination, to some observers the expanding reach of tribal power provides stronger arguments for subjecting tribal action to the scrutiny of federal courts. Externally, the increasing interaction of tribes with non–Indians participating in economic development has led to pressure for change including corporate, as well as individual, due process.[87]

Not surprisingly, one result of these post *Santa Clara* developments is the call for additional legislation to provide explicitly for federal court enforcement of constitutional rights against Indian tribes.[88] Since the Court in *Santa Clara Pueblo* left no doubt that Congress retained authority "expressly to authorize civil actions for injunctive relief [in federal court] or other relief to redress violations of [the ICRA], in the event that the tribes themselves prove deficient in applying and enforcing its substantive provisions,"[89] there is little question that such legislative initiatives would be upheld by the Court if they were supported by a federal record of tribal non-enforcement.

Reasons for the Difficulties of Tribal ICRA Enforcement

The shortcomings of tribal ICRA enforcement point to two separate but interrelated flaws in the Supreme Court's decision in *Santa Clara Pueblo*. The first is the failure of the Court to appreciate how closely enforcement of substantive constitutional values is tied to the existence of specific institutional arrangements, in particular the existence of separation of powers and an independent judiciary with the power of judicial review. The second flaw is the Court's failure to address the underlying question of the compatibility or incompatibility of constitutional norms and tribal values.[90]

Post-*Santa Clara Pueblo* Indian rights litigation in federal courts points toward a general pattern of deficient tribal ICRA enforcement. A closer look at these cases indicates that the single most important element of tribal noncompliance with ICRA requirements is the failure of tribal courts to implement the act. That failure, in turn, appears to result not from the tribal courts' unwillingness to apply civil rights standards but from their inability to enforce compliance with their decisions by tribal councils. That, at least, is the pattern in cases that reach the federal courts. For example, a tribal judge who invalidates rules barring an insurgent candidate for tribal office from the primary election is removed from office and replaced by a judge more compliant with the Tribal Executive Committee.[91] The term of office of a tribal judge ordering the implementation of an election redistricting scheme is terminated by tribal council resolution. When the removed judge competes successfully for tribal council office, he is barred from office by action of the tribal council.[92] A tribal judge indicates to non-Indians seeking a remedy against a tribal council's arbitrary reversal of a business license that he could not incur the displeasure of the council.[93] The disregard by a tribal court of a tribal council's resolution withdrawing court jurisdiction to determine the validity of any council resolution provokes a major crisis in tribal government.[94]

The reasons for the conflicts between tribal courts and tribal councils – and the general inability of tribal courts to maintain their independent authority in these conflicts – are readily apparent. The historical role of tribal courts in tribal government has been quite limited.[95] Traditional Indian justice systems were characterized by consensual and well-understood means for maintaining community harmony. More formal, Western-style judicial institutions like "Courts of Indian Offenses," introduced by the federal government in the second half of the nineteenth century to undercut traditional tribal leadership, lacked support and credibility. After 1934 many tribal governments attempted to reestablish traditional tribal justice systems under the auspices of the Indian Reorganization Act and by virtue of the inherent tribal sovereignty reconfirmed by that act.[96] As a result of their repeatedly disrupted development, the tribal courts operating in Indian country lack a firm foundation of independent political or communal support.

Most tribal courts function in the framework of tribal governments far more unitary than American government: they owe their very existence to the tribes' legislative bodies, the tribal councils who are the central repositories of power on the reservation. Tribal judges are generally appointed by tribal councils, and as a rule they have not been required to be attorneys nor to demonstrate special legal expertise. Recent testimony before the United States Commission on Civil Rights, however, indicates that tribal courts handle far more cases than in the years prior to *Santa Clara*, in part because they can no longer be bypassed easily by litigants seeking federal court review and have, subsequently, matured as institutions. Although by no means all of those called to testify before the commission concurred, many of the tribal and non-Indian people heard by the commission argued that given time and resources, a broad tribal willingness and capacity to enforce substantive civil rights will evolve.[97] Moreover, while the lack of separation of powers in most tribal constitutions theoretically limits neutral adjudication, it has been observed that "many tribes are sensitive to this problem and have moved to a policy of *de facto*, if not *de jure*, separation of powers."[98]

Conclusion: The Question of the Compatibility of Indian Culture and United States Constitutional Standards

The finding that the unworkability of the Court's *Santa Clara Pueblo* compromise results in significant part from the shortcomings of tribal courts that lack autonomy and independent power invites the conclusion that institutional reform of Indian justice systems can solve the dilemma addressed but not resolved by the Court. Such a conclusion, however, overlooks the underlying need to determine first whether American constitutional norms and the values of Indian culture and community are, or can be, in accord. For as long as the Court considers both constitutional values and

Indian self-determination to be legitimate governmental interests, the effectiveness of a solution allocating to tribes the enforcement of the Constitution depends, in the final analysis, on the compatibility of individual rights and Indian autonomy.

If these two sets of competing values are incompatible, tribal judicial reforms will not solve the problem. For even if, in theory, the shortcomings of tribal ICRA enforcement could be remedied by the creation of an independent tribal judiciary with powers of judicial review, the mandated creation of such a system would be at odds with the respect for tribal autonomy and self-determination that led the Supreme Court to reject federal court enforcement of the ICRA in the first place. If, in other words, the establishment of courts modeled on the American judiciary is the precondition for effective tribal ICRA enforcement, then the price for allocating ICRA enforcement authority to the tribes themselves may be abandonment of the very autonomy the Court sought to protect. It is the same conundrum Justice Thurgood Marshall tried to avoid when he concluded that external federal enforcement of ICRA standards would undermine Indian autonomy so pervasively that Congress could not have intended it consistently with a commitment to tribal self-determination.[99]

Neither Congress in enacting the ICRA nor the Supreme Court in interpreting the act in *Santa Clara Pueblo* asked – much less answered – the question whether respect for tribal self-determination was or could be congruent with substantive constitutional rights. Without an answer to that question the underlying tension of the Indian Civil Rights Act cannot be resolved, and federal courts, including the Supreme Court, are likely to make decisions that are both unsatisfactory in result and inconsistent in doctrine.

The courts should not be made to bear all the responsibility and all the blame for the apparent failure of the ICRA. Before they can resolve conflicts between Indian and Indian in a coherent and satisfactory manner, the larger conflict over the right and proper place of American Indians in their native land must be resolved. Any lasting resolution of that conflict will test the ability and readiness of American society to accept as valid the principles of law and politics, right and wrong that Indian nations have lived by since time immemorial and that only they themselves can affirm or disavow. The alternative is to insist that American constitutional choices be everyone's choices and that they be imposed on Indian people who are thought not to know what is good for them.

Even if – as is likely – the latter alternative is chosen, the Supreme

Court will still be left with the inherent contradiction of *Santa Clara Pueblo*: judicial confirmation of Indian sovereignty in the face of simultaneous judicial deference to Congress's unrestricted power to disregard Indian sovereignty, if only it does so explicitly and unequivocally. The attempt of Congress to impose what are held out to be universally valid constitutional standards on the relation of Indians to Indian governments stands in sharp contrast to the exemption from constitutional restraints of Congress's own exercise of plenary power over Indian tribes. A hundred years ago J.B. Thayer of the Harvard Law School observed that it would be futile to persuade Indian tribes of the need to establish Courts of Indian Offenses patterned on the American model as long as Indians were denied due process before American courts.[100]

Notes

1. Strickland, "Genocide-At-Law," 34 *U. Kan. L. Rev*. 713, 737 (1986).
2. 436 U.S. 49 (1978).
3. 25 U.S.C. §§ 1301–41 (1982). Senator Sam Ervin attached the ICRA to a housing bill certain for passage after the assassination of Dr. Martin Luther King. For a detailed analysis of the reasons for enactment of the ICRA, see Burnette, "An Historical Analysis of the 1968 'Indian Civil Rights Act'," 9 *Harv. J. Of Legis*. 557 (1972).
4. *Talton v. Mayes*, 163 U.S. 376 (1896) (holding that the Fifth Amendment does not apply to intratribal proceedings of the Cherokee Nation).
5. See, e.g., Ziontz, "After Martinez: Indian Civil Rights under Tribal Government," 12 *U. C. Davis L. Rev*. 1 (1979); S. Brakel, *American Indian Tribal Courts: The Costs of Separate Justice* (Chicago, 1978); and more recently, V. Deloria & C. Lytle, *The Nations Within* (New York, 1984); Gover & Laurence, "Avoiding *Santa Clara Pueblo v. Martinez*: The Litigation in Federal Court of Civil Actions under the Indian Civil Rights Act," 8 *Hamline L. Rev*. 497 (1985); Ball, "Constitution, Court, Indian Tribes," 1987 *Am. B.. Found. Res. J*. 1 (1987); Mackinnon, "Whose Culture? A Case Note on *Martinez v. Santa Clara Pueblo*," in *Feminism Unmodified: Discourses on Life and Law* (Cambridge, Mass.,1987); C. Wilkinson, *American Indians, Time, and the Law* (New Haven, 1987); Laurence, "Martinez, Oliphant, and Federal Court Review Of Tribal Activity under the Indian Civil Rights Act," 10 *Campbell L. Rev*. 411 (1988).

6. See, e.g., United States Commission on Civil Rights, Commission Meeting (February 11,1986), Transcript of Proceedings at 152–205. In 1988 Senator Orrin Hatch introduced legislation that would reverse the *Martinez* decision and extend the powers of the federal courts to entertain cases by any person against an Indian tribe, tribal organization, or official, alleging failure to comply with rights secured by the ICRA. Tribal remedies and appeals must first be exhausted. The bill would also eliminate sovereign immunity as a defense and would authorize the attorney general to initiate actions. S. 2747, "Indian Civil Rights Act Amendments of 1988," 100th Cong., 2d Sess.

7. Since the protections that the ICRA extends to individual tribal members derive from statute it is, strictly speaking, inaccurate to call them constitutional rights. With some exceptions, the act uses the same language as the U.S. Constitution, however, and covers the same rights and liberties. For a discussion of how the ICRA should not be considered to require a "jot-for-jot" incorporation and application of Bill of Rights guarantees, see Statement of Robert N. Clinton, Hearings Before the United States Commission on Civil Rights, *Enforcement of the Indian Civil Rights Act* 269–73 (Exhibit 11) (Washington, D.C., January 28, 1988).

8. *Cherokee Nation v. Georgia*, 30 U.S. 1 (1831) and *Worcester v. Georgia*, 31 U.S. 515, 559 (1832). In the 1980s the Supreme Court repeatedly confirmed the principle that Indian tribal governments "retain some of the inherent powers of . . . self-government." *National Farmers Union v. Crow Tribe*, 471 U.S. 845, 855–56 (1985) (holding that a tribal court should determine if it has jurisdiction over a civil matter between Indians and non-Indians before federal judicial review). See also *Rice v. Rehner*, 463 U.S. 713 (1983); *New Mexico v. Mescalero Apache Tribe*, 462 U.S. 324 (1983); and *Iowa Mutual Ins. Co. v. La Plante*, 480 U.S. 9 (1987).

9. 163 U.S. 376 (1896).

10. *Native American Church v. Navajo Tribal Council*, 272 F.2d 131 (10th Cir. 1959); *Toledo v. Pueblo de Jemez*, 119 F. Supp. 429 (D.C. 1954) (deprivation of religious liberties by tribal government could not be redressed by action under the Civil Rights Act).

11. F. Cohen, *Handbook of Federal Indian Law* 181 (Washington, D.C., 1942).

12. A Commission on the Rights, Liberties, and Responsibilities of the American Indian, established by the Fund for the Republic, in 1961, declared that the immunity of Indian governments from the Bill of Rights restraints jeopardizes "the very assumption on which our free society was established." Commission on the Rights, Liberties, and Responsibilities of the American Indian, *A Program for Indian Citizens* 24 (Albuquerque, 1961).

13. After World War II the Hoover Commission recommended that Indians should be brought into the mainstream of American society by terminating federal services to tribes and transferring jurisdiction over tribes to the states. *Report of the Committee on Indian Affairs to the Commission on Organization of the Executive Branch of the Government* (Washington, D.C., 1948). In 1953 Congress resolved that it was its policy "to make the Indians within the territorial limits of the United States subject to the same laws and entitled to the same privileges and responsibilities as are applicable to other citizens of the United States." H.R. Con. Res. 108, 83d Cong., 1st Sess., 99 Cong. Rec. 9968 (1953). Subsequently, Public Law 280 permitted certain states to assume jurisdiction over Indian affairs without even consulting the affected tribes. Act of August 15, 1953, 67 Stat. 588, as amended 18 U.S.C. § 1162 (1970) and 28 U.S.C. § 1360 (1970).

14. The policy of self-determination was formally propounded by President Nixon in his Special Message to Congress, July 8, 1970. It was expressed in law in the Indian Self-Determination and Assistance Act of 1975, 25 U.S.C. §§ 450–450n.

15. 113 *Cong. Rec.*, 90th Cong., 1st Sess., at 35473 (December 7, 1967).

16. See, e.g., De Raimes, "The Indian Civil Rights Act of 1968 and the Pursuit of Responsible Tribal Self-Government," 20 *S.D.L.Rev.* 59 (1975).

17. A series of hearings of the Senate Subcommittee on Constitutional Rights on the administration of justice by tribal governments, begun in 1961, brought together testimony accusing tribal officials of being tyrannical, arbitrary, and biased. The absence of guaranteed rights in tribal courts was illustrated in four critical areas of due process: right to counsel, right to remain silent, right to trial by jury, and right to appeal. Tribal members complained of police harrassment and employment discrimination on the basis of their religious beliefs. *Hearings on Constitutional Rights of American Indians Before the Subcomm. on Constitutional Rights of the Senate Comm. on the Judiciary*, 87th Cong., 1st Sess., pt. 1 (1961), cited in Burnett, *supra* note 3, at 577–82. But see R. Barsh & J. Henderson, *The Road* 254 (Berkeley, 1980).

18. See, e.g., The Indian Self-Determination and Education Assistance Act of 1975, 25 U.S.C. § 450 *et seq.* and the Indian Child Welfare Act of 1978, 25 U.S.C. § 1901 *et seq.*

19. One court described the consequences of decisions finding no subject matter jurisdiction for judicial intervention in "internal [tribal] controversies" as leaving the individual Indian in a "legal no man's land." *Solomon v. LaRose*, 335 F. Supp. 715 (D. Neb. 1971).

20. *Colliflower v. Garland*, 342 F.2d 369 (9th Cir. 1965).

21. *Id.* at 377 (emphasis added).

22. The court based its decision to extend federal habeas corpus jurisdiction over the Indian court detention order on a narrow exception

grounded on the particular method of federal financing of the tribal courts on Fort Belknap Reservation. *Id.* at 373–74.

23. *Id.* at 378.
24. *Id.* at 375.
25. *Id.* at 378.
26. See Burnett, *supra* note 3 and Note, "The Indian Bill of Rights and the Constitutional Status of Tribal Governments," 82 *Harv. L. Rev.* 1343 (1969) (hereinafter cited as "The Indian Bill of Rights").
27. Lazarus, "Title II Of The 1968 Civil Rights Act: An Indian Bill of Rights," 45 *N.D.L. Rev.* 337 (1969).
28. For a proposal of how judicial interpretation of the ICRA might avoid direct conflict with such traditional tribal values, see "The Indian Bill of Rights," *supra* note 26, at 1360–63.
29. "The Indian Bill of Rights," *supra* note 26, at 1355–60.
30. Burnette, *supra* note 3, at 603–17. See also V. Deloria & C. Lytle, *American Indians, American Justice* 125–30 (Austin, 1983).
31. Burnette, *supra* note 3, at 591; "The Indian Bill of Rights," *supra* note 26, at 1359.
32. Lazarus, *supra* note 27, at 340, 347.
33. This view was most persuasively argued by leaders from the New Mexico Pueblos who reiterated their opposition again and again in congressional hearings:

> Our whole value structure is based on the concept of harmony between the individual, his fellows, and his social institutions. For this reason, we simply do not share your society's regard for the competitive individualist. In your society, an aggressive campaigner is congratulated for his drive and political ability. In Pueblo society, such behaviour would be looked down upon and distrusted by his neighbours. Even the offices themselves, now so respected, would be demeaned by subjecting them to political contest. The mutual trust between governors and governed, so much a part of our social life, would be destroyed.

Hearings on S. 211 Before the Subcomm. on Constitutional Rights of the Senate Comm. on the Judiciary, 91st Cong., 1st Sess. (1969), cited in Burnett, *supra* note 3, at 614.

34. *Settler v. Yakima Tribal Court*, 419 F.2d 486 (9th Cir. 1969).
35. See the Major Crimes Act (making enumerated serious offenses among reservation Indians into crimes punishable in federal courts.). Act of March 3, 1885, ch. 341, § 9, 23 Stat. 362 (codified, *as amended*, at 18 U.S.C. § 1153 (1964)). The Supreme Court upheld the constitutionality of the statute in *United States v. Kagama*, 118 U.S. 375 (1886).
36. *Santa Clara*, 436 U.S. at 116. Tribal criminal jurisdiction is limited to

offenses punishable by detention up to one year or a fine of up to five thousand dollars.

37. See *Dodge v. Nakai*, 298 F. Supp. 26 (U.S.D.C. Ariz. 1969); *Spotted Eagle v. Blackfeet Tribe of Black Feet Indian Res.*, 301 F. Supp. 85, 89 (U.S.D.C. Mont. 1969).

38. See, e.g., *Groundhog v. Keeler*, 442 F.2d 674 (10th Cir. 1971); *Pinnow v. Shoshone Tribal Council*, 314 F. Supp. 1157 (D. Wyo. 1970).

39. *Luxon v. Rosebud Sioux Tribe*, 337 F. Supp. 243 (D.S.D. 1971) *aff'd.*, 455 F.2d 698 (8th Cir. 1974); *Loncassion v. Leekity*, 334 F. Supp. 370 (D.N.M. 1971); *Solomon v. LaRosa*, 335 F. Supp. 715 (D. Neb.1971). See also Note, "Tribal Sovereign Immunity: Searching for Sensible Limits," 88 *Colum. L. Rev.* 173 (1988).

40. *Dry Creek Lodge, Inc. v. United States*, 515 F.2d 926 (10th Cir. 1975); *Crowe v. Eastern Band of Cherokee Indians, Inc.*, 506 F.2d 1231 (4th Cir. 1974); *Johnson v. Lower Elwha Tribal Community*, 484 F.2d 200 (9th Cir. 1973); *Luxon v. Rosebud Sioux Tribe*, 337 F. Supp. 243 (D.S.D 1971) *aff'd.*, 455 F.2d 698 (8th Cir. 1972).

41. By the time of the *Martinez* decision, twelve years after passage of the ICRA, fifty-eight published decisions were annotated in 25 U.S.C.A. § 1302 (West Cum. Supp. 1978). For critical analyses of the judicial interpretation of the ICRA in this first decade, see, e.g., Ziontz, "In Defense of Tribal Sovereignty: An Analysis of Judical Error in Construction of the Indian Civil Rights Act." 20 *S.D.L. Rev.* 1 (1975); Note, "Implication of Civil Remedies under the Indian Civil Rights Act," 75 *Mich. L. Rev.* 210 (1976).

42. *Martinez v. Santa Clara Pueblo*, 402 F. Supp. 5 (D.N.M. 1975). Martinez brought suit under 28 U.S.C. § 1343(4), which grants federal jurisdiction "[t]o recover damages or to secure equitable or other relief under any Act of Congress providing for the protection of civil rights, including the right to vote."

43. For arguments in support of Julia Martinez's position, see Brief as *amicus curiae* of the ACLU in *Santa Clara Pueblo v. Martinez*, 436 U.S. 49 (1978), and the Brief, *amicus curiae*, prepared by the Civil Rights Division, Department of Justice, but not filed because of lateness. See also *New York Times*, May 16, 1978, pp. 20–21.

44. *Martinez v. Santa Clara Pueblo*, 402 F. Supp. 5, 15–16 (D.N.M. 1975).

45. Brief of the ACLU as *amicus curiae* at 3–4, 20, *Santa Clara Pueblo v. Martinez*, 436 U.S. 49 (1978).

46. For arguments in support of the Santa Clara Pueblo and tribal sovereignty, see Briefs *amici curiae* filed by the Shoshone and Arapahoe Tribes and the National Congress of American Indians, by the National Tribal Chairmen's Association, by the Pueblo De Cochiti et al., and the All-Indian Pueblo Council.

47. *Martinez*, 402 F. Supp. at 5.

48. *Martinez v. Santa Clara Pueblo*, 540 F.2d 1039 (10th Cir. 1976).

49. The Supreme Court had previously declined to review ICRA decisions. See, e.g., *Means v. Wilson*, 522 F.2d 833 (8th Cir. 1974), *cert. denied* 424 U.S. 958 (1975); *United States ex rel. Cobell*, 503 F.2d 790 (9th Cir. 1975), *cert. denied*, 421 U.S. 999 (1975); *Thompson v. Tonasket*, 487 F.2d 316 (9th Cir. 1973), *cert. denied*, 414 U.S. 871 (1974).
50. *Santa Clara Pueblo*, 436 U.S. at 72.
51. *Id*. at 65–66.
52. *Id*. at 62.
53. *Id*. at 59.
54. *Id*. at 60.
55. *Id*. at 72.
56. *Id*. at 65–66.
57. Ziontz, "After *Martinez*: Civil Rights under Tribal Government," 12 *UCD L. Rev*. 1, 5 (1979).
58. "Non-judicial tribal institutions have also been recognized as competent law abiding bodies." *Id*. at 65–66.
59. *Santa Clara*, 436 U.S. at 72.
60. *Id*. at 72.
61. Between 1971 and 1978 the Department of Justice received 280 complaints of ICRA violations by tribal governments. The department participated in six federal civil lawsuits that raised ICRA issues, including two brought solely on ICRA claims. James M. Schermerhorn, Civil Rights Division, U.S. Department of Justice, Statement Before the Federal Bar Association's Indian Law Conference at 16 (April 3, 1986).
62. Although the department could have tried to distinguish its cases from *Santa Clara* by arguing that the Court's refusal to imply a private cause of action did not reach the government's cause of action, the decision was made not to litigate to establish a public right of action. Interview with James Schermerhorn, attorney, United States Department of Justice, Civil Rights Division, April 7, 1986.
63. Presidential Commission on Indian Reservations Economies, *Report and Recommendation to the President of the United States*, at 29 (November 1984); see also, various testimony, *Hearing Before the United States Commission on Civil Rights, Enforcement of the Indian Civil Rights Act* (July 31–August 1 and August 21, 1986; August 13–14, 1987; January 28, 1988; March 31, 1988; July 20, 1988) (hereinafter cited as Enforcement of the Indian Civil Rights Act).
64. According to the Department of Justice, seventeen of the forty-five complaints received allege tribal court irregularities; thirteen allege flaws in the tribal election process; six allege improper tribal hiring practices; four allege improper housing assignment policies by tribes; five complaints allege discrimination in the provision of tribal benefits and the existence of inadequate tribal jail conditions. Schermerhorn statement, *supra* note 62.

65. Cases appealed to federal court make up only a very small portion of the approximately 70,000 cases handled by tribal courts each year. While it is possible to see similar patterns of civil rights denial among the federal cases, it is impossible to infer that the same pattern exists with respect to the thousands of cases never brought to the attention of the federal courts. As a general rule there may be few records made or kept of tribal court proceedings. The latter may be handled to the full satisfaction of the tribal members or, alternatively, tribal members may lack the resources or knowledge to attempt to win access to an extratribal forum. The *Indian Law Reporter*, published by the American Indian Lawyer Training Program, collects and publishes some tribal court decisions. It is currently the only reporter reprinting tribal court opinions.

66. *Dry Creek Lodge, Inc. v. Arapahoe & Shoshone Tribes*, 623 F.2d 682 (10th Cir. 1980), *cert denied*, 449 U.S. 1118 (1981).

67. *Shortbull v. Looking Elk*, 677 F.2d 645 (1982).

68. *Id.* at 650.

69. *Id.*

70. *Id.* quoting *Santa Clara Pueblo*, 98 S. Ct. at 1684, 89 (White, J. dissenting).

71. 676 F.2d 1206, 1210.

72. *Id.* at 1210, n. 2.

73. *Runs After v. United States*, 766 F.2d 347, 353 (8th Cir. 1985).

74. *Committee to Save Our Constitution v. United States*, 11 Indian Law Rep. 3035 (D.S.D. 1984).

75. *Id.* Eventually, however, the complainants in *The Committee to Save Our Constitution* and *Runs After* were elected to office demonstrating the ability of tribal process to work for them. *Enforcement of the Indian Civil Rights Act* (July 31–August 1 and August 21, 1986), *supra* note 63, at 186–87.

76. *Kickapoo Tribe v. Thomas*, 10 Indian L. Rep. 3093, 3096 (D. Kan. 1983).

77. *Wells v. Philbrick*, 486 F. Supp. 807 (D.S.D. 1980).

78. *Sahmaunt v. Horse*, 11 Indian L. Rep. 3091, 3092 (W.D. Okla., 1984).

79. *Dry Creek Lodge v. Arapahoe & Shoshone Tribes*, 623 F.2d 682 (10th Cir. 1980), *cert. denied*, 449 U.S. 1118 (1981). See also Core, "Tribal Sovereignty: Federal Court Review of Tribal Court Decisions – Judicial Intrusion into Tribal Sovereignty," 13 *Amer. Ind. L. Rev.* 175; Gover & Laurence, *supra* note 5.

80. 623 F.2d at 684.

81. *Id.* at 685.

82. *Id.* at 685–86. (Holloway, J., dissenting).

83. *Trans-Canada Entreprises v. Muckleshoot Indian Tribe*, 634 F.2d 474 (9th Cir. 1980).

84. *R.J. Williams Co. v. Fort Belknap Housing Auth.*, 509 F. Supp. 933

(D. Mont. 1981); *Sahmaunt, supra* note 78, at 3092.

85. *White v. Pueblo of San Juan*, 728 F.2d 1307 (10th Cir. 1984).

86. *Trans-Canada Entreprises*, 634 F.2d at 476. At the same time legal analysts point out – in what is, perhaps, dramatic language – that the use of *Oliphant's* "unwarranted intrusions" exception "threatens to swallow the principle of inherent [tribal] sovereignty." Gover & Laurence, *supra* note 5, at 507.

87. *Enforcement of the Indian Civil Rights Act, supra* note 63, at 93 (August 13–14, 1987).

88. From 1986 to 1988, the U.S. Commission on Civil Rights held five sets of hearings on tribal justice and the ICRA. United States Commission on Civil Rights, *Enforcement of the Indian Civil Rights Act: Hearing Held in Rapid City, South Dakota, July 31–August 1 & August 21, 1986*; United States Commission on Civil Rights, *Enforcement of the Indian Civil Rights Act: Hearing Held in Flagstaff, Arizona, August 13–14, 1987*; United States Commission on Civil Rights, *Enforcement of the Indian Civil Rights Act: Hearing Held in Portland, Oregon, March 31, 1988*; United States Commission on Civil Rights, *Enforcement of the Indian Civil Rights Act: Hearing Held in Flagstaff, Arizona, July 20, 1988*; and United States Commission on Civil Rights, *Enforcementt of the Indian Civil Rights Act: Hearing Held in Washington, D.C., January 28, 1988*. These sessions inquired into reported Indian rights violations by tribal governments. *Enforcement of the Indian Civil Rights Act, supra* note 63. In 1988 Senator Orrin Hatch introduced S. 2747, "A Bill to provide Federal court authority to enforce rights secured by the Indian Civil Rights Act of 1968." See *supra* note 6.

89. *Santa Clara Pueblo*, 436 U.S. 49 at 72.

90. For a discussion of the general issue of aboriginal rights and individual equality, see Crawford, "The Aborigine in Comparative law," in *Law & Anthropology: Internationales Jahrbuch für Rechtsanthropologie* 18–23 (Vienna, 1987).

91. *Shortbull v. Looking Elk*, 677 F.2d 695 (8th Cir. 1982).

92. *Committee to Save Our Constitution v. United States*, 11 Indian L. Rep. at 3035.

93. *Dry Creek Lodge v. The Arapahoe & Shoshone Tribes*, 623 F.2d at 684.

94. For details of the confrontation between tribal courts and tribal council in the Navajo tribe in the 1970s, see Ziontz, *supra* note 57, at 18–25. For more recent examples of Navajo and Hopi judicial decisions in internal tribal political cases, see 16 *Indian Law Reporter (ILR)*, e.g., *Kavena, et al. v. Hopi Indian Tribal Court, et al.*, 16 ILR 6061 (1989); *In Re Bowman: Navajo Nation, et al. v. MacDonald, et al.*, 16 *ILR* 6085 (1989); *In Re Certified Question II: Navajo Nation, et al. v. MacDonald et al.*, 16 ILR 6086 (1989); *MacDonald et al. v. Yazzie, et al.*, 16 *ILR* 6069 (1989). See also Tso, "The Process of Decision Making in Tribal Courts," 31 *Ariz. L. Rev.* 225. (1989) (review of

recent changes in Navajo Nation by the chief justice of the Navajo Supreme Court).

95. For a short history of Indian tribal justice systems, see American Indian Review Commission, U.S. Congress, *Final Report* (1977). See also W. Hagan, *Indian Police and Judges* (New Haven, 1966); Collins, Johnson, & Perkins, "American Indian Courts and Tribal Self-Government," 63 *A.B.A. J.* 808 (1970); Ziontz, *supra* note 57, at 10–24; various testimony, *Enforcement of the Indian Civil Rights Act, supra* note 63.

96. 25 U.S.C. 461.

97. *Enforcement of the Indian Civil Rights Act, supra* note 63. For example, see testimony July 31–August 1 and August 21, 1986, at 190; August 13–14, 1987, at 83–91; January 28, 1988, at 79–80 and 275–76; March 31, 1988, at 106; July 20, 1988, at 96–99.

98. Pommersheim, "The Contextual Legitimacy of Adjudication in Tribal Courts and the Role of the Tribal Bar as an Interpretive Community: An Essay," 18 *N.M.L. Rev.* 49, at 66 and n. 85 (1988).

99. *Santa Clara Pueblo*, 436 U.S. at 72. There is no better way to explore the complexity of the ICRA issue and the diversity of proposed policy solutions than to read the testimony offered at the hearings on enforcement of the act. *Enforcement of the Indian Civil Rights Act, supra* note 63. The verbal testimony, debate, and written comments of Robert N. Clinton, Robert Laurence, Stephen L. Pevar, and Suzan Harjo are instructive and suggest the range of remedies argued by public-interest law practitioners and law school faculty with expertise in federal Indian law. *Enforcement of the Indian Civil Rights Act, supra* note 63 (Washington, D.C., January 28, 1988).

100. 15 *Reports of the American Bar Association* (1892); *Report of the Committee on Law and Courts for the Indians*, 423–27 (Annual Meeting, August 1982).

Conclusion:
The Two-Tier Structure of
Federal Indian Law and the
Impossibility of Partial Justice

The Two-Tier Structure of Federal Indian Law

The result of the successful adaptation of original principles of federal Indian law to political demands for the dispossession of the Indian was the development of a two-tiered approach to questions of Indian rights. By the end of the nineteenth century judicial decisions had created two different levels or layers of legality. On one level, the higher level, the courts perfected the principle that the relationship of the federal government and Indians was exceptional and, therefore, exempt from ordinary constitutional standards and procedures. Based on the twin pillars of plenary power and the political question doctrine – the one granting Congress near absolute power over Indian affairs, the other exempting the uses of that power from judicial review – Indian affairs were conducted within an extra- or supraconstitutional framework. The simultaneous evolution of a trust theory that gave the United States as trustee an unchallengeable monopoly of authority over its Indian wards served to buttress the exceptional nature of federal power over Indians.

Within this extraconstitutional framework the most fundamental choices Congress and the executive made about the rights and resources of Indian people were exempt from external standards and immune from judicial review. Whether the political choices thus made entailed the protection or the expropriation of Indian land, whether they entailed the forcible relocation of entire tribes, or the restitution of land lawlessly taken was left entirely to the good grace or ill will of the dominant majority – with neither redress nor remedy for Indians. On this first, or higher, tier of federal Indian law the courts condoned a system of rule in which the power of the federal government was limited neither by concepts of the inherent rights of Indians nor the imposition of external constitutional standards or institutional restraints.

The courts did not, however, abdicate judicial responsibility for the entire field of federal-Indian relations. Though not confining the scope and substance of political choices open to the federal government, the courts did impose on a second, or lower level, legal standards of regularity, calculability, and due process consistent with liberal principles of formal legal rationality. On this second level the implementation and administration of such policies *as the federal government had chosen to adopt* were subjected to – often exacting – judicial scrutiny.[1] It is on this tier of legality that courts have established legal rules insisting that unclear treaty language be interpreted in favor of the Indian signatories, demanding that congressional treaty abrogation be based on explicit choice and full notice,[2] and guaranteeing compensation for the extinguishment of Indian title.[3] It is also on this second level that courts enforce traditional constitutional rules of the separation of powers between the executive and Congress.

The most important result of the two-tiered approach to Indian affairs is that judicial decisions on the second level imposing legal principles of fairness and due process on the way in which the federal government implements its policies can never breach the larger framework – the first tier – of the unlimited power of the federal government over Indians. Judicial decisions on the second level – no matter how exacting they are in enforcing rules and standards set by Congress and how biased toward the protection of Indian rights – leave to the federal government alone the judgment of what rights Indians have.

The trust doctrine embodies the contradictions of the two-tier structure of federal Indian law particularly clearly. On the first tier United States trusteeship over Indian tribes is neither subject to external constitutional standards nor tied to ordinary common-law fiduciary standards. Yet the absence of principled limits on the exercise of federal trust powers on the first tier of federal Indian law has not always prevented courts from applying exacting fiduciary standards to the conduct of the federal trustee. Particularly during the two and a half decades from 1955 to 1980, judicial decisions have condemned the government's abuse of its paternalistic powers in scathing terms. In response to Indian suits seeking to enforce fiduciary duties on the conduct of the federal trustee, courts have awarded equitable relief and even money damages to tribes for the mismanagement of tribal resources and other breaches of trust.[4]

Yet the courts' condemnation of the trustee's misconduct never set firm and enforceable standards for the exercise of federal trust power over Indians. Instead trust responsibility was imposed only where Congress had chosen to provide for it by making the trustee liable by special statute or where legislation specifically required application of the common-law fiduciary standards to the federal government.[5] Litigation under the Indian Claims Commission, for example, could build on breach of trust because of the enabling legislation Congress had specifically provided.[6]

Reliance on the trustee's own consent to be sued proved to be an uncertain foundation, however, for consistent enforcement of meaningful fiduciary standards. It was well within keeping with the two-tier structure of federal Indian law, therefore, that the handful of successes in which the strict standards applicable to a private trustee had been applied to the government during the last two decades[7] proved ephemeral. They were but a fleeting acknowledgment of what federal trust policy would have to be if it were not exempt on the first tier – in the name of exceptionalism – from the prohibition on self-dealing and conflict of interest and from the requirements of reasonable care incumbent on ordinary trustees. The two-tier standard of federal Indian law thus leaves tribes in the unenviable position of having no clearly defined or generally available legal or equitable remedies to hold their trustee accountable for mismanagement and with a trustee whose powers are as ill defined in scope as they are vague in foundation.

Within the framework of two-tiered legality courts could condemn as an unwarranted abuse of executive authority the military custody of an Indian leader resisting forced relocation, while at the same time confirming that the exercise of such arbitrary military authority would be legal if only Congress chose formally to provide for it. Habeas corpus was granted to Chief Standing Bear of the Poncas – but only as long as Congress did not act to allow General Crook to imprison him again.[8] In 1883 the Supreme Court confirmed that Indian tribes had always had autonomy to deal with crimes committed by their own members and categorically denied, under current law, the federal government's authority to prosecute Crow Dog for the slaying of his chief, Spotted Tail.[9] But only three years later when Congress, in response to that unpopular decision, chose to abandon the formerly unquestioned policy of respecting tribal criminal jurisdiction and imposed federal criminal jurisdiction on tribes, the Supreme Court confirmed the plenary power of Congress to do so.[10] After Congress decided in 1865 to bar Indian tribes from access to the newly established Court of

Claims, it subsequently enacted jurisdictional acts granting particular tribes ad hoc access. By the same logic courts impose stringent standards of explicitness and notice on the procedures of congressional abrogation of Indian treaties[11] but do not question the unrestricted power of Congress to abrogate treaties unilaterally and arbitrarily.[12] While courts enforce compliance with federal ground rules regulating Indian land cessions to states,[13] they have left Congress free to change those ground rules whenever it seems convenient.[14] Where the power of any one branch of the government over Indians is limited, it is done in the name of traditional separation-of-powers principles. But the totality of the federal government's power over the tribes is not questioned, not limited by rights that inhere in Indian tribes.

The "Standing Bear phenomenon," the combination of ringing judicial disapproval of the abuse of governmental authority over Indians along with the exercise of complete deference to a subsequent choice by Congress to authorize the very abuse deplored by the courts, is at the core of federal Indian law. Whenever Congress chooses to change the ground rules or framework for Indian rights, courts defer to the plenary power of the legislature to decide whether to respect or nullify Indian rights; it "has never held a congressional exercise of power over Indian tribes to be illegal."[15] Wherever courts protect Indian rights in land or sovereignty they do so on the premise that these rights exist only as long as the government permits.

The stark dualism resulting from this two-tiered structure of federal Indian law that evolved during the second half of the nineteenth century continues to the present. It is the basis of Supreme Court decisions both ten years ago and in the last several years. In *Santa Clara Pueblo v. Martinez*, decided a decade ago,[16] the Supreme Court shielded tribal autonomy from expanding federal court intervention by reading the 1968 Indian Civil Rights Act narrowly to limit federal court jurisdiction to criminal and not civil tribal jurisdiction. The decision protected what is left of tribal self-determination. Yet in so doing, Justice Thurgood Marshall stressed emphatically that the Court in no way intended to preclude Congress from extending the civil jurisdiction of federal courts over that of the tribes – if Congress so chose.[17] Montana's attempt to tax tribal royalties from gas and oil leases was rejected in 1985 as violating the prohibition against state taxation of Indian tribes, but the Court left no doubt that Congress's "plenary" power over Indians was extensive enough to authorize Montana taxation of tribes.[18]

There are in the post-*Cherokee* judicial doctrines of the nineteenth century few remnants of the early decisions of John Marshall's Court. Where that Court had defined the limits of the federal government's power over Indian tribes at the beginning of the nineteenth century by reference to the inherent rights possessed by, and vested in, Indians under international law, judicial doctrine by the end of the nineteenth century saw no limits to the federal power over Indians other than those the United States government had chosen to impose on itself. The courts found no rights vested in Indians other than those the government had been beneficent enough to grant. It followed from this premise that the federal government could also choose to remove the limits it had chosen to impose on itself and that it was free to take the rights it had chosen to grant.[19]

The two-tiered nature of federal Indian law explains the paradox of decisions that allow tribes – the Passamoquoddy and Penobscot among them – to seek enforcement of hundred-year-old promises in court but that will not bar Congress from changing its promise *ex post facto*; that narrowly interpret congressional legislation asserting federal power over internal tribal affairs but confirm at the same time that Congress is free to extend its authority as far as it pleases; that sanction the extinguishment of Indian title at will but demand compensation.

That federal Indian law is deeply flawed can no longer be questioned by students of the origins and development of federal Indian law. Little research, however, has addressed the question of why such a deeply flawed body of law can exist unchallenged today, why the exceptionalism of federal Indian law is accepted. Recognition of the deviation of federal Indian law does not address the question of why a body of law so flawed can persist at a time when consciousness over issues of human rights is raised.

The origins and disabilities of Native American legal status lie in the politics and culture of the last century, when notions of white supremacy and manifest destiny were dogma and when neither politicians nor judges shied from translating their prejudices into law. Yet while the causes of the exceptional legal status of Indians in the nineteenth century are not difficult to find, it is more difficult to determine why U.S.-Indian relations today continue to be governed by maxims of law that have long been rejected as invalid in other areas of legal relations. The Supreme Court's decision in *Lone Wolf* was reached at the same time as the Court's "separate but equal" decision in *Plessy v. Ferguson*.[20] Yet while *Plessy* has been overturned[21] and the principles underlying it have been rejected as reflecting an unabashed racism and intolerance that we neither would, nor could, accept today, *Lone Wolf* continues to be controlling law, its underlying principles still unchallenged in legal briefs[22] and unquestioned by the courts.[23] While the law governing relations between other minorities and the political system has changed dramatically, Native Americans are still subject to legal principles untenable in the light of modern doctrines of equality, our professed commitment to human rights, and our firm disavowal of racism.

The Impossibility of Partial Justice

The immeasurable advantage of the two-tier structure of federal Indian law was that it accommodated both law and power. It allowed questions of Indian rights to be decided according to the preponderance of white power without giving the appearance of lawlessness. The dualism of the legal rules that evolved from this structure explains why federal Indian law is praised for its protection of Indian interests and condemned for its capitulation to political and economic pressure.

The legal consequences of perpetuating the validity of federal plenary power in a context antithetical to its legal origins were an increase in the imbalance of power in federal Indian law and confirmation of the dependence of Indian tribes. A rule of law founded on the acknowledgment of Indian power became the basis of Indian powerlessness. That it managed to do so by reference to legal principles reflecting the original power and autonomy of Indians was an invaluable contribution to the legitimization of uses of power that could not otherwise be justified by constitutional or international legal standards. In few areas has legal formalism so successfully veiled such irreconcilable contradictions.

That it happened gradually made it less visible. So much so, that while the campaign of African-Americans and women to reverse the most egregious of their legal disabilities has been successful, the "Indian's Dred Scott decision," among others, continues to find affirmation in the last quarter of the twentieth century.

The rules of formal legal rationality developed and applied on the second level of judicial decision making fulfilled the central need of the liberal legal system to demonstrate its autonomy and integrity. Decisions supporting the assertion of Indian rights could serve to demonstrate the independence of law from gross manipulation. Judicial decisions censoring Congress or the executive for their

195

shameful mistreatment of the Indian serve as ostensible proof of the impartiality of the law. More than that, the commitment to rules of legal consistency and procedural fairness has allowed Indians at times to hold the law to its own promises and pretensions of justice – and to win. The legal victories thus won have often held real and substantial benefits for Indian litigants.[24] The Passamoquoddy and Penobscot Indians of Maine successfully invoked the legal process over the loss of millions of acres of their land more than a century and a half ago.[25] The settlement of their claim imposed costs on the United States that were neither materially nor politically insignificant. Although they settled for less than they might have been entitled to, the results of their lawsuit may have brought them closer to creating conditions for a decent life for themselves.

While the Sioux people did not win the return of their sacred homelands in the Black Hills, there is the possibility that the hundred million dollars in damages imposed for the government's "ripe and rank deceit" will enable them to blunt some of the hard edges of poverty and despair of their existence. What Indians have won by reliance on the law is a reminder that the legal process is not a sham and that legalism is an achievement.[26]

Legal developments altering the original principles of Indian sovereignty and property rights were successful from the perspective of American society in accommodating the contradictory needs for legal autonomy with the political demand for a massive transfer of Indian land to white ownership. Although the appearance of justice has, on occasion, made it possible for Indians to resist the wrongful taking of their land or allowed them to collect money for its loss, it has not protected the Indian's right and duty – as the Cherokee movingly argued in an 1823 letter to U.S. commissioners – "to preserve the rights of posterity to the lands of their ancestors." Yet it is uncertain whether the legal victories Indians have won by relying on the promises of procedural fairness and legal consistency have truly been "occasions of justice," whether the appearance of justice can satisfy the substantive requirement of justice. The imbalance of persistent injustice and occasional justice in federal Indian law suggests that the appearance of justice is no substitute for the substance of justice.

The open violation of the Cherokee's political and property rights was, in the 1830s, an exception. It made their case notorious and sparked protest. Despite President Jackson's disregard of its decision, the Supreme Court reaffirmed that the "rights of the Indian to his soil are as sacred as the fee simple of the white man."[27] By the end of the nineteenth century the taking of Indian land without Indian consent was no longer the exception but the rule. Respect for Indians "as rightful occupants of the soil, with a legal as well as a just claim to retain possession of it," ended when Indian tribes insisted on their right to retain it. Recognition of the tribes' corollary right to use the land according to their own discretion was withdrawn when tribes used their discretion in ways contrary to the economic and political maxims of white society. Indian land, it turned out, was protected by the law only as long as Indians were ready to give it up; Indian autonomy was assured only as long as tribes would accept dissolution.

The consequences of this legal paradox for Indians are that the legal gains they make are never final nor are they secure from political manipulation. The legal victory of the Maine Indians was immediately threatened by legislative proposals to abrogate retroactively the legal basis for their lawsuit. Had such legislation passed, it would have been shielded from judicial review by the political question doctrine. Congressional power to eliminate the legal basis of successful lawsuits hangs like the sword of Damocles over all Indian efforts to rely on the law. By confining Indian rights of redress to the second level of federal Indian law, where courts will limit their inquiry to the internal consistency and fairness of governmental action but exempt from review the underlying policy – be it based on the arrogance of power or such "benevolence and mercy as behooves a Christian people" – the courts have created a legal framework for lawlessness. It provides the occasion for partial but not lasting justice.

The law, then, has not been "a better way" for Indians despite the Ponca chief's faith. It is, nevertheless, not without meaning that Indians have relied on the law and have articulated their grievances and needs in terms of rights thought to be promised or owed by law. The faith in the law of a disenfranchised and dominated people nourishes the mystique of the neutrality and autonomy of the law, even as it denies them justice. Federal Indian law ought to be praised for inspiring the Indians' faith in the law but cursed for betraying the believer.

Notes

1. Chambers, "Judicial Enforcement of the Federal Trust Responsibility to Indians," 27 *Stan. L. Rev.* 1213 (1975).
2. Wilkinson & Volkman, "Judicial Review of Indian Treaty Abrogation," 63 *Calif. L. Rev.* 601 (1975).
3. *Washington v. Fishing Vessel Ass'n,* 443 U.S. 658 (1978); *Choctaw Nation v. United States,* 318 U.S. 423, 431–32 (1943); *Choate v. Trapp,* 224 U.S. 665, 675 (1912). See also Wilkinson & Volkman, *supra* note 2.
4. Newton, "Enforcing The Federal-Indian Trust Relationship after Mitchell," *Cath. U.L. Rev.* 635, 636 n. 10 (1982).
5. Many of the special jurisdictional acts that granted Indian tribes access to the Court of Claims provided specifically for judicial remedies for mismanagement of tribal resources. Tribes needed special congressional authorization because they had been barred from access to the Court of Claims by a special 1865 amendment to the Claims Act. See also Newton, *supra* note 4, at 636 n. 10.
6. Newton, *supra* note 4, at 642 n. 47.
7. Newton, *supra* note 4, at 639 n. 23–25.
8. *United States ex. rel. Standing Bear v. Crook,* 5 Dill. 465; 25 F. Cas. 695 (C.C.D. Neb. 1879) (No. 14,891).
9. *Ex Parte Crow Dog,* 109 U.S. 556 (1883).
10. *United States v. Kagama,* 118 U.S. 375 (1886).
11. *County of Oneida v. Oneida Indian Nation,* 470 U.S. 226, 247 (1985); *Kerr-McGee Corp. v. Navajo Tribe,* 471 U.S. 195, 200 (1985); *Montana v. Blackfeet Tribe,* 471 U.S. 759 (1985). See also Wilkinson & Volkman, *supra* note 2.
12. Wilkinson & Volkman, *supra* note 2.
13. *Joint Tribal Council of Passamaquoddy v. Morton,* 522 F.2d 270 (1st Cir. 1975).
14. *United States v. Wheeler,* 435 U.S. 313, 328 (1978). In the aftermath of the initial legal success of the Maine Indians, innumerable bills were introduced in the U.S. Congress that would terminate the ongoing litigation and extinguish Passamoquaddy and Penobscot title retroactively as of 1820. See Shattuck & Norgren, "Indian Rights: The Costs of Justice," *The Nation,* (July 22–29, 1978).
15. Ball, "Constitution, Court, Indian Tribes," 1987 *Am. B. Found. Res. J.* 1, 12 (1987).
16. 436 U.S. 49 (1978).
17. "As we have repeatedly emphasized, Congress' authority over Indian matters is extraordinarily broad . . . Congress retains authority expressly to authorize civil actions for injunctive or other relief to redress violations" *Id.* at 72. In the absence of congressional action, the Court has since then reaffirmed the vitality of tribal civil jurisdiction, including a tribe's authority to determine its own civil jurisdiction. *National*

Farmers Union Insurance Co. v. Crow Tribe, 471 U.S. 845 (1985).
18. *Montana v. Blackfeet Tribe*, 471 U.S. 201.
19. *Tee-Hit-Ton Indians v. United States*, 348 U.S. 272 (1955).
20. 163 U.S. 537 (1896).
21. *Brown v. Board of Education*, 347 U.S. 483 (1954).
22. See, e.g., Brief for Defendant-Appellant, *Oglala Sioux Tribe v. United States*, No. 80–1878 (8th Cir., filed February 1981); Brief for Appellants, *United States v. Sioux Nation*, No. 79–639 (S. Ct. filed February 2, 1980).
23. *Santa Clara Pueblo v. Martinez*, 436 U.S. 49 (1978).
24. *United States v. Mitchell*, 463 U.S. 206 (1983).
25. *Joint Tribal Council*, 522 F.2d 370 (1st Cir. 1975).
26. E. Thompson, *Whigs and Hunters* (New York, 1975).
27. *Mitchel v. United States*, 34 (9 Pet.) 711 (1835).

Select Bibliography

The literature in the field of Native American studies is extensive. This bibliography includes only sources basic to our book. It should be used in conjunction with the chapter notes.

In addition to the standard indexes to legal, social science, and humanities publications, readers should consult Francis Paul Prucha, *A Bibliographical Guide to the History of Indian-White Relations in the United States* (Chicago, 1977); The Newberry Library Center for the History of the American Indian critical bibliographical series (Bloomington, Ind.); and A. Hirschfelder, M. Byler, and M. Dorris, *A Guide to Research on North American Indians* (Chicago, 1983).

The records and documents of the Bureau of Indian Affairs, the U.S. Congress, and, in particular, the Office of Indian Affairs, Record Group 75 (National Archives, Washington, D.C.) are essential primary source materials, as are judicial opinions published in federal and state court reporters. The *Indian Law Reporter* (American Indian Lawyer Training Program) reprints some, although not all, opinions from tribal courts. Also important are the records of the Indian Claims Commission. Several journals specialize in Native American studies. These include the *American Indian Culture and Research Journal*, the *American Indian Law Review*, and the *European Review of Native American Studies*. The various publications of the Indian Law Resource Center (Washington, D.C.) and the Native American Research Fund (Boulder, Colo.) provide contemporary information about political and legal events in Native American and federal Indian law.

Casebooks in the field of federal Indian law include F. Cohen, *Handbook of Federal Indian Law* (Washington, D.C., 1942 and more recent editions); D. Getches & C. Wilkinson, *Federal Indian Law* (2d ed. St. Paul, 1986); M. Price, R. Clinton & N. Newton, *Law and the American Indian* (3d ed. Charlottesville, 1990).

Ball, Milner S. "Constitution, Court, Indian Tribes." *Am. B. Found. Res. J.* 1 (1987).

Barsh, Russel Lawrence, and James Youngblood Henderson. *The Road: Indian Tribes and Political Liberty*. Berkeley, 1980.

Berkhofer, Robert F. *Salvation and the Savage: An Analysis of Protestant*

Missions and American Indian Response, 1787–1862. Lexington, Ky., 1965.
——. *The White Man's Indian: Images of the American Indian from Columbus to the Present.* New York, 1978.

Brodeur, Paul. *Restitution: The Land Claims of the Mashpee, Passamaquoddy, and Penobscot Indians of New England.* Boston, 1985.

Burnett, Donald L. "An Historical Analysis of the 1968 'Indian Civil Rights Act'." 9 *Harv. J. on Legis.* 557 (1972).

Cadwalader, Sandra L., and Vine Deloria, Jr., eds. *The Aggressions of Civilization.* Philadelphia, 1984.

Cahn, Edgar S. *Our Brother's Keeper: The Indian in White America.* Washington, D.C., 1969.

Canby, William C. *American Indian Law.* (2d ed. St. Paul, 1988).

Clinton, Robert N. "The Proclamation of 1763: Colonial Prelude to Two Centuries of Federal-State Conflict over the Management of Indian Affairs." 69 *Bost. U. L. Rev.* 329 (1989).

Debo, Angie. *And Still the Waters Run: The Betrayal of the Five Civilized Tribes.* Princeton, 1940. Reprint. Norman, Okla., 1984.

——. *A History of the Indians of the United States.* Norman, Okla., 1970.

Deloria, Vine, Jr. *The Nations Within.* New York, 1984.

Deloria, Vine, Jr., and Clifford M. Lytle. *American Indians, American Justice.* Austin, 1983.

Driver, Harold E. *Indians of North America.* 2d ed. Chicago, 1975.

Green, Michael D. *The Politics of Indian Removal: Creek Government and Society in Crisis.* Lincoln, Nebr., 1985.

Hagan, William T. *Indian Police and Judges.* Lincoln, Nebr., 1966.

——. *The Indian Rights Association.* Tucson, 1985.

Harmon, George D. *Sixty Years of Indian Affairs: Political, Economic, and Diplomatic, 1789–1850.* Chapel Hill, 1941.

Hertzberg, Hazel W. *The Search for an American Indian Identity: Modern Pan-Indian Movements.* New York, 1971.

Hoxie, Frederick E. *A Final Promise: The Campaign to Assimilate the Indians, 1880–1920.* Lincoln, Nebr. 1984.

——. ed. *Indians in American History.* Arlington Heights, Ill., 1988.

Jennings, Francis. *The Invasion of America.* Chapel Hill, 1975.

——. *Empire of Fortune: Crowns, Colonies, and Tribes in the Seven Years' War in America.* New York, 1988.

Indian Law Symposium, 31 *Ariz. L. Rev.* 191 (1989).

Institute for Government Research, *The Problem of Indian Administration.* Ed. L. Meriam. Baltimore, 1928.

Kappler, Charles J., ed. *Indian Affairs: Laws and Treaties.* Washington, D.C., 1904.

Kawashima, Yasuhide. *Puritan Justice and the Indian: White Man's Law in Massachusetts, 1630–1763.* Middletown, Conn., 1986.

Kennedy, John P. *Memoirs of the Life of William Wirt.* Rev. ed. Philadelphia, 1856.

Kickingbird, K., and K. Ducheneaux. *One Hundred Million Acres*. New York, 1973.

Laurence, Robert. "Learning to Live with the Plenary Power of Congress over the Indian Nations," 30 *Ariz. L. Rev.* 413 (1988). In same issue, see reply by Robert A. Williams, Jr. and rejoiner by Laurence.

Lurie, Nancy O. "The Indian Claims Commission," 436 *Annals of the American Academy of Political and Social Science* 97 (1978).

McLoughlin, William G. *Cherokees and Missionaries, 1789–1839*. New Haven, 1984.

——. *Cherokee Renascence in the New Republic*. Princeton, 1986.

Newton, Nell Jessup. "Federal Power over Indians: Its Sources, Scope, and Limitations." 132 *U. Penn. L. Rev.* 195 (1984).

Norgren, Jill L., and Petra T. Shattuck. "Limits of Legal Action: The Cherokee Cases." 2 *Amer. Ind. Culture and Res. J.* 14 (1978).

Otis, D.S. *The Dawes Act and the Allotment of Indian Lands*. Ed. F. Prucha. Norman, Okla., 1973.

Perdue, Theda. *Slavery and the Evolution of Cherokee Society: 1540–1866*. Knoxville, 1979.

Philp, Kenneth R. *John Collier's Crusade for Indian Reform, 1920–1954*. Tucson, 1977.

Priest, Loring Benson. *Uncle Sam's Stepchildren: The Reformation of United States Indian Policy, 1865–1887*. New Brunswick, N.J., 1942. Reprint. Lincoln, Nebr., 1975.

——, ed. *The New American State Papers: Indian Affairs*. 13 vols. Darby, Pa., 1973.

Prucha, Francis Paul. *The Great Father: The United States Government and the American Indian*. Lincoln, Nebr. 1984.

——, ed. *Americanizing the American Indians: Writings by the "Friends of the Indian," 1880–1900*. Cambridge, Mass., 1973.

——, ed. *Documents of United States Indian Policy*. Lincoln, Nebr., 1975.

Schmeckebier, Laurence F. *The Office of Indian Affairs: Its History, Activities, and Organization*. Baltimore, 1972.

Shattuck, Petra T., and Jill Norgren, "Political Use of the Legal Process by Black and American Indian Minorities," 22 *How. L.J.* 1 (1979).

Strickland, Rennard. "The Absurd Ballet of American Indian Policy or American Indian Struggling with Ape on Tropical Landscape: An Afterword." 31 *Me. L. Rev.* 213 (1980).

——. *Fire and the Spirits: Cherokee Law From Clan to Court*. Norman, Okla., 1975.

——. "Genocide-At-Law: An Historic and Contemporary View of the Native American Experience." 34 *U. Kan. L. Rev.* 713 (Summer 1986).

Sutton, Imre. *Indian Land Tenure: Bibliographical Essays and a Guide to the Literature*. New York, 1975.

——, ed. *Irredeemable America: The Indian's Estate and Land Claims*. Albuquerque, 1985.

Tibbles, Thomas Henry. *The Ponca Chiefs: An Account of the Trial of Standing Bear.* Ed. K. Graber. Lincoln, Nebr., 1972.

Tullberg, S., and R. Coulter. "The Failure of Indian Rights Advocacy." In National Lawyers Guild, *Rethinking Indian Law.* New York, 1982.

United States Commission on Civil Rights. *Indian Tribes: A Continuing Quest for Survival.* Washington, D.C., 1981.

United States Congress, American Indian Policy Review Commission, *Final Report.* Washington, D.C., 1977.

United States Indian Claims Commission. *Final Report.* Washington, D.C., 1978.

Vanderwerth, W.C., ed. *Indian Oratory.* New York, 1972.

Washburn, Wilcomb. E. *The Assault on Indian Tribalism: The General Allotment Act (Dawes Act) of 1887.* Philadelphia, 1975.

——. *Red Man's Land/White Man's Law: A Study of Past and Present Status of the American Indian.* New York, 1971.

——, ed. *The American Indian and the United States: A Documentary History.* 4 vols. New York, 1973.

——, ed. *The Indian and the White Man.* New York, 1964.

White, G. Edward. *History of the Supreme Court of the United States.* Vols. 3–4, *The Marshall Court and Cultural Change, 1815–1835.* New York, 1988.

Wilkins, Thurman. *Cherokee Tragedy: The Story of the Ridge Family and the Decimation of a People.* 2d rev. ed. Norman, Okla., 1986.

Wilkinson, Charles F. *American Indians, Time, and the Law.* New Haven, 1987.

Williams, Robert A., Jr. *The American Indian in Western Legal Thought: The Discourses of Conquest.* New York, 1990.

Young, Mary Elizabeth. *Redskins, Ruffleshirts, and Rednecks: Indian Allotments in Alabama and Mississippi.* Norman, Okla., 1961.

Index

Abbott, Lyman, 79, 96
Aboriginal land title, 24
Act of 1877, 8
American Civil War, 82
Americanizing the Indian, 101
American land policy, 113
Apache, 82
Articles of Confederation of 1777, 29

Bank of the United States, 42
Beeson, John, 79, 83
"Bill of Rights"
    of Indian Tribes, 28
Bingo. *See also* Tribal Gaming
    as an Indian employment, 10
Black Hills, 7, 196
Blackmun, Justice, 128
Bland, Dr. Thomas A., 90, 91, 97
Board of Indian Commissioners, 79
Boldt, Judge George, 8, 9
    1974 decision, 7
Boston Citizenship Committee, 79, 99
Bradwell v. Illinois, ix
Brule Sioux, 92
Buck v. Bell, ix
Bureau of Indian Affairs (BIA), 83, 92,
    93, 98, 132–133, 134, 147

Canfield, George, 91
Card games. *See also* Tribal gaming
    as an Indian employment, 10
Carlisle Indian Industrial School, 96
Carroll, Lewis, 23
Carter, President Jimmy, 12
Cherokee Cases, The, 38–50
Cherokee Nation v. Georgia, 3, 43, 46,
    47, 49, 52, 69, 110, 130–131, 131,
    131–132, 132, 133, 138, 182
Cherokee, 3, 4, 16, 39, 98, 100, 113,
    114, 119, 196
    resistance, 39
Cherokee Tobacco, 54

Chickasaws, 100
Choctaws, 7, 100
Christian Science Monitor, 7
Citizenship
    extended by Dawes Act, 99
Claims process
    and Indian interest, 150–153
    monetary-compensation-only, 150
Cleveland, President Grover, 91
Cohen, Felix, 27, 59, 167, 182
Comanches, 5, 6, 81, 125
Commerce
    regulation of, 28
Committee to Save Our Constitution, 176
Conflict of interest, 150
Constitution, of the U. S.
    Article i, Section 8, 123
Continential Congress, 28
Corn Tassel, 3, 43. *See also* Tassel,
    George
Court, The
    entrance of, in Native American
        cases, 30
Court of Claims, 5, 7, 143, 157, 193,
    198
Creeks, 100
Crook, General George, 90, 192
Crow Dog, 92, 93, 192
Custer, General George, 7

Dartmouth College, 81
Dawes, Senator Henry, 97, 98
Dawes (General Allotment) Act, 57,
    91, 97–99, 107, 116, 124, 144
Delaware Indians, 33
Delaware Tribe, 28, 128
Department of Interior, 117
Department of Justice
    Civil Rights Division, 174
Doctrine, development of, 30–38
Doctrine of Discovery, 31, 110, 111
Documents of Indian Policy, 156–157

Domestic, dependent nation, 47
Draper, Solomon, 84
Dry Creek Lodge, 176, 177
Dundy, Judge Elmer S., 3, 86, 87

Elk, John, 95
Elk v. Wilkins, 92, 95
Emancipation Proclamation, 90
Ervin, Senator Sam, 167
European law
  as applied to Native Americans,
    24–27
Ex Parte Crow Dog, 92, 93, 94, 96, 106

Federal Indian Law. *See also* two-tiered
  structure, 190–197
Fishing Rights, 19–20
Fishing Treaty, 9
Fletcher v. Peck. See also "Yazoo"
  Case, 29, 30, 32, 34, 35, 36, 37, 43,
    46, 63, 110, 112, 138
  vested rights in property, 30
Foreign nation status of Indian tribes,
  123
Fort Belknap Reservation, 168
Fort Berthold
  "good faith effort," 119
Fort Niobrara, 93

Garreaus v. Andrus, 175
Gates, Merrill E., 102
General Allotment Act, The, 4
General Allotment Act of 1885, 92.
  See also Dawes General Allotment
  Act of 1885
Gray, Justice, 95
Grossman, Prof. Joel, xiii
Guardianship, 47, 100, 115. *See also*
  Trusteeship

Harsha, William J., 89
Holden v. Joy, 54
Holloway, Judge, 177
Holmes, Judge Oliver Wendell, ix
Hoover Commission, 183
Hopi, 154, 162, 163
Hruska, Senator Roman, 167

Indian Citizenship Bill, 84
Indian
  acknowledged as a person, 3
Indian Civil Rights Act (ICRA), 164,
  165, 166, 167, 169, 172, 173, 174,
  176, 180, 185, 188, 189, 193

application in lower courts, 170–171
difficulties of tribal enforcement,
  178–179
enactment of, 166–170
interpretation in lower court,
  170–171
problems of tribal enforcement,
  174–177
Supreme Court, in, 171–174
Indian Claims Commission (ICC),
  5, 7, 103, 141, 143, 151, 154,
  158–61, 192
  as "legal conscience," 141
  independent investigative division,
    147, 148
Indian consent, 37, 38, 48, 113, 114,
  115, 119, 134
Indian Immunity
  from state law, 43
Indian Law
  early federal, 29
Indian Law Resource Center, xiii
Indian occupancy, 37, 54
  tenant for life, 54
  title, 51
  unlimited duration, 54
Indian Property Rights, 61, 61–63
Indian removal bill, 39. *See also*
  Removal Act
Indian Rights Association (IRA), 89,
  90, 92, 96, 99, 105, 125
Indian Rights Committee, 79
Indians as separate and distinct political
  entities, 110
  as wards of U.S., 116
"Indian's *Dred Scott* Decision," ix, 127,
  195
Indian sovereignty, 88
Indian title, 37
  to land, 35
Indian Trade and Intercourse Act of
  1790, 6, 29, 73, 123
Indian tribes
  as domestic dependent nations,
    43–46
Individual rights
  vs. state sovereignty, xi
Innocent IV, 25
Inter Caetera of May 3, 1493, 25
Interior Department, 122
International law
  as applied to Native Americans, 29

Jackson, Justice Robert, 109

Jackson, President Andrew, 38, 40, 41, 114, 196
Jackson, Senator Henry, 156
Jefferson, President Thomas, 29, 39
John Elk v. Wilkins, 96
Johnson, Justice, 32, 46
Johnson v. M'Intosh, 34, 35, 36, 45, 47, 48, 49, 50, 51, 76, 112, 119, 130, 138
Judicial decisions
  regarding Indian tribes, 191
Judiciary Act of 1789, Section 25, 45

Kiowas-Apache, 125
Kiowa Tribe, 125
  treaty with, 138
Kluger, Richard, xi
Knox, 29

Lake Mohonk Conference, 79, 96, 101, 102
Lake Mohonk Conference of Friends of the Indian and Other Dependent Peoples, 101
Lamar, L. Q. C., 97
Lamberton, Genio, 86, 97
Land allotment, 51, 98
Land allotment legislation, 4, 84. *See also* Dawes (General Allotment) Act
Las Casas, Bartolome de, 26
Law of Discovery, 112
Law of Nations, 101
Lawyers, role of, 148–150
Lincoln, President Abraham, 83
Little Big Horn, 7
Lone Wolf v. Hitchcock, 76–77, 107, 118, 119, 125, 126, 127, 128, 138–139, 140, 194, 195
Louisiana Purchase, 39, 67
Lynch, Gerald, xiii

Maine Indians Claims Settlement Act, 12
Major Crimes Act of 1885, 92, 94, 95
Major Crimes and Allotment Act, 127
Manifest Destiny, 41, 79, 194
Manypenny, George W., 91
Marshall, Chief Justice John, xi, 4, 23, 31, 32, 33, 34, 36, 37, 43, 44, 47, 48, 49, 56, 71, 112, 129–130, 167, 194
Marshall Court, The
  national character of Indian governments, 55

Marshall, Justice Thurgood, 172, 180, 193
Martinez, Julia, 171, 172
Matthews, Judge, 93, 94
Meriam Report, 144, 154
Miccosukee Seminoles, 152
Mitchel v. United States, 51, 75, 135–136
  Mitchell I, and *Mitchell II*, 120, 121
Monroe Doctrine, 32, 41, 44, 65–66
Moody, Judge G. C., 93
Morton v. Marcari, 128, 139–140

National character of Indian governments, 55
National Indian Defense Association, 79, 90, 91
Native American Church v. Navajo Tribal Council, 167
Native American nations
  as autonomous, 25
Native American Rights Fund, xiii
Natural inferiority
  of Native Americans, 79
Nevada v. U. S., 118
New England Mississippi Land Company, 30
New Jersey v. Wilson, 33
Nichols, Judge, 150
Nixon, President Richard, 167
Northwest Ordinance of 1787, 28, 49, 61, 112, 131

Oglala, 152
Oglala Sioux, 175
Omaha Committee, 88
Omaha Nation, 3, 85
Organized Crime Control Act of 1982 (OCCCA), 10
Osage Nation, 151

Pacific Northwest Indians, 8
Paine, Thomas, 1
Painter, C. C., 96
Pancoast, Henry S., 90, 96
Passamaquoddy Nation, 6, 17, 120, 194, 196, 198
Penn, William, 81
Penobscot Nation, 6, 120, 194, 196, 198
Plenary authority, 126
Plenary power, 121–127
  of Congress, 13
  Power Doctrine, 129

Plessy v. Ferguson, 195
Plowman, A. J., 93
Political Question Doctrine, 121–127
Ponca tribe, 82, 192. *See also* Standing
  Bear chief of, 1
Poppleton, Andrew J., 85, 87
Power, unlimited
  of Federal government, 13
Power of Law, 102
Pratt, Captain Richard Henry, 96, 97
Presidential Commission of 1984, 174
Property tax
  state, imposed on Indian land, 11
Public Law, 280
  Jurisdiction of, 10
Pueblos, 169
Pueblo of Santo Domingo, 152
Pyramid Lake Paiute, 117
Pyramid Lake Paiute Tribe v. Morton,
  117

Raw Power, 102. *See also Worcester v.*
  Georgia
  limits on use of, 78–102
Rehnquist, Justice, 117, 118
Removal Act, The, 40, 41, 42, 49, 68
Removal Policy, 82–84
Requerimiento, 26
Roosevelt, President Theodore, 97
Rosebud Sioux, 152
Rule of Law, 78–102

Santa Clara Pueblo v. Martinez, 22,
  164, 165, 171, 172, 173, 174, 175,
  176, 177, 178, 179, 180, 181, 182,
  185, 186, 189, 193
  as a compromise, 165
Santo Domingo Pueblo, 150
Sargeant, John, 42
Second Great Awakening, 81
Seminole, 152, 154
Senate Indian Affairs Committee, 97
Sexter, Provost Jay, xiii
Shoshone, 6. *See also* Western
  Shoshone
Schurz, Secretary of the Interior Carl,
  85
Sioux, 5, 7, 82, 84, 93, 119, 132, 196
Sioux Nation of Indians v. United States,
  17–18, 128
South Carolina's Nullification
  Ordinance, 50
Spotted Tail, 92, 192
Standing Bear, 1, 3, 13, 84, 90, 97,

104, 192, 193.
  See also Ponca tribe
  trial of, 84–88
Storrs, Henry
  New York Whig, 40
Strickland, Rennard, 164
Supreme Court, 3

Talton v. Mayes, 167
Tassel, George, 42
Taylor Grazing Act of 1934, 152
Tee-Hit-Ton Band of Tlingit, 6
Tenant for life, 54
Thayer, James, 99, 181
The Case of John Elk, 94. *See also Elk*
  v. Wilkins
Tibbles, Thomas, 85, 88
Tocqueville, Alexis de, 78, 82
Trade and Intercourse Act of 1834, 52,
  53
Transcontinental railroad, 103
Treaty of Holston in 1791, 38, 48
Treaty of Hopewell, 48
Treaty of Medicine Lodge, 125
Tribal autonomy, 115, 122
Tribal consent, 51
Tribal Councils. *See also* Tribal Courts
  and tribal courts, conflicts between,
  178
Tribal Court of the Cheyenne River
  Sioux Tribe, 176
Tribal Courts. *See also* Tribal Councils
  and tribal councils, conflicts
  between, 178
Tribal Executive Committee, 178
Tribal gaming, 10
Tribal sovereignty, 8, 18, 21, 23, 24,
  26, 52, 94, 129, 167, 169, 174
  basic claims of, 24
  and the Federal courts, 164–181
  limits of, 4

Tribal treaty rights, 89
Truman, President Harry, 103, 141
Trust Doctrine
  of Congress, 13
Trusteeship, 115–121
  over Indian tribes, 191
Two-tiered structure, *See* Federal Law
  of Federal Indian Law, 190–197

United States assimilation program,
  144
  termination and relocation, 144

Index

United States Bureau of Reclamation
irrigation project, 117
United States Court of Appeals, 176
United States Court of Claims, 142
United States' Trust Doctrine, 116
*United States ex. rel Standing Bear v.
Crook*, 86
United States v. Celestine, 100
United States v. Cook, 54, 75, 76
United States v. Dann Sisters, See
Western Shoshone
*United States v. Forty Three Gallons of
Whiskey*, 53
United States v. Holliday, 53
United States v. Kagama, 94, 10
United States v. Rogers, 4, 51, 52, 54,
72, 73, 74
United States v. Sioux Nation, 128
United States v. Washington, 8
U. S. Commission on Civil Rights,
156, 156–157
U. S. jurisdiction over claims, 145. *See
also* Indian Claims Commission
(ICC)

Victoria, Franciscus de, 26, 31, 37, 101

War Department, 122

Washington, George, 29
Washington, State of
Native American tribes, 8
Watkins, Senator Arthur V., 144
Webster, John L., 85, 87
Western Shoshone, 4, 15, 15–16, 152,
162
Dann sisters, 15, 16, 163
Whipple, Henry, 79, 83
White, Justice, 126, 175
White, Justice Edward, 109, 126, 175
Wilkins, Charles, 95
Williams, Roger, 27
Wirt, William, 42
Witt, Chief Commissioner, 147
Women's National Indian Association,
79
Worcester, Samuel, 46
Worcester v. Georgia, 3, 8, 18, 23, 33,
46–50, 48, 49, 50, 51, 54, 55, 56, 71,
73, 92, 110, 119, 138, 182. *See also*
Raw Power
"Indian Independence," 47
Writ of habeas corpus, 168
re: Standing Bear, 86

"Yazoo" case, *See Fletcher v. Peck*